National Version

Study Guide

Raymond L. Lee
Indiana University of Pennsylvania

Dorothy Palmer
Indiana University of Pennsylvania

Larry Elowitz
Georgia College

16th Edition

GOVERNMENT BY THE PEOPLE

James MacGregor Burns
University of Maryland,
College Park
and
Williams College

J.W. Peltason
University of California

Thomas E. Cronin
Whitman College

David B. Magleby
Brigham Young University

Prentice Hall, Englewood Cliffs, New Jersey 07632

©1995 by PRENTICE-HALL, INC.
A Simon and Schuster Company
Englewood Cliffs, New Jersey 07632

10 9 8 7 6 5 4 3 2 1

ISBN 0-13-303991-9
Printed in the United States of America

CONTENTS

CHAPTER

PREFACE

The basic goal of this new edition of Study Guide to **GOVERNMENT BY THE PEOPLE** is that of its predecessors — to offer the reader a rational way to learn about American Government. To that end, we have tried to focus on the most significant aspects of each chapter of the text. In the final analysis, we believe that all true education is self-education. Students can claim no concept as their own until they can use it. We hope to shorten that process by making students their own tutors. This new edition is a greatly expanded version of its immediate predecessors.

We owe a long-term debt to those students and teachers who have taken the time to write us about the strengths and weaknesses of this Study Guide since it was first published in 1963. But obviously, our greatest indebtedness is to Professor James MacGregor Burns of Williams College, President J.W. Peltason, University of California System, Thomas E. Cronin, Whitman College and Professor David B. Magleby, Brigham Young University. Their lively, insightful approach to American Government is the basis of this Study Guide. **GOVERNMENT BY THE PEOPLE** is in its fifth decade and the sixteenth edition, still displaying all of its original zest.

We also owe a debt to our collegues, whose ideas we have shamelessly pirated. Especially worthy of mention is Professor Emeritus Bert A. Smith of IUP, a skillful, seasoned teacher who used various versions of the guide for over a quarter of a century. Also vital to the enterprise was Larry Elowitz, who did the Political Science Today and Data Analysis sections.

Indiana, Pennsylvania

Raymond L. Lee
Dorothy A. Palmer

CHAPTER 1
CONSTITUTIONAL DEMOCRACY

I n the mid 1990s American Constitutional democracy has captured world-wide attention that results in a strange dilemma. European, Hispanic and Latin American students often study the origins of our constitutional system more than do our own students, who take it for granted. Unfortunately, the path to democracy is apt to have many pitfalls and rocky places. It may be of some comfort to remember that we have had similar difficulties over the last two centuries.

Two contrasting ideas have dominated American political thought since the nation was founded — liberty and order. In one sense they are in conflict; in another sense they reinforce each other.

The Founders had no ready-made blueprint for their new government. Their first effort produced a weak government that could not preserve order (the Articles of Confederation). Slowly and reluctantly they moved toward stronger government (The Annapolis Convention). Then, spurred by Shay's Rebellion, they assembled in Philadelphia in May, 1787, and throughout a long hot summer compromised their differences to draft a new Constitution that was adopted only by paper-thin majorities in many of the mutually antagonistic states.

This original document has been amended and interpreted since 1787 to make it conform more nearly to American goals of openness, representation, and responsibility. That search in one sense is the very essence of American democracy. In this chapter, we look at how the framers approached the problem of building a strong national government and at the background from which the federal Constitution came. Above all, our Constitution is a living, changing document, rather than a faded parchment scroll.

PART I — GUIDEPOSTS

1. Defining Democracy
    a. What is a constitutional democracy?
    b. How are these democratic values linked:
        individualism? equality of opportunity? personal liberty?
    c. How do the above conflict?
    d. How did the Bill of Rights supplement the original Constitution?
    e. What balance is necessary between liberty and equality?
    f. What are the essential elements for a democratic election?
    g. What is meant by federalism?
    h. How is power separated?

2. Making Democratic Principles a Reality
    a. How do each of these conditions promote democracy: education? the economy? social conditions? and ideology?
    b. What conditions did we overcome to survive as a democracy?
    c. What potential threats still remain?

3. America's Constitutional Roots
    a. What incidents provoked opposition to British rule?
    b. Why were the Articles of Confederation inadequate?

c. What prompted the Annapolis Convention?

d. Why was Shay's Rebellion a catalyst for revision of the articles?

4. The Philadelphia Convention, 1787

a. What was the background of the convention delegates?

b. Why are they described as "well-read, well-fed, well-bred, and well-wed"?

c. What groups were missing from the convention?

d. Why did the convention impose a rule of secrecy?

e. What consensus existed among the delegates?

f. On what issues did they compromise?

g. Why was the Connecticut Plan adopted over those proposed by Virginia and New Jersey?

h. How did the convention compromise the issue of slavery?

i. What evidence exists to prove that the framers were moral philosophers? Practical men?

5. The Struggle Over Adoption

a. What restrictions on the revision of the articles had the convention violated? Why?

b. Who were the supporters of the Federalists?

c. Who supported the anti-Federalists?

d. What impact did the *Federalist* papers have in the debate?

e. How did the lack of a Bill of Rights help opponents of ratification?

f. How did the Federalists meet this objection?

g. What factors favored the Federalists?

6. Into the Twenty-first Century

a. Is our democratic system sufficiently open? Responsive? Representative? Responsible? Effective?

b. What was Benjamin Franklin's response when he was asked if the government he had helped to draft was a republic or a monarchy? What did he mean?

PART II — GLOSSARY

CONSTITUTIONAL CONVENTION, 1787 - The convention held in Philadelphia that drafted our basic government document, the Constitution.

REPUBLIC - A form of democracy where elected officials govern as agents of the people.

SEPARATION OF POWERS - Deliberate division of governmental powers between the legislative, executive, and judicial branches to check arbitrary rule.

ARTICLES OF CONFEDERATION - The first constitution of the newly independent American states, drafted in 1776, ratified in 1781, and replaced by the present Constitution in 1789.

SHAY'S REBELLION - The rural rebellion of 1786-1787 in western Massachusetts, protesting mortgage foreclosures, that engendered conservative support for a stronger national government.

VIRGINIA PLAN - A proposal in the Constitutional Convention that provided for a strong legislature with representation in each house determined by population, thus favoring the large states.

BICAMERALISM - A two-house form of legislature.

NEW JERSEY PLAN - A proposal in the Constitutional Convention that provided for a single-house legislature with equal representation, thus favoring the small states.

CONNECTICUT COMPROMISE - A blending of the New Jersey and Virginia Plans that gave equality of representation in one house, representation based on population in the other.

THREE-FIFTHS COMPROMISE - An agreement in the Constitutional Convention that counted slaves as three-fifths of a person for both representation and taxation purposes.

FEDERALIST - Originally, a supporter of the new Constitution; later, a political party that favored strong central government.

DEMOCRACY - Government by the people, either directly or indirectly, with free and frequent elections.

INDIVIDUALISM - In a political sense, the belief that the welfare of the citizen is more important than that of the state.

STATISM - A political theory that holds that the welfare of the nation has topmost priority, transcending the welfare of any or all individual citizens.

CONSTITUTIONAL GOVERNMENT - A government restricted by a written or unwritten statement (constitution) under which it functions.

PART III — PRETEST

1. One of the following words is not at the heart of American beliefs.
   a. competition
   b. freedom
   c. liberty
   d. equality

2. When democracy is described as a process, we emphasize
   a. equal voting rights.
   b. worth of the individual.
   c. individual freedom.
   d. liberty and justice.

3. Advocates of democracy argue that the public interest is best discovered by
   a. consulting top social scientists.
   b. permitting all adults to have a vote.
   c. entrusting decision making to political party leaders.
   d. the creation of philosopher-kings.

4. Democracy as a theory of government is centered on
   a. the individual.
   b. political parties.
   c. interest groups.
   d. an independent judiciary.

5. Constitutionalism as a part of democratic government serves to
   a. define and limit the government's power.
   b. expand the authority of officials.
   c. protect the rights of the majority.
   d. safeguard against revolution.

6. Freedom of the press was furthered by the case of New York printer
   a. John Paul Jones.
   b. Daniel Shay.
   c. John Hancock.
   d. John Peter Zenger.

7. Franklin D. Roosevelt's Four Freedoms did not include
   a. freedom of speech.
   b. freedom of religion.
   c. freedom of fear.
   d. freedom from oppressive taxes.

8. The American Revolution is best described as
      a. conservative.
      b. bloody.
      c. radical.
      d. reactionary.

9. The best characterization of the framers of the Constitution would be
      a. visionary idealists.
      b. political philosophers.
      c. experienced, practical politicians.
      d. spokesmen for the average person.

10. The Three-fifths Compromise did *not* deal with
      a. counting slaves.
      b. taxation.
      c. representation.
      d. treaty ratification.

PART IV — PROGRAMMED REVIEW

Knowledge Objective : To review the many meanings of democracy
      1. In a democracy government derives its authority from its _____ .
      2. Ancient Greek city-states had a _____ democracy which often turned to mob rule.
      3. Democracy has taken on a _____ meaning only in the last one hundred years.
      4. The word _____ is not used in the Declaration of Independence or in the Constitution.
      5. Framers of the Constitution favored the use of _____ rather than democracy.
      6. Democracy can be viewed as a system of _____ political structures.
      7. _____ is the term used to describe government by the many.
      8. A representative democracy is commonly called a _____ .
      9. A constitutional government normally _____ the power of officials.
     10. The central measure of value in a democracy is the _____ .
     11. The doctrine of _____ makes the community or state the measure of value.
     12. _____ or _____ are terms used to describe the right of an individual to set his own goals.
     13. In modern America the two major values that are in a state of tension and interaction are _____ and _____ .
     14. The basic democratic principle involved in elections is one person, _____ vote.
     15. In democracies, elections are decided by _____ vote.
     16. To have a truly democratic election, citizens must have the right to _____ .

Knowledge Objective: To examine conditions necessary for democracy to survive
     17. New democracies generally have a (slim/good) chance of surviving.
     18. When faced with difficult times new democracies are tempted to back a strong _____ to solve their problems.
     19. Democracies are most likely to survive when there are positive _____ , _____ , and _____ conditions.

Knowledge Objectives: To explore America's Constitutional Roots

20. The Founding Fathers insisted that the rights they had as English subjects be spelled out in _____ form.
21. In most American colonies _____ freedom had not been guaranteed.
22. Our Declaration of Independence asserted that the basic rights of all men included _____ , _____ and _____ .
23. During the period 1781-89, Americans were governed under their first constitution, the _____ .
24. Under the Articles of Confederation, a _____ was created rather than a national government.
25. The need to strengthen the machinery of government was demonstrated during the winter of 1786-87 by a debtor's protest known as _____ .

Knowledge Objective: To discover how the Constitutional Convention of 1787 went about creating a "more perfect union"

26. The framers of the Constitution were guided chiefly by _____ rather than theory.
27. At the Constitutional Convention of 1787, _____ presided; _____ was the highly respected elder statesman.
28. To encourage open discussion and compromise, proceedings of the Constitutional Convention were _____ .
29. To break the deadlock over representation, the Connecticut Compromise provided that one house of Congress be based on _____ ; the other on _____ .

Knowledge Objective: To examine the political strategy that led to adoption of the new Constitution

30. Adoption of the new Constitution required ratification by _____ states.
31. Those who opposed adoption of the Constitution were called _____ .
32. Hamilton, Jay, and Madison wrote a series of essays urging adoption of the Constitution that is known collectively as _____ .
33. Opposition to the new Constitution was largely concentrated in the _____ region.
34. The strategy of those who favored adoption of the Constitution was _____ .
35. The Bill of Rights was demanded by the _____ .

PART V — POST-TEST

1. A democratic government is one in which all citizens have equal
   a. political influence.
   b. voting power.
   c. social status.
   d. economic benefits.

2. Believers in democracy do *not* accept
   a. statism.
   b. equality.
   c. individualism.
   d. liberty.

3. In modern America, two concepts once thought to be opposites exist in an uneasy relationship are
   a. equality and liberty.
   b. federal and unitary government.
   c. oligarchy and autocracy.
   d. socialism and capitalism.

4. Only one of these revolutionary leaders was present at the Constitutional Convention.
   a. Thomas Jefferson
   b. Sam Adams
   c. Patrick Henry
   d. Alexander Hamilton

5. The incident that did most to destroy faith in government under the Articles of Confederation was
    a. the Whiskey Rebellion.
    b. Shay's Rebellion.
    c. the Loyalist revolt.
    d. the Indian uprising.

6. The Founding Fathers favored *all but one* of the following ideas.
    a. a unicameral legislature
    b. a strong executive
    c. an independent judiciary
    d. a more powerful Congress

7. The Connecticut Compromise found a middle ground on the issue of
    a. representation.
    b. slavery.
    c. the court system.
    d. the electoral college.

8. The authors of *The Federalist* include all but one of the following.
    a. Hamilton   c. Madison
    b. Jefferson   d. Jay

9. To secure ratification, supporters of the Constitution promised
    a. presidential veto power.
    b. Bill of Rights.
    c. a federal income tax.
    d. a Homestead Act.

10. Only one of the following statements is true of the ratification process.
    a. The opponents tried to get a quick "no" vote
    b. Most newspapers were Federalist opponents
    c. Most of the opponents were in rural areas
    d. Opposition was concentrated in the small states

PART VI — POLITICAL DIALOGUE: THE CLASH OF ISSUES AND IDEAS

1. Defenders of democracy quote Aristotle, who wrote "The guest can judge the banquet better than the chef, though he might not be able to cook the meal." What is the thrust of this quotation? Does it make a valid point?

2. The renowned Spanish political philosopher, Jose Ortega y Gasset has written that the role of the common man in politics has everywhere meant a decline in standards. Is there evidence to support his thesis? What rebuttal could you offer?

3. Former Secretary of State, George Schultz wrote in 1986 that on the world scene a massive movement toward democracy had set in. Have events since then confirmed his prediction? Cite examples.

4. In *Framing a Constitution*, Sir William Gladstone, the famous British Prime Minister, once described the American Constitution as "the greatest work that was every struck off at a given time by the brain and purpose of man."

Without detracting in any way from the Constitution-makers of 1787, how can it be argued that Americans were engaged in writing a constitution from 1607 to 1787? Can a case be made for the idea that the American Constitution is not yet written — although we have been engaged in that project from 1787 to the present date?

PART VII — POLITICAL SCIENCE TODAY

1. Try to imagine what a second Constitutional Convention would be like if it were held in the 1990s. The 1787 Convention was conducted in total secrecy in order to prevent disruptions from external hostile forces and the possible rallying of opposition to the convention itself. Today, a new constitutional convention would take place in the glare of the modern media. It would be virtually impossible for "secrets" to be kept. Given the media attention, could a new convention actually accomplish any structural changes in our government? Also, would a new convention possibly become radicalized due to media pressures? Speculate on what could and could not be accomplished given our media-oriented age.

2. The question as to the economic motives of the constitutional framers is still debated. Some contemporary scholars uphold the Beard thesis in one form or the other, i.e., economics and self-interest were the factors behind the formation of our Constitution.

   Thus, in Michael Parenti's book *Democracy for the Few* (New York: St. Martin's Press, 1988, fifth edition), the following contention is asserted:

   "The Constitution was framed by financially successful planters, merchants, and creditors, many linked by kinship and marriage and by years of service in Congress, the military, or diplomatic service. . . . Most troublesome to the framers of the Constitution was the increasingly insurgent spirit evidenced by the people. Fearing the popular takeover of state governments, the wealthy class looked to a national government as a means of protecting their interest.

   The nationalist conviction that arose so swiftly among men of wealth during the 1780s was not the product of inspiration; it was not a 'dream of nation-building' that suddenly possessed them. . . . Rather, their newly acquired nationalism was a practical response to material conditions affecting them in a most immediate way. Their like-minded commitment to federalism was born of a common class interest that transcended state boundaries." (p. 56)

   Parenti also sees the Constitution as an elitist document, property-oriented, and ratified by unscrupulous means:

   "More important than to conjecture about the framers' motives is to look at the Constitution they fashioned, for it tells us a good deal about their objectives. The Constitution was consciously designed as a conservative document, elaborately equipped with a system of minority checks and vetoes, making it easier for entrenched interests to endure. It provided ample power to build the services and protections of state needed by a growing capitalist class but made difficult the transition of rule to a different class. . . .

   The Constitution championed the rights of property over the rights and liberties of persons. For the founders, liberty meant something different from and antithetical to democracy. It meant liberty to invest, speculate, trade, and accumulate wealth and to secure its possession without encroachment by sovereign or populace. The civil liberties designed to give all individuals the right to engage in public affairs won little support from the delegates. . . ." (p. 65)

   "If the Constitution was so blatantly elitist, how did it manage to win ratification? Actually, it did not have a wide backing, initially being opposed in most of the states. But the same superiority of wealth, organization, and control of political office and the press that allowed the rich to monopolize the Philadelphia Convention enabled them to orchestrate a successful ratification campaign. The Federalists used bribes, intimidation, and other discouragements against opponents of the Constitution. What's more *the Constitution never was submitted to a popular vote*. Ratification was by state convention composed of delegates drawn mostly from the same affluent strata as the framers. Those who voted for these delegates were themselves usually subjected to property qualifications." (p. 66)

The assertions made by Parenti would furnish some excellent debate material to be used in class discussion. Find other sources (consult your chapter) which refute the Parenti charges. After doing this, arrive at your own conclusions about the motivations of the framers.

3. During the ratification struggle, the new Constitution was barely ratified in such important states as New York, Massachusetts, and Virginia. Imagine that these three states had voted not to ratify the Constitution. What strategies would the Federalists have then been forced to follow to try and salvage a difficult political position? Would they have called a new constitutional convention? Try to list some possible political strategies that the Federalists might have considered and assess the merits and demerits of each strategy.

PART VIII — DATA ANALYSIS

1. Look at the text material dealing with "Democracy as a System of Interacting Values." Take each of the values and express your own understanding of them at this point in the course. After you have completed the course, come back to your original conceptions and modify them, if need be, according to what you have subsequently learned. This "before and after" comparison should prove interesting in terms of honing your analytical skills.

2. In a similar way to data exercise #1 above, look at the twelve questions posed at the end of Chapter 1. Write down your opinions at this early point in the course, even if you feel unsure about the "answers." At the end of the course, compare your original responses with your subsequent modifications.

3. Speculate on this question: What would have happened to the young American nation if the Articles of Confederation had only been modified slightly, rather than completely overturned?

4. After the liberation of Eastern Europe, the reunification of Germany (East and West Germany), and the demise of the Soviet Union during the 1989-1991 period, there was hope among American leaders that democracy would be strengthened and even expanded in these former communist nations along with other communist nations such as China. However, it is apparent that creating a political democracy along with a capitalistic free market in a short period of time is no easy task. Why is it so difficult to make the transition from an authoritarian form of government to a democratic one? Hint: Democracy rests upon shared cultural values and certain psychological predispositions. Can you identify these values or predispositions? Which of these might be lacking in a formerly totalitarian-authoritarian nation? Jot down your thoughts now and return to this question at the end of the course.

PART IX — TEST ANSWERS

Pretest

1. a
2. a
3. b
4. a
5. a

6. d
7. d
8. a
9. c
10. d

Programmed Review

1. citizens
2. direct
3. positive
4. democracy
5. Republic
6. interdependent
7. democracy
8. republic
9. limits
10. individual
11. statism
12. liberty; freedom
13. liberty; equality
14. one
15. majority
16. organize
17. slim
18. leader

19. educational, economic, social
20. written
21. religious
22. life; liberty; pursuit of happiness
23. Articles of Confederation
24. league of friendship
25. Shay's Rebellion
26. experience
27. Washington; Franklin
28. kept secret
29. population; equality
30. nine
31. Antifederalist
32. The Federalist
33. back country
34. quick ratification
35. Antifederalists

Post-test

1. b
2. a
3. a
4. d
5. b

6. a
7. a
8. b
9. b
10. c

Data Analysis

Responses to the data analysis exercises will vary according to the student's background and type of information gleaned from the entire course.

But what did liberty (or freedom) mean when not governments but other individuals — employers, lynch mobs, plantation owners — deprived persons of this right? Slavery forced Americans to rethink their ideas. "The world has never had a good definition of the word liberty," Abraham Lincoln said during the Civil War, "and the American people, just now, are in want of one." We all declare for liberty, but in using the same word we do not all mean the same thing. With some the word liberty may mean for each man to do as he pleases with himself, *and the product of his labor, while with others the same word may mean for some men to do as they please with other men.*

With the coming of industrialization, urbanization, and agrarian and labor discontent of unions, depressions, and social protest; and of leaders like William Jennings Bryan, Theodore Roosevelt,

Robert LaFollett, Eugene Debs, and Woodrow Wilson, liberty came to have far more positive meanings. Americans slowly came to understand that men and women, crowded more and more together, lived amid webs of all kinds; personal and private, institutional and psychological. To abolish one type of restraint (such as black slavery) might mean increasing another type of restraint (such as wage slavery). To cut down on governmental restraint *of liberty might simply mean increasing private economic and social power. The question was not simply how to liberate people from government; it was how to use government to free people from nongovernmental curbs on liberty as well.*

But what about the idea of *equality*, next to liberty probably the most vital concept in American thought. "All men are created equal and from that equal creation they derive rights inherent and unalienable, among which are the preservation of liberty and the pursuit of happiness." So read Jefferson's first draft of the Declaration, and the words indicate the primacy of the concept. Alexis de Tocqueville, James Bryce, Harold Laski, and other foreigners who investigated American democracy were struck by the strength of egalitarian thought and practice in both our political and social lives.

What did equality mean? What kind of equality? Economic, political, legal, social, or something else? Equality for whom? For blacks as well as whites?

The completion of two centuries of self-government — a major accomplishment — is a time of national celebration. However, it is also appropriately a time of national questioning. The questions that are being asked have no easy answers. They are questions to which there is no single logical response, no answer that stems easily from an analysis of facts; they are basic questions that deal with value choices. The following questions may help stimulate your thinking as we proceed with a more detailed investigation of the operations of the American Republic:

1. Is the system *sufficiently open* to persons of all races, sexes, classes, and political views who wish to participate in making decisions?

2. Is the system sufficiently responsive? Is the leadership accountable to the voters?

3. Is the system sufficiently representative? This concept of representation is one of the most difficult in political science. Here we mean to focus not on whether those who govern precisely mirror divisions of class, race, interest, and region, but on whether those who govern are sensitive to the needs and opinions of differing groups.

4. Is the system sufficiently responsible? Does the leadership keep in mind the long-term needs of the entire nation and not merely respond to the short-term demands of the most vocal or most prosperous special interests?

5. Is the system effective? Does it permit us to solve our most pressing problems?

Is it relevant to the challenges of the 1990s and the coming new century?

We must remember, as we consider these questions, that the framers did not favor a government in which the mass of people would participate directly, or one that would be representative of or responsive to the people at-large. Rather, they sought to control both the spirit of faction and the thrust of majorities. Their prime concern was how to fashion a viable, but limited, government. The framers had not seen a political party in the modern sense and would not have liked it if they had. They did not favor an arousing, mobilizing kind of leadership, but preferred instead a stabilizing, balancing, magisterial leadership, the kind George Washington was expected to (and did) supply. Today we have high-pressure politics characterized by strongly organized groups and political-action committees, potent and volatile public opinion dominated by opinion-making agencies, parties vying to mobilize nationwide majorities, and celebrity-leaders intimately covered by the media. How responsive are our political agencies to fast-moving changes in public attitudes and moods? Will our Constitution and the system it created be able to deal with the problems of our third century?

According to an old story, Benjamin Franklin was confronted by a woman as he left the last session of the Constitutional Convention in Philadelphia in September 1787.

"What kind of government have you given us, Dr. Franklin?" she asked, "a Republic or a Monarchy?"

"A Republic, Madam," he answered, "—if you can keep it."

CHAPTER 2
THE LIVING CONSTITUTION

While it is true that many Americans venerate the Constitution chiefly because they hear it mentioned in reverent tones, the student of government must dissect this document to discover why it has survived while other charters fade away. Is the Constitution an idealistic document? Or does it make a rather "hard-boiled" appraisal of people and try to check human weakness with human weakness? Is the Constitution great because it is majestic and unshakable — a kind of Ten Commandments good for all places and times? Or is it great because it is vague and flexible — a work of art that may mean different things to different generations?

Obviously, the Constitution of the 1990s is not that of the 1780s, if only because of the amendment process. Twenty-seven amendments have both increased and restricted the scope of national power; state power has been limited; the democratic basis of American life has been undergirded by giving the vote to Blacks, women, and residents of the District of Columbia; selection of the President and Senate has been altered to give greater popular control.

But probably the most provocative question concerning the Constitution is that contained in the chapter title — "The Living Constitution." The original document itself is carefully preserved under glass in the National Archives and is an old, somewhat faded parchment in eighteenth-century handwriting.

Question: Why is the Constitution a living document?
One answer: The Constitution is alive because it has received new blood through amendment.
Another answer: The Constitution has retained its vitality because of informal changes — custom, tradition, interpretation.
Another answer: The Constitution is alive because its roots go deep into the American heritage, making it a document for the ages.

PART I — GUIDEPOSTS

1. Checking Power With Power
    a. The Constitution is both a symbol and an instrument. How does it function at each level?
    b. Explain with examples the manner in which separation of powers and checks and balances were combined by the Constitution makers? Why did they adopt this device?

2. Judicial Review
    a. What is it?
    b. How does it differ from British precedent?
    c. Who originally supported it? Who opposed it?
    d. What role was played by John Marshall in <u>Marbury</u> <u>v.</u> <u>Madison</u>? Why is it a landmark decision?

3. Checks and Balances
   a. Why was inefficiency built into our political system?
   b. What modifications of the original American system resulted from the rise of national political parties; the shift in presidential election arrangements; the appearance of administrative agencies; the increased importance of the presidential office?
   c. Contrast the British and American systems of government in the following respects:
      (1) British Prime Minister-American President
      (2) British Cabinet-American Cabinet
      (3) British Courts-U.S. Supreme Court
      (4) House of Lords-Senate
      (5) House of Commons-House of Representatives

4. The Constitution as an Instrument of Government
   a. In what four ways has our original written Constitution been modified informally? Give examples of each change.
   b. In what sense can it be argued that the Constitution has changed only slightly?
   c. Why has our Constitution managed to survive with relatively few amendments since 1787?

5. Changing The Letter of the Constitution
   a. What are two methods of proposing amendments? Why has one never been used?
   b. How are amendments ratified? Which is the more common method?
   c. What changes in national power have been made by amendment of the Constitution?
   d. How has state power been limited?
   e. How has the power of the voters been altered?
   f. How did the Twelfth and Twentieth Amendments change our constitutional structure?

6. Ratification Politics
   a. ERA, why did it fail adoption?
   b. The D.C. Amendment, why has it been opposed?

PART II — GLOSSARY

SEPARATION OF POWERS - A theory applied to the national government by the Constitution, dividing power between the three branches.

CHECKS AND BALANCES - The constitutional arrangement that makes the three branches of the American government politically independent of each other but requires that they carry out many of their functions in collaboration.

JUDICIAL REVIEW - The power exercised by the Supreme Court in determining the constitutionality of congressional or state legislation and the authority exercised by the president.

INTERDEPENDENCE - The constitutional arrangement that requires branches of the national government to share power rather than to operate independently of each other.

INFORMAL CONSTITUTION - Customs and practices of government, developed over two centuries, that carry authority equal to that of the written Constitution.

BROAD CONSTRUCTION - An interpretation of the Constitution and laws that grants officials great authority and flexibility.

NARROW CONSTRUCTION - A restricted interpretation of the Constitution and laws that closely limits officials actions.

IMPEACHABLE OFFENSE - Improper conduct involving dereliction of duty or violation of constitutional responsibilities.

WRIT OF MANDAMUS - A Court order directing an official to perform a duty.

MARBURY V. MADISON - Supreme Court decision of 1803 that established practice of judicial review.

PART III — PRETEST

1. The branch of government most likely to have dominated the framers' opinion was the
   a. bureaucracy.
   c. judicial.
   b. executive.
   d. legislative.

2. The Nixon impeachment process is a good example of constitutional development by way of
   a. judicial review.
   c. congressional elaboration.
   b. presidential practice.
   d. custom and usage.

3. The presidential nominating convention is a good example of constitutional development by way of
   a. presidential practice.
   b. congressional elaboration.
   c. custom and usage.
   d. judicial interpretation.

4. With one exception, ratification of constitutional amendments has been by action of
   a. the president.
   c. state conventions.
   b. the Supreme Court.
   d. state legislatures.

Match the items in the left column with the correct items from the right column.

5. separation of powers
6. checks and balances
7. shared powers
8. Marbury v. Madison
9. impeachment
10. informal Constitution

a. based on custom
b. lame duck Congress
c. allocates power among three branches
d. independent branches that are interdependent
e. established principle of judicial review
f. charges brought by House of Representatives
g. president signs congressional bill

PART IV — PROGRAMMED REVIEW

Knowledge Objective: To analyze the original constitutional arrangements that diffused political power

1. In the United States, the symbol of national loyalty and unity has been the _____ .
2. The constitutional arrangement that delegated certain powers to the national government and reserved the rest for the states is called _____ .
3. The framers of the Constitution did not fully trust either _____ or the _____ .
4. The allocation of constitutional authority among three branches of the national government is known as _____ _____ _____ .
5. The framers devised a system of shared power that is described by the term _____ _____ _____ .
6. The varying terms of office for national officials were intended to prevent rapid changes by a popular _____ .
7. In the United States the ultimate keeper of our constitutional conscience is the _____ _____ .
8. The court case that established the practice of judicial review was _____ v. _____ .

Knowledge Objective: To examine the developments that have modified the original checks and balances system

9. The president, Congress, and even judges have been drawn together in the American system by _____ _____ .
10. Originally neither the _____ nor _____ were elected directly by the people.
11. Legislative, executive, and judicial functions are combined in some agencies, weakening the concept of _____ _____ _____ .
12. In the modern United States, the branch of government that has acquired the greatest power is the _____ .
13. The British system concentrates power and control in the _____ _____ .

Knowledge Objective: To trace evolution of the Constitution by custom and interpretation

14. The customs, traditions, and rules that have evolved over the past two centuries are referred to as a(an) _____ Constitution.
15. The structure of the national judicial system was defined by action of _____ .
16. The most discussed example of congressional elaboration of the Constitution during the Nixon years was the _____ process.
17. _____ realities have increased the importance of the presidency.
18. The Constitution has been adapted to changing times largely through judicial _____ .

Knowledge Objective: To analyze the amendment process and the constitutional changes made by it

19. To initiate a constitutional amendment requires a _____ vote by both houses of Congress.
20. Although it has never been used, an amendment can be proposed by a _____ _____ .
21. A proposed amendment must be ratified in three-fourths of the states by either their _____ or _____ _____ .
22. Congress (has, has not) _____ proposed a great number of amendments.

Knowledge Objective: To examine politics of the amendment process in cases of ERA and the D.C. Amendments

23. In the case of _____ Congress altered the normal process by extending the time for ratification.
24. Equal Rights Amendment ratification has been blocked chiefly by a group of _____ states.
25. Opposition to the D.C. Amendment has come from _____ and _____ _____ districts.

PART V — POST-TEST

1. The framers of the Constitution depended heavily on which of the following assumptions about human behavior?
    a. Ambition will serve to check ambition.
    b. Most people want to do the right thing.
    c. People are normally apathetic.
    d. Human savagery always lurks below the thin veneer of civilization.

2. The Founding Fathers created a system that
    a. encouraged participatory democracy.
    b. favored the popular majority.
    c. restricted decision making by popular majority.
    d. emphasized prompt, decisive government action.

3. The British democratic system differs from the American system in that
 a. the queen reigns but doesn't rule.
 b. Parliament has only one house.
 c. government authority is concentrated in Parliament.
 d. the High Court exercises judicial review.

4. The original checks and balances system has been modified by *all but one* of the following.
 a. the rise of political parties
 b. creation of regulatory agencies
 c. direct election of senators
 d. giving representatives a four-year term

5. As originally drafted, the Constitution was expected to
 a. cover all foreseeable situations.
 b. be a legal code, combining the framework of government and specific laws.
 c. be a general framework of government.
 d. be a philosophical statement of the relationships between individuals and society.

6. The Constitution of the United States has been altered without formal amendment by *all but one* of the following methods.
 a. congressional elaboration
 b. presidential practice
 c. custom and usage
 d. interposition by states

7. Compared to many state constitutions, the national constitution is more
 a. recent. c. specific.
 b. complicated. d. flexible.

8. The major tool of the courts in checking the power of other government branches has been
 a. impeachment. c. judicial review.
 b. *habeas corpus.* d. common law.

9. The constitutional arrangement that limits the power of American officials is known as
 a. separation of powers. c. sharing of powers.
 b. prohibitions on authority. d. implied powers.

10. During the Revolutionary period, legislatures
 a. were curbed by the checks and balances system.
 b. became the dominant branch of government.
 c. suffered from a steady decrease in power.
 d. governed firmly and wisely.

PART VI — POLITICAL DIALOGUE: THE CLASH OF ISSUES AND IDEAS

1. Comment on the following statement:
 "Every nation needs certain semi-mystical symbols around which all men can rally — a flag, a man, a national anthem, the sacred writings of their forefathers. The Constitution as a symbol is such a common rallying point for Americans, be they Jew, Catholic, Protestant, atheist; be they Slav, Italian, Scot, or Swede; be they Democrat or Republican."

Do nations need symbols? Why? What problems of this nature do the new African nations face?

Suggest a symbolic device used by a nation other than the United States.

2. Thomas Jefferson advocated that a new Constitution be adopted by every generation so that it belonged to the living, rather than the dead.

Would you approve of an automatic Constitutional Convention scheduled at 30 year intervals?

What advantages would such an arrangement have?

What would be apt to happen to the symbolic value of the Constitution?

3. "Beyond the Bill of Rights, few Constitutional amendments have radically altered the American system of government. Slavery was actually abolished by warfare, rather than legislation. In all probability a new Supreme Court majority would have authorized the graduated income tax. Senators were actually chosen by the people long before the amendment was passed; women would today have the vote, Nineteenth Amendment or no."

Is this analysis valid? Can you find further evidence to make this point? Can you think of evidence that contradicts this thesis?

4. React to the following extract from a modern political speech:

"Today we live in perilous times, dominated by such doctrines as relativity. Our forefathers, the Founding Fathers, authored a great document, as valid for all time as the Ten Commandments. But modern judges, clever lawyers, have made of this Rock of Gibraltar a weathervane, which swings to the prevailing political winds. Instead of the Old Constitution, which stood four-square, they have constructed a barometer that rises and falls with every sentiment of the mob, every changing whim of the sociologists or psychologists."

Is this a fair charge? Why?

5. "In a very fundamental sense the Constitution is undemocratic. It originally became operative when adopted by simple majorities of the conventions called in nine of the thirteen states."

"Yet the amendment process was filled with traps and pitfalls that thwarted the majority will. All proposals for amendment were dependent on a two-thirds majority: ratification was dependent on lopsided three-fourths majorities. In other words, the Constitution was an iron trap — easy to enter; almost impossible to alter."

Do you agree? Why? What explanation can be offered for the amendment process? Can it be defended? How have most modifications in our fundamental law been achieved?

PART VII — POLITICAL SCIENCE TODAY

1. Once again, review Madison's famed constitutional admonition that "ambition must be made to counteract ambition." Now look through recent issues of your local or a national newspaper and see if you can find examples of this "ambition checking" either by the respective branches of government being pitted against each other or even powerful interest groups being checked by other powerful interest groups. Try to compile a list of these actions with a brief description as to how Madison's principle was actually being realized.

2. Not every "observer" is enamored of those amendments to the Constitution which followed the original Bill of Rights. Russell Baker, in The New York Times Magazine issue of September 13, 1987 (a special issue devoted to the 200 years of the Constitution), argues that the last 10 amendments, all adopted since 1913, are a collective testimonial to the "ruin and decay" of the 20th century (p. 28).

In a column entitled "Amendment Addendum," Baker asserts that the 17th amendment involving direct election of U.S. Senators has led to candidates needing massive amounts of funding for television and a corresponding dependence on PACs. As Baker puts it, "is it not disgraceful that the Senate should be a society of the rich whose riches, increasing daily as the PACs churn out the moola, makes them invulnerable to challenge from any but the absolutely filthiest rich? The 17th Amendment created this blight."

Baker applauds the 19th Amendment (woman's suffrage), the 23rd (giving the vote to the District of Columbia), and the 24th (abolishing the poll tax, a restriction on voting), but derides the many years it took for these amendments to become a reality. He reserves his greatest scorn for the 20th, 22nd, 25th, and 26th Amendments by stating that the Constitution would be better off without them:

(1) *20th* - This moves the inauguration of Presidents forward from the old date of March 4 to January 20. A terrible idea. At present, candidates spend two years campaigning, leaving the winner exhausted by Election Day. Just when they desperately need a six-week vacation, he is given 10 weeks to create a government capable of directing one of the planet's most complex societies and get his Christmas shopping done.

It is a silly system that devotes two years to campaigning but only 10 weeks to creating a government. A sensible system would have a skilled governing group (like the British 'shadow cabinet') already in place. Barring that, we might at least give the winning candidate six or eight months to prepare himself for the work before taking office. The 20th Amendment makes a bad situation impossible.

(2) *22nd* - Limiting Presidents to two terms was not only a shoddy act of retroactive spite against four-termer Franklin Roosevelt that cheapens the Constitution, but had also prevented two popular Presidents, Eisenhower and Reagan, from sustaining their power and possibly running for third terms.

(3) *25th* - A nightmare of lawyers on picnic, this tries to lay down rules of conduct for coping with the unforeseeable. The subject is Presidential disability. Who decides what it is? How do you replace a President without elections? This is a bomb ticking in the Constitution. If it explodes, we could end up with two feuding Presidents and only one button.

(4) *26th* - This grants the vote to 18-year olds in an era when 18 is much younger than it was 200 years ago. Then, men in their 30's helped draft the Constitution. Nowadays, you find people in their 30's still at school and dependent on parental remittances. Does it make any sense to let people vote before they've had to pay the bills?

Keep Russell Baker's criticisms of these amendments in mind as you progress through your course in American Government. You may wish to debate the merits of Baker's views now or even incorporate them into an analytical research paper or oral report. At the very minimum, jot down your impressions of his arguments now and return to them at a later point in the course.

3. The *27th* Amendment was added to the U.S. Constitution in 1992. It deals with the issue of congressional pay raises. What is unique about this amendment is that it took about 200 years to

become part of the Constitution. Research the background of this amendment by looking at 1992 articles from Time, Newsweek, U.S. News and World Report, etc. that covered this amendment's passage. In particular, try to find out what the reaction of members of Congress was to the amendment and what controversy surrounded its ratification (hint: did it violate the traditional time for ratification?).

4. What other amendments have been considered in recent years? Investigate the balanced-budget and school-prayer possibilities as well as their respective pros and cons.

PART VIII — DATA ANALYSIS

1. One of the most fundamental premises in the Constitution is that there are three major governmental powers which, if government is to be constrained, must be placed into the hands of three separate institutions. Accordingly, the Constitution established the Congress, the Presidency, and the Supreme Court and empowered them with the legislative, executive, and judicial powers, respectively.

   Read Articles I, II, and III of the Constitution. Determine which branch has primary control over each of the powers listed below. Place the letter "C" (for Congress), "P" (for President), or "S" (for Supreme Court) in the space provided.

   _____ power to declare war
   _____ power to command the armed services
   _____ power to lay and collect taxes
   _____ power to hear legal cases arising under the U.S. Constitution and U.S. laws
   _____ power to grant pardons for federal offenses
   _____ power to negotiate treaties
   _____ power to receive ambassadors from other countries
   _____ power to appoint ambassadors
   _____ power to hear controversies between two or more states
   _____ power to establish courts inferior to the Supreme Court
   _____ power to propose amendments to the Constitution

2. Upon reading the Constitution and the text, you may see that the separation of powers is not a neat, clean system. Each branch is given some responsibility in the functioning of the other branches, and so each branch has the potential power to control or constrain the actions of the others. This is the concept of checks and balances.

   Provide at least two examples for each of the following.

   (a) Congressional checks on the President
   (b) Congressional checks on the Supreme Court
   (c) Presidential checks on the Congress
   (d) Presidential checks on the Supreme Court
   (e) Supreme Court checks on the Congress
   (f) Supreme Court checks on the President

PART IX — TEST ANSWERS

Pretest

1. d	6. d
2. c	7. g
3. c	8. e
4. d	9. f
5. c	10. a

Programmed Review

1. Constitution	14. informal
2. federalism	15. Congress
3. public officials; majority	16. impeachment
4. separation of powers	17. global
5. checks and balances	18. interpretation
6. majority	19. two-thirds
7. Supreme Court	20. constitutional convention
8. <u>Marbury</u> v. <u>Madison</u>	21. legislatures; ratifying conventions
9. political parties	22. has not
10. president; senators	23. ERA
11. checks and balances	24. southern
12. executive	25. rural; small town
13. legislative branch	

Post-test

1. a	6. d
2. c	7. d
3. c	8. c
4. d	9. a
5. c	10. b

Data Analysis

1. In order to encourage you to read the Constitution, not all the answers will be provided for in exercise 1. As a start however, the "power to declare war" should have a "C" for Congress and the "power to command the armed services" is a "P" for president since he is commander-in-chief of all armed forces according to the Constitution.

2. Data Analysis #2 requires research as well. But to help you get started, you should consider the power of the veto, judicial review, and ratification of treaties as all being involved in the system of checks and balances. Good luck on completing the exercise!

CHAPTER 3
AMERICAN FEDERALISM

The United States has a federal type of government, with power divided between the states and the nation. This division is spelled out in general terms in the Constitution. It is also an endless source of conflict. As this chapter demonstrates, a federal government is a good deal more complicated than one in which power is centralized or decentralized.

Federalism is more than a remote constitutional theory. It is also a day-by-day political issue involving money, influence, power, and people. The various levels of government intermesh to provide a total government for Americans. In recent years the big debate has been over the disbursement of national funds to states and communities — who gets what, when, where, and how.

Question: Can a case be made for "states rights" today?

One Answer: Yes! In spite of improvements in communication and transportation, the United States is still a diverse land which is governed best when there is a great deal of regional autonomy. Our federal system is a happy compromise that provides both unity and diversity.

Another Answer: Our policy of leaving great blocs of power with the state governments has made it possible to do a great deal of regional experimentation. Our states should be viewed as political science laboratories.

Another Answer: No! "States rights" has become a slogan used to defend otherwise indefensible practices — to oppose positive action by the national government and to prevent parallel action by the state governments. Behind the "states rights" facade is a philosophy of "do nothing."

Many of our great political debates have centered around the question of the future of national-state relationships. In an elementary form, the issue becomes:

Question: Is our present federal system threatened by current trends and policies? What is the future of states rights?

One Answer: If present trends are extended, the state governments will gradually wither away. We should fight any expansion of the power of the national government and guard against any parallel expansion of government at the state level.

Another Answer: Both state and national governments of necessity have expanded their activity in this century. If state governments are to maintain their present position in the federal equation, they must assume a more aggressive role in solving modern social-economic problems.

Another Answer: As we become more unified, the necessity for local government will decline. Most of our problems will be national problems, beyond the competence of regional governments.

PART I — GUIDEPOSTS

1. Why Federalism?
    a. Distinguish between a federal government and a confederation and give an example of each.
    b. Why was federalism rather than a unitary state the only realistic arrangement in 1787?
    c. What advantages has federalism offered with respect to:
    (1) American expansion

(2) diversity
(3) social-economic experiments
(4) political leadership

2. Constitutional Structure of Federalism
    a. What is meant by expressed national powers? Implied powers? Inherent powers?
    b. How have each of the following powers contributed to expansion of the national government?
        (1) war
        (2) commerce
        (3) taxation - general welfare
    c. What powers are left to the state?
    d. What constitutional restraints were put on the national government? The state government?
    e. What forms does horizontal federalism take? Give an example of full faith and credit; interstate privileges and immunities; extradition.

3. The Politics of Federalism
    a. How have each of the following factors brought a demand for expanded national government:
        (1) urbanization and population growth
        (2) world power status
        (3) transportation - communication changes
        (4) concentration of private economic power
    b. What was the original nationalist position on federalism?
    c. What was the states rights position?

4. The Role of the Federal Courts
    a. What issues were at stake in McCulloch vs. Maryland? How were they decided?
    b. What was the impact of the Garcia decision?
    c. Over the years when has the Supreme Court favored a position that makes it, rather than Congress, the ultimate umpire in contests between the states and the national government?

5. Federal Grants and Regulations
    a. What is the distinction between categorical formula grants, project grants, and block grants?
    b. Why was revenue sharing eliminated?
    c. What groups favor the various types of grants?
    d. What does the term "iron triangle" mean as applied to grant policy?
    e. What has been the result of grant consolidation under Reagan, Bush, and Clinton?
    f. What four types of regulations are involved in federal grants?

6. Federalism: a Look to the Future
    a. How has direct aid to subordinate governments affected federalism? What is the current trend?
    b. How have ideological positions been involved in federal power contests?
    c. What was the impact of federal deficits during the Reagan-Bush years in grant policy?
    d. What is the long-range prognosis on the durability of the states?

PART II — GLOSSARY

FEDERAL GOVERNMENT - A government with power divided between the national and constituent governments by a Constitution. Commonly used as a synonym for "national government."

CONSTITUENT GOVERNMENT - One of the units composing a federation.

UNITARY GOVERNMENT - A government in which all power is held by the central authority.

CONFEDERATION- A government in which the central authority derives all its powers from the member states.

EXPRESS POWERS - Powers specifically granted to the national government by the Constitution.

IMPLIED POWERS - Powers that by inference belong to the national government as a result of its enumerated powers.

INHERENT POWERS - Undelegated powers belonging to the national government by virtue of its existence.

CONCURRENT POWERS - Powers shared by the national and state governments.

RESERVED POWERS - All powers not delegated to the national government or prohibited to the states.

STATES' RIGHTS DOCTRINE - The theory that the national government is a creation of the state governments, with very limited powers, narrowly defined.

MCCULLOCH V. MARYLAND (1819) - Supreme Court decision that established the doctrine of National Supremacy as a guiding principle.

FULL FAITH AND CREDIT - Clause in the Constitution that requires each state to recognize civil judgments rendered by courts of other states.

EXTRADITION - Legal process whereby an alleged criminal is surrendered by one state to the one in which he/she committed the crime.

INTERSTATE COMPACT - Agreement among states on some question of common interest.

PROJECT GRANT - A national grant to a state, community, or college or other institution to carry out an approved project.

BLOCK GRANT - A federal allotment for a general program made to a state or local government with no strings attached.

IRON TRIANGLE - The three groups (executive agencies, interest groups, Congressional committees) involved in shaping grant policy.

PART III — PRETEST

1. The best argument for retention of our federal system would be that it
   a. prevents the centralization of power.
   b. provides cheap, efficient government.
   c. simplifies political party organization.
   d. provides both unity and diversity.

2. The national government has *all but one* of the following powers.
   a. implied
   b. inherent
   c. reserved
   d. delegated

3. The state governments have *only one* of the following sets of powers.
   a. delegated and reserved
   b. reserved and concurrent
   c. direct and inherent
   d. expressed and implied

4. The states' rights interpretation of the Constitution conflicts with one of these concepts.
   a. broad construction
   b. reserved powers
   c. treaty among sovereign states
   d. state governments closer to people

5. The power of the national government that has not been a chief source of its expansion is
   a. to coin money.
   b. to declare war.
   c. to regulate interstate commerce.
   d. to levy taxes.

6. Currently one of the following best defines the power of the national government.
   a. all power specifically delegated by the Constitution
   b. delegated powers plus powers implied from the delegated ones
   c. whatever needs to be done to promote the general welfare
   d. dependent on which party is in power

7. In our history, northerners, southerners, business people, and workers have
   a. consistently agreed on the role of the state governments.
   b. held to a single opinion with respect to national powers.
   c. changed sides in the debate over national-state powers.
   d. shown no discernible pattern of opinion at all.

8. Any group that "has the votes" in Washington is almost certain to favor
   a. a strong national government.
   b. states' rights.
   c. a Supreme court critical of congressional power.
   d. local government as being closer to the people.

9. The great expansion of our grant-in-aid system occurred during
   a. the New Deal.   c. World War I.
   b. the 1960s.   d. World War II.

10. A federal grant that gives a state the right to spend money within a broad category is called a
   a. project grant.   c. community action grant.
   b. block grant.   d. grant-in-aid.

PART IV — PROGRAMMED REVIEW

Knowledge Objective: To contrast federalism with alternate forms of government and to discover what advantages it offers Americans

1. A _____ government divides power between a central government and constituent governments.
2. The central government of a confederation exercises no power over _____ .
3. A _____ government vests all power in the central government.
4. The relationship between American state and city governments is an example of the _____ form of government.
5. A federal government provides for _____ without uniformity.
6. Under our federal system such questions as divorce, gun control, and school dress codes are _____ issues.
7. The American people are most concerned with _____ politics.

Knowledge Objective: To define how the Constitution allots power and the limitations it imposes

8. The three major powers of Congress upon which national expansion is based are _____ , _____ , and _____ .

9. The Constitution delegates to Congress both _____ powers and _____ powers.

10. As an independent nation, the national government has certain _____ powers.

11. The powers shared by the national and state governments are called _____ powers.

12. The Constitution requires that the national government guarantee to every state a _____ form of government.

13. The _____ clause requires states to enforce civil judgments of other states.

14. The process by which a criminal is surrendered by one state to another is called _____ .

15. A binding agreement among states that is approved by Congress is known as an _____ _____ .

Knowledge Objective: To trace and explain the growth of the national government and the expanding role of the federal courts

16. Today Congress has the power to deal with (any, delegated) _____ issues.

17. The _____ interpretation of the Constitution argued that the national government was created by the states.

18. The nationalist interpretation of the Constitution argued that the national government was an agent of the _____ rather than the states.

19. The concept of implied powers for the national government was first established by the Supreme Court in _____ _____ _____ .

20. The Chief Justice of the Supreme Court who first set forth the doctrine of national supremacy was _____ _____ .

21. The umpire of the Federal system that has favored the national government is the _____ _____ .

22. The expansion of the national government can be explained in large part by our evolution from an agrarian society to an _____ society.

23. Our urban society has created a demand for programs operated by the _____ government.

24. Today many Americans identify closely with the national government because of their daily exposure to _____ .

25. In the Garcia case the Court declared _____ , not the federal courts, should decide which state actions should be regulated.

26. The court action giving Congress the right to assume total power over a state issue is called _____ .

Knowledge Objective: To differentiate among the various types of federal grant programs and controls

27. _____ _____ grants involve matching federal-state funds for a specific program.

28. Local communities can receive federal funds directly outside any formula distribution under _____ grants.

29. Federal funds distributed according to formula for a broad purpose are called _____ grants.

30. The federal grant program phased out by the Reagan administration was _____ _____ .

31. Federal regulations that bar state-local discrimination in employment are an example of _____ _____ .

32. The national government has indirectly regulated automobile speed limits and minimum drinking ages through its financing of _____ construction.

33. Under the Reagan administration, national control of state and local governments (was, was not) _____ diminished significantly.

Knowledge Objective: To consider the relationship that has developed between national and urban government

34. During the 1960s federal grant policy created a financial bond between the national government and _____ .

35. In recent years city officials have found state governments to be (more, less) _____ responsive to their problems.

36. _____ ideology normally favors state-local government.

37. The expansion of national grant programs has been curbed in recent years by budget _____ .

38. In recent years the quality of state government has (improved, deteriorated)_____ .

PART V — POST-TEST

1. The "states' righters" basic premise is that the Constitution is a
    a. statement of principles.
    b. union of people.
    c. treaty among sovereign states.
    d. document inspired by God.

2. The basic nationalist premise is that the Constitution is a supreme law established by the
    a. people.   c. Creator.
    b. state.   d. Continental Congress.

3. Federalism can be defended in *all but one* of the following ways.
    a. Political experimentation is encouraged.
    b. Governed and governors are in closer contact.
    c. Allowances are made for differences.
    d. A national majority can more easily implement its program.

4. The supreme law of the land is composed of *all but one* of the following.
    a. the Supreme Court   c. U.S. law
    b. the U.S. Constitution   d. U.S. treaties

5. John Marshall's decision in <u>McCulloch</u> <u>v</u>. <u>Maryland</u> was that
    a. the government did not have authority to operate a bank.
    b. state tax powers are unlimited within their boundaries.
    c. Scottish naturalized immigrants can sit on the Supreme Court.
    d. the national government has the authority to carry out its powers in a variety of ways.

6. In interstate relations each state must accept without question
    a. a demand for extradition.
    b. enforcement of civil judgment.
    c. a Nevada divorce.
    d. immediate voting rights for the other state's citizens.

7. The average citizen of the United States today
    a. follows closely the activities of the state legislature.
    b. regards the citizens of other states as foreigners.
    c. is in close contact with local and state officials.
    d. is best informed about the national political scene.

8. Throughout our history, business had advocated
     a. states' rights.
     b. national supremacy.
     c. neither a nor b
     d. both a and b

9. The present mood of the country with respect to federalism is best described as
     a. confused.
     b. pro city hall.
     c. less revenue-sharing.
     d. states' rights.

10. Under its partial preemption regulations, the national government has sought to control
     a. surface mining.
     b. air quality standards.
     c. highway speed limits.
     d. occupational safety.

PART VI — POLITICAL DIALOGUE: THE CLASH OF ISSUES AND IDEAS

1. "Lord Acton wrote long ago that 'power corrupts; absolute power tends to corrupt absolutely.' The growth of the national government can largely be explained by pursuing this theory. Government always expands; government never grows smaller. Public officials always reach for more power. This, rather than the growing need for governmental services, explains the consolidation of power in Washington."

   Do you find this rather common explanation of the expansion of government persuasive? Try to arrive at your answer by testing it against national powers of regulation developed under the commerce clause in this century. Why do we have a federal law prohibiting adulterated goods? Automobile theft? Bank robbery? Kidnapping? Transportation of women for immoral purposes? Was such legislation the result of a ground swell of popular demand, or was it imposed from above by government officials?

2. "Even though we concede that inadequate communication, transportation, and parochialism in 1787 precluded anything but a federal government, that type is as antiquated as the dinosaur in the 1990s. We fly across the United States more rapidly than a horseman of 1787 could cross Rhode Island. Our communication system is characterized by split-second radio and T.V. transmission. We no longer think of ourselves as New Mexicans, Michiganders, or Virginians."
     a. What basic assumption does the author make regarding the origin and necessity for federalism?
     b. If this assumption is granted, is his analysis correct?
     c. What other factors or assumptions, if any, do you feel that he has overlooked?

3. Ronald Reagan labeled his revenue sharing proposals as the New Federalism. He pictured millions of Americans as resentful of the idea that "a bureaucratic elite in Washington knows best what is best for people everywhere and that you cannot trust local governments . . . Local government is the government closest to the people; it is most responsive to the individual person; it is people's government in a far more intimate way than the government in Washington can ever be."
     a. In what sense can it be argued that government at the local level is closer to and more responsive to the people? Which people?
     b. What does your text suggest regarding the relative knowledge of citizens about the men and issues at the national and local levels?
     c. Why don't all local and state governments tax their people heavily enough to operate their own governments?

4. Discuss:
   a. "State governments today are providing effective, responsive government."
   b. "Before too long the only people interested in state boundaries will be Rand-McNally."
   c. "The expansion of direct federal aid has given local governments unmistakable status as a third component of the system."
   d. "The good sense and practical judgment of Americans (helps them) evade numberless difficulties resulting from the Federal Constitution."

PART VII — POLITICAL SCIENCE TODAY

1. Check with your local government — perhaps the mayor's office or the office of a city councilman — to see if your hometown has ever received a federal grant of any kind. If so, research how much money was in the grant, for what purpose the grant money was allocated, and what procedures the local government had to follow in order to apply and receive the grant. The whole research process may help you to understand better the politics of fiscal federalism.

2. Review the chapter question which follows the respective arguments made by the centralists vs. the decentralists, i.e., "Look closely at the operation of your state and city government. Do the facts as you know them support the contentions of the centralists?" In order to answer the chapter query even more effectively, show the list of arguments to local political officials. Their responses could be tabulated and used in compiling a data base on attitudes toward federalism. In addition, do any of the respective arguments, be they on the centralist or decentralist side, strike you as particularly compelling? If so, explain why?

3. One of the advantages of federalism is the ability of state and local governments to take policy initiatives or political actions well before the federal government. In this way, the political "grass-roots" of the nation can become a valuable wellspring of political efficacy and renewed citizenship.

   A typical example of this process was documented in a July 2, 1989 New York Times article entitled "Grass-Roots Groups Show Power Battling Pollution Close to Home" written by reporter Roberto Suro (p. 1, 12). Suro began his analysis with the following lead paragraph:

   A new form of environmental protest is spreading through the country as thousands of people band together in small community groups. Their target is usually pollution by local industrial plants, employers traditionally respected but not reviled as prisoners of the neighborhood.

   People with no previous interest in environmental issues or other civic affairs are often the leaders of these grass-roots efforts. Since their targets are frequently smokestacks visible from their front doors, the new protesters include many from the working poor in addition to more affluent people who can afford to live farther away. (p. 1)

   Gerry Poje, chief environmental toxicologist at the National Wildlife Federation, said: "A reordering of priorities, a rethinking of strategy and tactics is taking place throughout the entire environmental movement because of the increased activism by the very people who are most at risk. Here in Washington it is becoming increasingly obvious that true change will occur at the local level." (p. 1)

   Suro pointed out that the proliferation of grass-roots environmental groups reflected the growing concern of Americans with environmental hazards and the dangers to health they pose. Suro describes what specific actions these groups were taking to protect the environment:

Many of the new community groups are seeking relief through traditional channels like filing suits or petitioning legislative and regulatory bodies. But at the same time new avenues are also being explored, as local organizations try to negotiate directly with the management of individual plants. (p. 12)

In addition, many of these groups were enlisting the support of employees in the polluting plants, gaining information which could then be used in lawsuits or petitions. In short, an era of much stronger environmental activism was emerging, reflecting a traditional strength of federalism.

Are there any similar environmental groups working in your local community, state, or even region of the country? If so, try to find out more about their activities.

PART VIII — DATA ANALYSIS

1. In recent years, critics of American education have argued that the federal government should establish national standards for all fifty states in the form of uniform testing and even curriculum. These critics assert that American schools vary too much from state to state, and even from locality to locality. American schools must improve and become more demanding of students across the entire nation. Only in this way can America compete with other nations such as Japan.

   What would tighter federal controls over education do to the traditional American ideal of local autonomy? How would a "federalized school system" impair the structure of federalism? Finally, do you think greater federal supervision is the answer to America's school problems—why or why not?

2. Given the challenges that America faces in the 21st century, should American federal and state officials consider transforming the nation into a unitary system? What would be three advantages and disadvantages of such a move?

PART IX — TEST ANSWERS

Pretest

1. d
2. c
3. b
4. a
5. a

6. c
7. c
8. a
9. b
10. b

Programmed Review

1. federal
2. individuals
3. unitary
4. unitary
5. unity
6. state
7. national
8. war, commerce, tax
9. express; implied
10. inherent
11. concurrent
12. republican
13. full faith and credit
14. extradition
15. interstate compact
16. any
17. states' rights
18. people
19. McCulloch v. Maryland

20. John Marshall
21. Supreme Court
22. industrial
23. national
24. television
25. Congress
26. preemption
27. categorical formula
28. project
29. block
30. revenue sharing
31. direct orders
32. highway
33. was not
34. cities
35. more
36. Conservative
37. deficits
38. improved

Post-test

1. c
2. a
3. d
4. a
5. d

6. b
7. d
8. d
9. a
10. b

Data Analysis

Both data analysis questions do not have specific answers. They are open-ended and will vary depending upon each student's research effort.

CHAPTER 4
FIRST AMENDMENT RIGHTS

The First Amendment, by general agreement, is the most sweeping part of the Bill of Rights. Here, in a single sentence, Madison defined those rights that were beyond the reach of the new Congress: the establishment of a national church, freedom of religious belief, a free press, free speech, and rights of assembly and petition. Although at the outset, these prohibitions did not apply to the individual states, through Court interpretation and action of the state legislatures themselves they were extended to embrace the states as well. Nine of the original thirteen colonies had established churches, taxation for their support and membership as a requirement for office holding. Jefferson, who played an active role in eliminating the Virginia establishment had inscribed on his tombstone: "Here lies buried Thomas Jefferson, author of the American Declaration of Independence, the Virginia statute for religious freedom, and founder of the University of Virginia."

Other rights embedded in the same amendment had been subject to controversy in the Mother Country and the colonies for centuries. They were established as fundamental freedoms by the stroke of a quill pen.

Of course, the definition of the scope of these rights is a never-ending subject of controversy. What does the concept of a "wall of separation" mean? How does freedom of the press apply to TV? How does freedom of assembly and right of petition apply to shopping malls? But such questions should not obscure the central fact — that Americans have fundamental rights on these issues embedded in their Constitution in written form.

PART I — GUIDEPOSTS

1. Basic Supports of a Free Society
    a. What rights are guaranteed to U.S. citizens by the First Amendment?
    b. To what government did the Bill of Rights originally apply?
    c. How was that interpretation expanded by Gitlow v. New York?
    d. Today, which trend has developed at the state level to enlarge the national Bill of Rights?

2. Religion: A Wall of Separation
    a. What is meant by an "establishment of religion?" Why did our colonial experience prompt this prohibition?
    b. How have we attempted to walk the fine line between "accommodation," "nonpreferential" and "nonestablishment" positions? How is this balancing act applied to nativity scenes, devotional exercises, teaching evolution, Bible study, parochial schools, and taxation?
    c. How has the right to freedom of worship been interpreted?

3. Free Speech and Free People
    a. Why did Justice Holmes believe that free speech was the best test of truth?
    b. What distinction exists between speech, belief, and action?
    c. Distinguish between protected and unprotected speech under the:
        • bad tendency doctrine
        • clear and present danger doctrine
        • preferred position doctrine

d. Why is the Court skeptical of all forms of prior restraint?

e. Why does the Court challenge restrictions on speech that it regards as vague or overly broad?

4. Freedom of the Press

a. Why does the press believe it has special rights? Does the Court agree?

b. What is a sunshine law?

c. What has been the impact of the Freedom of Information Act?

d. How is the claim of executive privilege restricted?

e. Why do reporters want "shield laws"?

f. Does TV coverage prevent a fair trial?

g. Are there special restrictions that are applied to the mails, motion pictures, handbills, sound tracks, billboards, picketing, and advertising?

h. How has the Fairness Doctrine been modified? The equal time requirement?

i. What exceptions to the equal time rule have been applied to presidential debates?

j. What developments during recent years have thrown the special status of TV broadcasters into question?

k. Where does cable TV fit into the free press guarantee?

l. What problems have FAX, 900 telephone numbers and auto dialers created?

5. Libel, Obscenity and Fighting Words

a. What is libel? Why are public and private persons treated differently under libel laws?

b. Do we have evidence that pornography has a relationship to behavior patterns?

c. How much authority do local communities have in declaring materials obscene?

d. What groups have formed a coalition to oppose pornography?

6. Peaceable Assembly, Petitions, and Associations

a. Cite several "assemblies" that led to concern for public order. What sort of statutes are necessary to deal with such issues?

b. How does the place that a rally is held have a bearing on its legality?

c. Can restrictions be placed on the expenditures of private groups to back a candidate for office?

d. What constitutional rights, if any, do each of these persons have: traitors, terrorists, spies, saboteurs, revolutionaries, and flag burners?

e. What events prompted the Sedition Act of 1798? What actions were proscribed by the Smith Act of 1940?

PART II — GLOSSARY

LIBEL - A written defamation of another person. Public figures have less protection than private citizens.

SEDITION - Written or oral criticism of government, or urging its forceful overthrow.

FAIRNESS DOCTRINE - A regulation, not now enforced, that required TV and radio stations to air conflicting opinions.

EQUAL TIME REQUIREMENT - A regulation that would require all candidates for public office equal access to radio and TV. As now applied, this requirement involves only TV debates of the two major party Presidential candidates.

FREEDOM OF INFORMATION ACT - Legislation that makes records of federal officials and agencies available.

SUNSHINE LAWS - Required public agencies to open their meetings to the general public.

SHIELD LAW - A state law that protects the sources used by a reporter from questioning in a trial.

EXECUTIVE PRIVILEGE - A right claimed by presidents to withhold information that would jeopardize national security.

NONPREFERENTIALIST VIEW - Court doctrine that allows government to support religious activities that favor no specific faith.

ACCOMMODATIONIST DOCTRINE - Permits government support of activities that are only incidentally religious.

NEW JUDICIAL FEDERALISM - The doctrine that states may extend freedoms guaranteed by the national Bill of Rights.

ESTABLISHMENT CLAUSE - The clause in the First Amendment that states "Congress shall make no law respecting the establishment of religion . . ."

WALL OF SEPARATION - The doctrine that holds that the Constitution prohibits both the state and national governments from aiding any and all religions and religious activities.

EXCESSIVE GOVERNMENT ENTANGLEMENT - The ruling in <u>Lemon</u> v. <u>Kurtzman</u>* (1971) that a statute, to be constitutional, must not foster "an excessive government entanglement with religion."

FIGHTING WORDS - Words that have traditionally been recognized as likely by their very nature to inflict injury or incite an immediate breach of the peace.

CLEAR AND PRESENT DANGER - A test requiring that speech can be inhibited only when it constitutes a clear and imminent danger to substantial interests.

DANGEROUS TENDENCY - The doctrine which holds that speech may be prevented if it tends to lead to substantive evil.

PREFERRED POSITION - A formula that gives a special or privileged position to the First Amendment freedoms in our constitutional system.

PRIOR RESTRAINT - The requirement that prior approval, usually in the form of a permit or license, must be obtained before communication is permitted. The Court has been highly critical of this type of regulation.

EXECUTIVE PRIVILEGE - The right of the president to withhold information if he feels the release would jeopardize security or confidentiality. The Court upheld a limited executive privilege.

*For Further information on this case, see *The New York Times*, November 2, 1994, p. A5.

PART III — PRETEST

1. Specifically, the Bill of Rights was aimed at
    a. the national government.
    b. the state governments.
    c. both national and state government.
    d. providing unlimited freedom to the people.

2. The due process clause, interpreted to mean that the states could not abridge the First Amendment freedoms, is part of the
    a. Fifteenth Amendment.   c. Eighteenth Amendment.
    b. Fourteenth Amendment.   d. Thirteenth Amendment.

3. Because of the Establishment Clause, states may not
    a. teach the Darwinian theory of evolution.
    b. study religion in public schools.
    c. permit religious instructors to teach in public schools during the day.
    d. establish Blue Laws.

4. The Supreme Court has held that tax funds may not be used to
    a. furnish secular textbooks in parochial schools.
    b. furnish guidance and remedial help in parochial schools.
    c. pay fares to send children to church-operated schools.
    d. pay parochial teachers' salaries.

5. The doctrine that free speech cannot be restricted unless there is a close connection between a speech and illegal action is called
    a. the clear and present danger test.
    b. the speech and dangerous result test.
    c. the speech and action test.
    d. absolutist doctrine.

6. Of all forms of government interference with expression, judges are most suspicious of those that
    a. trespass on First Amendment freedoms.
    b. limit freedom of speech of any kind.
    c. impose prior restraints on publication.
    d. impose *a posteriori* restraints.

7. The current standards for obscenity are made
    a. by the Supreme Court.   c. at the community.
    b. at the state level.   d. by Congress.

8. Persons may be convicted for
    a. possessing obscene materials.
    b. selling obscene literature.
    c. importing obscene literature from abroad.
    d. writing obscene material.

9. Street marches by protest groups are protected by the First Amendment right to
    a. assemble.   c. demonstrate.
    b. petition .   d. boycott.

10. The formula which imposed on licensees the obligation to see that issues of public significance are covered adequately on radio and television is called
    a. equality doctrine.   c. coverage doctrine.
    b. fairness doctrine.   d. broadcasting code.

PART IV — PROGRAMMED REVIEW

Knowledge Objective: To examine constitutional safeguards of freedom
    1. The first ten amendments to the Constitution are known as _____ _____ _____.
    2. The Bill of Rights originally limited only the _____ government.
    3. The _____ _____ clause of the Fourteenth Amendment protects freedom of the press and of speech from impairment by the states.

Knowledge Objective: To inquire into the meaning of the wall of separation between church and state
    4. The _____ clause is designed to prevent three main evils: sponsorship, financial support, and active involvement of the sovereign in religious activity.
    5. Chief Justice Rehnquist has supported the _____ concept that government may support religion if it avoids favoritism.
    6. The Court has held that a publicly sponsored Nativity scene (is, is not) _____ constitutional if the basic purpose is commercial.
    7. Because of the Establishment Clause, states may not prohibit the teaching of Darwin's theory of _____ .
    8. The Supreme Court has ruled that tax funds (may, may not) _____ be used for teacher salaries and instructional materials in religious schools.

9. Sponsorship of prayer in school buildings by public school authorities (is, is not) _____ constitutional.

10. The Supreme Court (has, has not)_____ upheld the right of parents to deduct from their state taxes expenses incurred in sending children to public/private schools.

Knowledge Objective: *To analyze the relationship between free speech and a free people*

11. Government's constitutional power to regulate speech involves three forms: beliefs, speech, and _____ .

12. The limits of free speech were set forth as the _____ _____ _____ _____ test by Justice Holmes in <u>Schneck</u> v. <u>United</u> <u>States</u>.

13. The _____ position doctrine takes the view that freedom of expression has the highest priority.

14. Of all forms of governmental interference with expression, judges are most suspicious of those that impose _____ restraint on publication.

15. When people of common intelligence differ on the requirements of a law, it is unconstitutional on the grounds of _____ .

Knowledge Objective: *To investigate the scope of freedom of the press*

16. In a recent decision the Supreme Court (did, did not) _____ support barring of the press from a criminal case.

17. The Supreme Court has rejected press requests for a "shield" ruling, declaring that this is a _____ decision.

18. Supreme Court decisions (have, have not) _____ recognized a limited right of the president to withhold information under executive privilege.

19. Censorship of the mails is _____ .

20. The _____ _____ _____ acts make most nonclassified records of federal agencies public.

21. Many states have passed so-called _____ laws requiring most public agencies to open their meetings to the public and the press.

22. Television (has, has not) _____ the same First Amendment rights as newspapers.

Knowledge Objective: *To define limits on speech (libel, obscenity) that are constitutional*

23. The First Amendment (does, does not) _____ prevent the FCC from refusing to renew a radio license if, in its opinion, a broadcaster has not served the public interest.

24. The _____ doctrine imposed on broadcasters an obligation to see that issues of public significance reflect differing viewpoints.

25. The mere fact that a statement is wrong or even defamatory is not sufficient to sustain a charge of _____ .

26. Under the current test a jury determines whether or not a work appeals to prurient interests or is patiently offensive to _____ standards.

27. Obscenity (is, is not) _____ entitled to constitutional protection.

28. Pornographic books and X-rated movies are entitled to (less, the same) _____ protections than/protections as political speech.

29. The Supreme Court (has, has not) _____ given encouragement for the creation of speech codes in public universities.

30. Leadership in efforts to ban the sale of pornographic materials has come from _____ groups.

Knowledge Objective: *To examine the right of the people peaceably to assemble and to petition the government*

31. The right to assemble peaceably applies not only to meetings in private homes, but to gatherings held in _____ _____ .

32. The right to assemble and to petition does not include the right to _____ on private property.

33. The rights of Iranian students in the United States and American Nazis to march on the streets (has, has not) _____ been upheld by the courts.

34. _____ consists only of the overt acts of giving aid and comfort to the enemies of the United States or levying war against it.

35. In the late eighteenth century the _____ Act made it a crime to utter false, scandalous, or malicious statements intended to bring the government or any of its officers into disrepute.

36. The first peacetime sedition law since 1798 was the _____ Act of 1940.

PART V — POST-TEST

1. Concerning free speech, Justice Holmes wrote that the best test of truth is the power of thought to
    a. endure over time.
    b. be accepted by the majority.
    c. get itself accepted in the competition of the market.
    d. reflect the wisdom of the forefathers.

2. The bad tendency doctrine gives to _____ the power to decide what kinds of speech can be outlawed.
    a. courts
    b. legislatures
    c. the people
    d. local communities

3. Constitutional restrictions on establishment of religion include
    a. persons praying in school buildings.
    b. classes observing a moment of silence.
    c. public officials sponsoring prayer.
    d. studying the Bible.

4. The Freedom of Information Act of 1966 concerns
    a. censorship.
    b. press responsibility and fairness.
    c. abuses in the overclassification of documents.
    d. the right to privacy.

5. Legislation that would protect the confidential information of journalists from police and court investigations is called a _____ law.
    a. sunshine
    b. umbrella
    c. shield
    d. covert

6. In <u>Miller</u> <u>v.</u> <u>California</u> (1973), Chief Justice Burger defined obscenity as a work that
    a. lacks serious artistic, political, or scientific value.
    b. does not apply traditional standards of morality.
    c. is utterly without redeeming value.
    d. graphically describes sex relations.

7. The distributions of religious and political pamphlets, leaflets, and handbills to the public is
    a. constitutionally protected.
    b. under almost all circumstances locally prosecuted.
    c. constitutionally ignored.
    d. prohibited without a license.

8. Of the following, which has the greatest restrictions placed upon it by the Constitution.
   - a. speech
   - b. assembly
   - c. picketing
   - d. petitions

9. Persons may be restrained from assembling in
   - a. any area designed to serve purposes other than demonstrations.
   - b. courthouses.
   - c. schools.
   - d. privately owned shopping malls.

10. In an effort to protect children from indecent telephone calls, Congress passed a law, —approved by the Supreme Court—that
   - a. banned all 900 calls.
   - b. let consumers block all 900 calls.
   - c. require proof of age to get access to 900 lines.
   - d. doubled rates for 900 calls.

PART VI — POLITICAL DIALOGUE: THE CLASH OF ISSUES AND IDEAS

Comment on the following remarks and where appropriate cite an illustration:

1. People can vote with their feet as well as with the ballot.

2. There never was and never will be a complete separation of church and state.

3. Violence in attempting to secure a redress of grievances is always counterproductive.

4. The Supreme Court opens each day with a prayer; yet the Court refused to allow public school classes to open with a prayer.

5. Granting tax credits to patrons of parochial schools will destroy the American public school system.

6. Do anti-abortion protestors have a moral right to wreck abortion clinics?

7. Does a 1986 Supreme Court decision upholding a Georgia sodomy law indicate a trend toward state restrictions on private sexual practices?

8. Old restrictions on pornography, sexually explicit motion pictures and public nudity have largely been abolished in contemporary America. Homosexuals and lesbians have come out of the closet. "Anything goes," say critics of the new morality. Many Americans regard this absence of restrictions as a constitutionally guaranteed freedom. Conservatives look upon the current scene as one of outright license rather than liberty.

9. Evaluate the Supreme Court yardstick of judging obscenity by community standards. How can such standards be determined? Are a community's standards reflected by a jury selected in hit-or-miss fashion? Do adult book stores have a right to set up shop anywhere? Can the sale of "kiddy porn" movies (child actors involved in sexually explicit scenes) be banned? Can certain "deviant" sexual activities be made punishable? Should male and female prostitutes have the right to practice their profession? Can their customers be charged with law violation?

PART VII — POLITICAL SCIENCE TODAY

1. Do you believe that a local community has the right to censor films, books, magazines, etc. under the guise of "community standards"? As your text chapter points out, the Supreme Court has had great difficulty in defining obscenity, preferring to leave such a determination to local governing units.

   Does your community have a film preview board or some governmentally sanctioned structure which has the power to ban reading materials? If so, how is this structure constituted (membership, elected or nominated, etc.)? Even if your community does not have institutionalized censorship, would you favor such a development — why or why not? Finally, what would happen to American society, in your opinion, if there were no censorship at all? For example, if pornography were not restricted in any way, would this policy hurt society or would individuals soon become bored with these materials? Speculate, perhaps in a report or research paper.

2. A truly controversial application of the First Amendment occurred in a 1989 Supreme Court ruling concerning the burning of the American flag. In the case of <u>Texas</u> v. <u>Johnson</u>, the Court decided in a 5-4 vote that burning the flag as political protest was a form of expression protected by the First Amendment. States could therefore not prosecute individuals who engaged in this form of protest. A storm of protest followed this ruling. There were calls from President Bush and a large number of congressmen for a new constitutional amendment which would reverse the ruling.

   Examine the aftermath of this ruling. What happened to the proposed amendment? What factors led to its eventual passage or defeat? Did the amendment ever clear Congress, etc.? Finally, after dealing with these issues, reflect upon your own feelings about the flag-burning controversy. In your opinion, does freedom of speech permit such actions? You might wish to examine the arguments on each side of the question before you arrive at any firm conclusions.

3. Another Supreme Court ruling in 1989, <u>County of Alleghany</u> v. <u>American Civil Liberties Union</u>, revealed the Court's changing views on separation of church and state. By another 5-4 vote, the Court restricted the ability of state and local governments to exhibit displays of religion vis-a-vis such holidays as Christmas.

   In this case, a local Catholic group had placed a nativity scene or creche inside the county courthouse. The creche which proclaimed "Glory to God in the Highest" in Latin was tantamount to a government sanctification of religion according to the Court's majority. However, the Court also ruled by a 6-3 vote that a city display featuring a Christmas tree and Hanukkah menorah a block away from the city office building did *not* mean an improper endorsement of religion.

   However, Justice Kennedy argued that the First Amendment should allow local government far greater discretion in celebrating holidays with both secular and religious significance.

   Since this decision, have there been other Supreme Court rulings touching upon the church-state separation issue? Research whether subsequent rulings have moved the Court toward the Kennedy position or not.

4. In November of 1994, a federal judge ruled that CNN had been in contempt of court when it had aired taped conversations of telephone calls made by General Noriega, former leader of Panama, while he was in a Miami jail awaiting trial for drug trafficking. (The conversations were between Noriega and his lawyers.) Despite being ordered by the judge not to play those tapes over the air, CNN did so, claiming that the order was contrary to freedom of the press under the first Amendment. The judge ruled that airing those tapes violated the traditional confidentiality relationship between lawyer and client.

Based upon this brief summary, do you agree with the judge's reasoning? Or was it more important for the public to have full information about the Noriega case as suggested by CNN? (Noriega was eventually sentenced to 40 years in prison.) Was the judge's original admonition to CNN a form of judicial censorship—why or why not?

PART VIII — DATA ANALYSIS

The First Amendment is, of course, only one amendment of the ten amendments which collectively comprise the Bill of Rights. In order to analyze your understanding of the Bill of Rights, please read the first ten amendments to the Constitution. In the spaces below match the phrase (these phrases are frequently used in current political controversies) with the number of the amendment to which it applies. You should understand that the phrases themselves are not necessarily constitutionally correct or incorrect; they are simply phrases that are often heard. After trying this test, consult the answers in the Test Answers section. (You may wish to consult other text chapters.)

1) _____ The government cannot take my land for that new road without paying me a fair price for it.

2) _____ Gun control is unconstitutional.

3) _____ If a magazine wants to publish instructions on how to build an atomic bomb, the government can't stop it.

4) _____ You can't be tried for the exact same crime twice if you were once found innocent of that crime.

5) _____ The government should not be able to keep a woman from having an abortion.

6) _____ Execution is cruel and unusual punishment.

7) _____ The police can't enter my house without a search warrant.

8) _____ I refuse to answer on the grounds that it may tend to incriminate me.

9) _____ At my public high school, we can't open the assembly period with a prayer.

10) _____ In a criminal case, an attorney will be provided for you if you can't afford one.

11) _____ There are other rights besides those mentioned in the Constitution.

12) _____ I believe in states' rights; the Constitution reserves most governmental powers to the states.

PART IX — TEST ANSWERS

Pretest

1. a
2. b
3. c
4. d
5. a
6. c
7. c
8. c
9. a
10. b

Programmed Review

1. Bill of Rights
2. national
3. due process
4. Establishment
5. nonpreferentialist
6. is
7. evolution
8. may not
9. is not
10. has
11. action
12. clear and present danger
13. preferred
14. prior
15. vagueness
16. did not
17. congressional
18. have
19. unconstitutional
20. Freedom of Information
21. sunshine
22. has not
23. does not
24. Fairness
25. libel
26. community
27. is not
28. less
29. was
30. feminist
31. public streets
32. trespass
33. has
34. treason
35. Sedition
36. Smith

Post-test

1. c
2. b
3. c
4. c
5. c
6. a
7. a
8. c
9. d
10. b

Data Analysis

1. 5
2. 2
3. 1
4. 5
5. 9
6. 8
7. 4
8. 5
9. 1
10. 6
11. 9
12. 10

CHAPTER 5
EQUAL RIGHTS UNDER THE LAW

The fundamental meaning of equal rights has shifted since the Bill of Rights was drafted over 200 years ago. Then there was general agreement that the phrase was restricted to white males over 21 years of age. Reasoned more closely, it was probably applied only to property owners.

Our entire history is an expansion of that original definition. At the close of the Civil War the vote was granted to African-American males, although as a practical matter full voting rights were not won until the Civil Rights Act of 1965, nearly one hundred years later. After over a century of protest, suffrage was granted to women in 1919. Young people, aged 18 to 21 gained the right to vote over forty years later. Meanwhile, Native Indians were given the ballot, somewhat grudgingly in several states that had originally barred them. On the voting front, then, we seem to have opened the doors wide, except for prison inmates.

Meanwhile, the very definition of equality has been expanded, with an emphasis on opportunity. All Americans do not begin life's race at an even starting line. Some have educational, social and economic advantages not shared by their fellows. Although the "American Dream" asserts there are no ceilings on success, a hard look at results suggests that certain factors do give some persons an advantage on an uneven playing field. This fact holds true, despite many stories of success despite great handicaps. The black child, born in a ghetto to an unwed mother, starts with several strikes against it. Similar handicaps are faced by Native Americans, Hispanics, a wide span of Asiatics, and women. Discrimination takes many forms. The Civil Rights Act of 1964 attempts to deal with discrimination in a variety of situations. The greatest success has been in breaking down barriers in public accommodations. Jobs have been opened by affirmative action programs. Schools no longer experience legal segregation, but housing largely remains separated by race. Although a small minority of Americans believe in equality of result (equal incomes), the great majority accept only equality of opportunity.

PART I — GUIDEPOSTS

1. Equality and Equal Rights
   a. What are the different concepts of equality?
   b. Trace the struggle of women to secure the suffrage and equal rights.
   c. Why did the Civil War amendments fail to give blacks equality?
   d. Why did the federal government become involved in African-American protests in the 1960s?
   e. What forms of pressure did African Americans use in their struggle for equality?
   f. Why was the demand by Native Americans for equal rights so long delayed?
   g. Into what four groups can Hispanics be classified? What complexities blur Hispanic protests?
   h. How are Asian-American demands for equality fragmented?

2. What Does Equal Protection of the Law Mean?
   a. What is the rational basis test?
   b. Differentiate between suspect and quasisuspect classifications of groups?
   c. Are age and poverty proper classifications?

d. List fundamental rights of Americans. What rights are not fundamental?

e. What essential criteria proves that a law is discriminatory?

3. The Life and Death of Jim Crow in Education

a. Why was the Court's decision in Plessy v. Ferguson so significant?

b. In what fundamental way was the Plessy decision reversed by Brown v. Board of Education?

c. How does affirmative action affect school programs and activities?

d. What conflicting forces have been involved in school busing?

4. Barriers to Voting

a. What devices were used by Southern states to circumvent the 14th and 15th amendments?

b. How were these devices curbed in 1965?

c. What changes in political life did the 1965 law bring?

d. What constitutes diluting of minority voting power?

5. Barriers to Public Accommodations, Jobs and Homes

a. Upon what constitutional basis did Congress justify laws against discrimination?

b. What national impact did the 1964 Civil Rights Act have on public accommodations? Employment?

c. Why has housing legislation against discrimination been less successful?

d. Is affirmative action constitutional?

e. What was the significance of the Bakke case?

f. What fundamental conflict lies at the base of the affirmative action issue?

g. What conclusions did the Kerner Commission reach? Are they still valid a generation later?

PART II — GLOSSARY

EQUALITY OF OPPORTUNITY - All persons have the right to compete and succeed, based on ability.

EQUALITY OF RESULTS - All persons should get equal financial rewards.

EQUALITY OF CONDITION - All persons should get an even start in the race for success.

KERNER COMMISSION - The Commission created by President Johnson that concluded that America was rapidly becoming two societies (black and white) separate and unequal.

BOAT PEOPLE - Refugees from Southeast Asia who escaped from their native lands in, overcrowded, makeshift vessels.

RATIONAL CLASSIFICATION - A classification lacking any discrimination and based on objective evidence.

SUSPECT CLASSIFICATION - Classification based on racial or national origin.

QUASISUSPECT CLASSIFICATION - A classification that categorizes persons in questionable ways, e.g. illegitimacy or sex.

BROWN V. BOARD OF EDUCATION - Supreme Court decision of 1954 that overturned Plessy v. Ferguson.

PLESSY V. FERGUSON - Supreme Court decision of 1896 that legalized the separate but equal doctrine.

VOTING RIGHTS ACT (1965) - Legislation that outlawed state laws that had effectively kept blacks from the polls.

CIVIL RIGHTS ACT (1964) - Legislation that forbade racial discrimination in a variety of ways.

KERNER REPORT - Report of President Johnson's National Advisory Commission on civil disorders. The report was submitted to the president in 1968, and recommended large programs and new approaches to combat frustration and poverty in the ghettos.

RACIALLY RESTRICTIVE COVENANTS - Clauses inserted in deeds restricting the sale of property to certain ethnic and racial groups. Such covenants are unenforceable in the courts.

JIM CROW LAWS - General name for all segregation laws.

DE JURE SEGREGATION - Segregation by law — now virtually a thing of the past.

DE FACTO SEGREGATION - Segregation that exists in fact, in reality, by virtue of residential patterns and other factors, even though it is legally banned.

POLL TAX - A head tax that was used as a prerequisite for voting. The Twenty-fourth Amendment abolished the poll tax as a prerequisite for voting in federal elections.

AFFIRMATIVE ACTION - Presidential executive orders and Congressional laws that required states to create programs to overcome past discrimination against women and minorities.

BAKKE CASE - Supreme Court decision (1978) that challenged affirmative action programs based on quotas.

CLASS ACTION - Judicial ruling that applied to a large group of plaintiffs (a class).

PART III — PRETEST

1. Since 1960 the women's movement has not concentrated on
      a. pay.
      b. pensions .
      c. parenthood.
      d. peace.

2. Only one of the following cities or states does not have an Hispanic mayor or governor.
      a. Miami
      b. Tampa
      c. Pittsburgh
      d. New Mexico

3. The civil rights gains of the 1960s chiefly benefitted
      a. young black males.
      b. black welfare mothers.
      c. the black middle class.
      d. poverty stricken blacks.

4. Major origins of Hispanics in the United States do not include
      a. Spain.
      b. Cuba.
      c. Puerto Rico.
      d. Mexico.

5. A state legislature may classify people only if the classification meets a _____ test.
      a. suspect
      b. almost suspect
      c. fundamental rights
      d. rational basis

6. In a famous dissenting opinion (<u>Plessy</u> v. <u>Ferguson</u>), Justice Harlan wrote
      a. most blacks are mentally inferior.
      b. the black family must be restructured.
      c. our Constitution is colorblind.
      d. busing promotes tolerance.

7. One of the following is unconstitutional as an age classification.
      a. Driver licenses may not be issued to those under 16.
      b. Alcohol may not be sold to those persons under 21.
      c. A state policeman is retired at age 55.
      d. An applicant for a teaching position (age 57) is rejected on the basis of age.

8. Slavery was abolished and black equal rights were granted by the _____ Amendments.
   a. Eighteenth, Nineteenth, and Twentieth
   b. Thirteenth, Fourteenth, and Fifteenth
   c. Sixteenth, Seventeenth, and Eighteenth
   d. Twelfth and Sixteenth

9. In the 1930s, African Americans resorted to which of these strategies to secure their rights?
   a. violence   c. litigation
   b. political power   d. persuasion

10. The civil rights movement produced it first charismatic leader during the Montgomery, Alabama bus boycott of 1955.
    a. James Baldwin
    b. Dick Gregory
    c. Martin Luther King
    d. Jesse Jackson

PART IV — PROGRAMMED REVIEW

Knowledge Objective: To examine the role of government in providing equal rights
1. Most of the equality debate in the United States is over equality of (opportunity, conditions) _____ .
2. The American Dream has not emphasized equality of _____ .
3. The focus of the modern women's rights movement has been to secure adoption of the _____ _____ Amendment.
4. The fastest growing minority in the United States is _____ .
5. A top priority of Hispanics is _____ education.
6. The three largest subgroups of Hispanics in the United States are _____ , _____ and _____ .
7. Native American tribes are _____ of the nation, subject to supervision by _____ .
8. After the Civil War, three "civil rights" amendments were added to the Constitution, the _____ , _____ and _____ Amendments.
9. The first branch of the national government to become sensitized to the aspirations of African-Americans was the _____ .
10. In the 1930s, blacks resorted to _____ to secure their rights.
11. In the 1960s, the use of litigation by blacks was supplemented by a widespread _____ , _____ and _____ movement.
12. The immediate origin of the black revolt occurred in 1955 when a _____ boycott was organized in Montgomery, Alabama.
13. A U.S. Civil Rights commission found that Asian-Americans (do, do not) _____ face widespread discrimination.

Knowledge Objective: To examine equal protection under the laws
14. The equal protection of the laws clause is part of the _____ Amendment and is implied in the due process clause of the _____ Amendment.
15. The Constitution forbids only _____ classification.
16. The traditional test of whether a law complies with the equal protection requirement is the _____ basis test.
17. Race and national origins are obviously _____ classifications.
18. The quasi-suspect classification includes _____ and _____ .
19. Justice Brennan, speaking for the Supreme Court, declared that much past legislation placed women in a _____ , rather than on a _____ .

20. Poverty, according to the Supreme Court, (is, is not) _____ an unconstitutional classification.
21. Age (can, cannot) _____ be used as a criterion in employment if it is related to proper job performance.

Knowledge Objective: To describe the life and death of Jim Crow in Education

22. In the 1954 case of _____ v. _____ the Supreme Court reversed its 1896 decision in <u>Plessy</u> v. <u>Ferguson</u>.
23. Segregation required by law is called _____ _____ segregation.
24. When segregation occurs without sanction of law, it is called _____ _____ segregation.
25. Busing across school district lines (is, is not) _____ required if the school district lines have been drawn to maintain segregation.

Knowledge Objective: To review barriers to voting

26. Most suffrage requirements, inside the U.S. constitutional framework, are fixed by the _____ .
27. The Voting Rights Act of 1965 has been (effective, ineffective) _____ .
28. The poll tax was abolished in federal elections by the _____ Amendment.
29. The Voting Rights Act of 1965 as amended set aside _____ tests throughout the country.
30. In attempting to give minorities a majority district, the result will probably be more minority districts and more safe _____ districts.

Knowledge Objective: To examine racial and sexual barriers to public accommodations, jobs, and homes

31. Private clubs restricted to Italians are (constitutional, unconstitutional) _____ .
32. The Fourteenth Amendment applies only to _____ action and not to private groups serving only their own members.
33. Segregation in places of _____ accommodation is unconstitutional.
34. A training program that gives preference to minorities or women (is, is not) _____ constitutional.
35. The Court (upheld/struck down)_____ the Richmond, Virginia plan to require nonminority contractors to subcontract work to minority business.
36. Attempts through legislation to end housing discrimination (have, have not) _____ been a great success.
37. In the Bakke case the Supreme Court held that a special admissions category from which whites were excluded was (constitutional, unconstitutional) _____ .
38. To redress the discrimination suffered by minorities, governments have adopted _____ _____ programs.
39. Affirmative action programs may temporarily set _____ but not _____ .
40. The Kerner Commission concluded that the nation was moving toward two societies, one black, one white, and _____ and _____ .

PART V — POST-TEST

1. Upon passage of the Nineteenth Amendment, women
   a. received equal pay
   b. received equal rights
   c. put an end to legal discrimination
   d. got the right to vote

2. Identify the unrelated word.
   - a. freedom rides
   - b. sit-ins
   - c. bus boycott
   - d. violence

3. The Kerner Report declared that
   - a. violence is as American as apple pie.
   - b. our nation is moving toward two societies, separate and unequal.
   - c. affirmative action is un-American.
   - d. black children should have neighborhood schools.

4. The fastest growing minority in the United States is
   - a. Indians.
   - b. Vietnamese.
   - c. Hispanics.
   - d. African Americans.

5. A reasonable government classification would be based on
   - a. age.
   - b. religion .
   - c. sex.
   - d. race.

6. Since 1960 the national government's role in the issue of equal rights has been to
   - a. support discrimination.
   - b. remain neutral.
   - c. take affirmative action.
   - d. defer to the states.

7. One of the following situations is outside government jurisdiction.
   - a. a restaurant bars men without jacket and tie
   - b. a hotel refuses to register a rock-and-roll star
   - c. a realtor refuses to sell property to an extended Vietnamese family
   - d. a theater refuses to seat a group with long hair and blue jeans

8. _____ is a fundamental right
   - a. Travel
   - b. Housing
   - c. Welfare
   - d. Education

9. Which of these cases marked the end of the separate but equal interpretation of the Constitution?
   - a. Plessy v. Ferguson
   - b. Weber v. Kaiser
   - c. Bakke v. California Regents
   - d. Brown v. Board of Education

10. Which method used to prevent African-Americans from voting was outlawed by the Voting Rights Bill of 1965?
    - a. literacy tests
    - b. threats of violence
    - c. poll taxes
    - d. white primary

Part VI — Political Dialogue:
The Clash of Issues and Ideas

1. What are reasonable objectives for those interested in women's rights? What discrimination do women face today in employment and salary? Is affirmative action working? Do present divorce laws discriminate against women?

2. The Kerner Report of twenty years ago declared that existing discrimination had led some blacks to the conviction that there was no alternative to violence and that America was rapidly becoming two societies: one white, one black, separate and unequal. What has been the end result of the intervening years? Has Kerner been confirmed? Or was it a false alarm?

3. Would you support a compensatory handicap bonus for all minorities on Civil Service exams? Should they get a special "break" in private employment, income taxes, and university admissions?

4. How have the goals of minority groups been thwarted by internal dissensions?

5. Several Asiatic minorities (Vietnamese, Japanese, Koreans, Chinese) appear to have entered the mainstream of American life more easily than have Hispanics, Native Americans and African-Americans. Is this actually the case? If so, what explanation can you offer?

6. Is the contemporary hue and cry over equality a false issue? Given the slow, grinding process by which permanent social change comes about, are we not moving as quickly as any reasonable person could expect? Who heads the noisy minority that is demanding total equality *now*?

Part VII — Political Science Today

1. The fundamental question as to whether black-Americans had made economic, social, and political progress since the civil rights legislation of the 1960s was addressed by the National Research Council of the National Academy of Sciences and Engineering in a four year study published in 1989. The study revealed that persistent discrimination and a lagging economy had kept blacks trailing whites in key facets of American life. The conditions cited by the study were serious according to the researchers, so serious that the real possibility of new urban riots was mentioned. The report called on Congress to narrow the gap between blacks and whites.

Some of the salient findings of the report were as follows:

(a) The poverty rate for blacks was two to three times as high as the poverty rate for whites. In 1986, the median income for black families stood at $17,604 vs. $30,809 for white families.

(b) In the area of education, black achievement scores had increased due to assistance from various government programs. However, academic performance standards for predominantly black schools vis-à-vis both teachers and students were lower than the same standards recorded for schools with predominantly white students. Also, high school drop-out rates for blacks were twice the level of white rates, and black-Americans were less than half as likely to enter college as whites within one year after high school graduation.

(c) Health statistics were depressing as well. Blacks had a shorter life expectancy than whites and black babies were twice as likely to die in infancy as white infants.

(d) The murder rate for blacks was twice as great as the white homicide rate. Also, blacks were twice as likely as whites to be victims of robbery, auto theft, or aggravated assault.

(e) Regarding housing, blacks were more likely to live in segregated circumstances than other minority groups. Finally, the report asserted that discrimination against blacks seeking housing had been conclusively demonstrated.

If you were a member of Congress reading the report's conclusions, what would be your reaction in terms of addressing these problems? What "causes" would you attach to these problems? Furthermore, how real would you deem the probability of new urban race riots in the near future if some or many of the ills delineated above were not addressed? Expand your thinking on the problems of the continuing civil rights struggle either in written or oral format.

2. The South Vietnamese are probably the newest Asian immigrant group to come to the shores of the United States after the fall of their country in 1975. Apparently, they have faced discrimination of their own as they have struggled to become acclimated to American life. Using the *Reader's Guide to Periodical Literature, The New York Times Index,* or other appropriate sources, find three or four representative articles on the Vietnamese and their own battles against discrimination, particularly over the last five to ten years. Can you find any evidence of discrimination which appears comparable to other minorities? A research paper could perhaps be written from these initial sources.

3. What would be your own position toward a bilingual school program for Hispanics, Cubans, etc.? As the text chapter asserts, some critics feel that English should be the only language taught, since it will allow minorities to be assimilated more rapidly into the mainstream of American society. Conversely, should it not also be the duty of the American schools to preserve the heritage of these groups by emphasizing both their native language and English? To perhaps gain a better "handle" on the issue, try to talk to a language teacher in the public schools who can comment on the advantages and disadvantages of the bilingual approach. A classroom debate on the issue would also be helpful and relevant to the chapter.

4. Have you or any of your friends ever been "bused" in your pre-college days to achieve racial integration? If so, what was your and/or your friends' reaction to the practice? Do you believe it helped to foster equal educational opportunity for both blacks and whites or not? You may wish to research the issue of busing further by consulting material both past and present.

5. As a possible research project, find out how many women, blacks, Hispanics, Cubans, or other minorities mentioned in the chapter are members of your local city government or state legislature. Are the numbers of minorities you uncover typical of other surrounding states in your region of the country? Finally, do you think democracy is strengthened or weakened if more minority representation in American politics is attained at all levels — why or why not?

6. In 1994, civil rights scholars assessed the status of school integration forty years after Brown v. Board of Education (1954). While a considerable amount of progress was noted in ending racially segregated schools throughout the nation, it was also true that racial divisions and disparities in education attainment had by no means vanished. As a further irony, black and white children were most likely to go to school together in the small towns and rural regions of the South, rather than in the central core areas of larger cities, such as Atlanta. From the data available, it appeared that the rural South, the area of greatest resistance to the original Brown decision in the 1950s, had created the most integrated school systems in the nation.

To test the validity of the above statement, review magazine or newspaper articles from the May-June period of 1994 to see if available data is supportive or not. Also, assuming you live near a large metropolitan area, check with school officials as to the status of integration in the public schools. Then try to contrast that status with the pattern of segregation/integration in smaller communities within your state. These research activities could form the basis of a term paper or outside project in your American Government course.

PART VIII — DATA ANALYSIS

1. In 1989, the Rehnquist Court delivered a number of rulings which alarmed pro civil rights groups, in that civil rights advocates saw those decisions as making it more difficult to carry out programs to redress past discrimination against minorities, as weakening the principle of affirmative action, and as generally curbing the rights of blacks and women. What were some of these cases and what was the content of their rulings?

   Look in the issues of *The New York Times* dated June 6, 13, and 30 (1989) to uncover the necessary information. The cases involved were <u>Richmond</u> v. <u>Croson</u>, <u>Wards Cove</u> v. <u>Antonio</u>, <u>Martin</u> v. <u>Wilks</u>, <u>Lorance</u> v. <u>A.T.&T.</u>, and <u>Richmond</u> v. <u>J.A. Croson Co.</u> After reviewing these cases, what conclusions can you reach regarding the status of civil rights principles as interpreted by the Rehnquist Court?

   As an update, research civil rights cases considered by the Supreme Court during the 1990-1994 period. Do any of these civil rights decisions indicate a change in the thinking of the Court since 1989? If so, which specific cases are especially prominent?

2. Ask a representative sampling of your classmates, both males and females, whether they believe women are "second-class citizens" in America. Do you find any differences between the sexes in terms of their fundamental underlying belief systems? Conversely, is there general agreement? Whatever your findings, speculate as to the reasons for the data you have uncovered.

3. On September 12, 1994, a federal judicial panel in Georgia ruled, by a 2 to 1 vote, that Georgia's 11th Congressional District was unconstitutional because it had been drawn in order to ensure that a black congressional district had been "racially gerrymandered." This lower court judgement was consistent with the 1993 Supreme Court ruling in the case of <u>Shaw</u> v. <u>Reno</u>. However, the dissenting judge argued that oddly-shaped legislative districts drawn to enhance minority representation in Congress should not automatically be condemned as constitutionally invalid.

   Follow up this event by analyzing whether this district was ever redrawn? If so, how did its revised "shape" differ? Also, do you believe that congressional districts should be created to encourage African-American representatives in the House of Representatives—why or why not?

PART IX — TEST ANSWERS

Pretest

1. c
2. c
3. c
4. a
5. d

6. c
7. d
8. b
9. c
10. c

Programmed Review

1. conditions
2. results
3. Equal Rights
4. Hispanic
5. bilingual
6. Mexicans, Puerto Ricans, Cubans
7. wards; Congress
8. 13th; 14th; 15th
9. executive
10. litigation
11. social; economic; political
12. bus
13. do
14. 14th; 5th
15. unreasonable
16. rational
17. suspect
18. sex; illegitimacy
19. cage; pedestal
20. is not

21. can
22. <u>Brown</u> v. <u>Board</u> of <u>Education</u>
23. de jure
24. de facto
25. is
26. states
27. effective
28. 24th
29. literacy
30. Republican
31. constitutional
32. government
33. public
34. is
35. struck down
36. have not
37. unconstitutional
38. affirmative action
39. goals, quotas
40. separate; unequal

Post-test

1. d
2. d
3. b
4. c
5. a

6. c
7. a
8. a
9. d
10. a

Data Analysis

1. As a way of helping you get started, note that the <u>Wards</u> <u>Cove</u> v. <u>Antonio</u> case, by a vote of 5-4, reversed an 18-year civil rights precedent by ruling that the plaintiff, not the employer, must prove that a job requirement is deliberate discrimination rather than a "business necessity."

CHAPTER 6
RIGHTS TO LIFE, LIBERTY AND PROPERTY

Perhaps there is no better way of introducing this chapter than to ask an historic question: What is *justice*? In Plato's Republic, justice was defined by some of Socrates, associates as "giving to each man what is proper to him . . . that justice is the art which gives good to friends when they are good and evil to enemies when they are evil."

In all civilizations a form of "just" retaliation has entered into the concept of justice. But our country has sought to abolish "cruel and unusual punishment," and it has aimed instead at the restoration of individual harmony through the rights of citizenship, life, liberty, and property. Surely, the Fifth and Fourteenth Amendments forbidding either national or state governments to deny any person his life, liberty or property without due process of law represents the Platonic maxim of justice. The two kinds of due process — procedural and substantive — aim at protecting the individual against unfair and vague punitive laws and against any presupposition of guilt "where there is no rational connection between the facts proved and the facts presumed." Whereas substantive due process makes sure that the content of a law is reasonable and fair, procedural due process is the ultimate method of justice which confronts those who would blindly punish the accused. Procedural due process as Daniel Webster said is "a procedure that hears before it condemns, proceeds upon inquiry, and renders judgment only after a trial."

We also have protection against punishment during or immediately after an alleged crime has occurred. These include protection against unreasonable seizure and searches. Also, the accused has the right to remain silent; to have an attorney present during questioning; to be permitted at any stage of police interrogation to terminate it. Our system has come a long way from the torture, detention and sustained interrogation of police states whose common practice has been full use of punishment. Furthermore, the *Writ of Habeas Corpus* insures a person held in custody from being unlawfully detained.

Persons accused of crime have a great many protective rights which guard against punishment: the right to the assistance of counsel; the right to be informed of the nature and cause of the accusation; the right to a speedy and public trial; the right to be confronted with the witnesses against them; protection against the levying of excessive fines; and, protection against cruel and unusual punishment.

Also, property is protected against arbitrary government seizure, and the government furnishes protection for property of the weak against the strong.

PART I — GUIDEPOSTS

1. The Constitution Protects Citizenship
    a. Explain *jus soli, jus sanguinas*, and collective naturalization.
    b. In what ways did the Fourteenth Amendment give constitutional protection to citizenship?
    c. What are the steps in naturalization?
    d. What are some of the privileges of national citizenship? Of state citizenship?
    e. Trace the American immigration program from the early "open door" policy through the 1924 and 1965 immigration acts.
    f. How was the 1965 immigration act a major turning point in our immigration policy?
    g. What changes were made by the 1986 immigration act?

2. Constitutional Protection of Property
    a. What is the difference between procedural due process and substantive due process?
    b. How do you explain the fact that substantive due process is no longer a serious check on legislative regulation of economic matters?
    c. What is eminent domain?
    d. What constitutional basis is used today to expand the right to privacy?
    e. How does the right to privacy restrict record-keeping by schools and universities?
    f. What rights to abortion were given to women by Roe v. Wade?
    g. How is private property protected by the contract clause?

3. Freedom From Arbitrary Arrest, Questioning and Imprisonment
    a. Under what restrictions do the police operate in making searches, arrests, and using deadly force?
    b. Explain: 1) *habeas corpus*; 2) *ex post facto*; 3) bill of attainder
    c. What controversy surrounds the exclusionary rule?
    d. What is the source of these rights: 1) to remain silent; 2) third-degree confessions?

4. Rights of Persons Accused of Crime
    a. What protection is provided to a person accused of a crime by the Fourth, Fifth, Sixth and Eighth amendments?
    b. How were these protections extended to John F. Crook in the text example?
    c. What restrictions on capital punishment have been imposed by the Court?

5. Nationalization of Civil Rights
    a. What parts of the Bill of Rights do not apply to the states?
    b. What is meant by double jeopardy?

6. How Just Is Our System of Justice?
    a. What arguments are advanced to prove that our system is just? Unjust?
    b. Why do some people believe that our justice system discriminates against ethnic and racial minorities?
    c. Ultimately, on what is our guarantee of freedom and liberty based?

PART II — GLOSSARY

JUS SOLI - Citizenship based upon place of birth.

JUS SANGUINIS - Citizenship based upon citizenship of parents.

NATURALIZATION - The process of conferring upon an alien the rights and privileges of citizenship.

PROCEDURAL DUE PROCESS - One aspect of due process, which stresses procedures based upon legal, accepted, and fair concepts of law.

SUBSTANTIVE DUE PROCESS - Another aspect of due process, which emphasizes the substance or content of the law.

EMINENT DOMAIN - The right of the state to take private property for public purposes with just compensation.

SEARCH WARRANT - A legal warrant issued for the purpose of examining a specific premise for evidence under specified conditions.

SELF-INCRIMINATION - Testifying against oneself in a court of law. The Fifth Amendment guarantees that "no person shall be compelled in a criminal case to be a witness against himself."

THIRD DEGREE - Methods at times used by the police in coercing confessions from suspects. These techniques include torture, detention incommunicado (isolation), and sustained interrogation. The Court has attempted to eliminate arbitrary and coercive methods of obtaining convictions by undergirding the rights of the accused.

WRIT OF HABEAS CORPUS - A court order to an official having a person in custody to produce the defendant and to explain why the person was taken and is being held.

EX POST FACTO LAW - A retrospective criminal law that works to the disadvantage of the individual.

BILL OF ATTAINDER - Judgment of guilt and the legislation of punishment by a legislature without judicial trial.

EXCLUSIONARY RULE - Evidence obtained unconstitutionally cannot be used in a criminal trial.

PLEA BARGAINING - The possibility of pleading guilty to a reduced charge rather than face trial on a more serious charge.

GREEN CARD - Document issued to an immigrant granting permanent status to work.

PART III — PRETEST

1. Identify the nationality not greatly involved in recent immigration.
   - a. Italians
   - b. Cubans
   - c. Mexicans
   - d. Salvadorans

2. Existing immigration laws do *not* include
   - a. deporting unmarried men.
   - b. higher immigration quotas.
   - c. giving permanent resident status to undocumented aliens.
   - d. filing charges against employers of undocumented aliens.

3. Conviction for one of the following actions has not been found to violate due process of law.
   - a. treating the flag contemptuously
   - b. to be on a public highway late at night without visible business
   - c. to be a "common night walker"
   - d. to carry a concealed pistol

4. Persons who are arrested by Federal officers at the scene of a crime are presumed to be
   - a. guilty.
   - b. innocent.
   - c. accomplices.
   - d. suspect.

5. Federally guaranteed rights include all of the following except
   - a. no double jeopardy.
   - b. application of *ex post facto* laws.
   - c. excessive fines and unusual punishments.
   - d. parole and/or probation.

6. The concept that private property cannot be taken for public use without just compensation is
   - a. eminent domain.
   - b. *habeas corpus.*
   - c. *ex post facto* law.
   - d. martial law.

7. Protection against self-incrimination should prevent
   - a. double jeopardy.
   - b. *habeas corpus.*
   - c. eminent domain.
   - d. the "third degree".

8. Aliens do not have the right to
    a. jury trial.
    b. freedom of religion.
    c. vote.
    d. attend school.

9. Faculties of state universities under the due process clause are guaranteed the right to
    a. tenure.
    b. hearings before dismissal.
    c. promotion.
    d. write uncensored books.

10. Substantive due process today is primarily concerned with
    a. property rights.
    b. social policy.
    c. civil liberties.
    d. economic regulation.

PART IV — PROGRAMMED REVIEW

Knowledge Objective: To analyze how the Constitution protects citizenship
1. Citizenship was given constitutional protection in 1868 with the adoption of the _____ Amendment.
2. The principle of _____ _____ confers citizenship by place of birth.
3. The principle of_____ _____ confers citizenship by blood.
4. The immigration law of 1986 attempted to deal with _____ aliens.
5. Current immigration law has permitted the admission of 100,000 refugees each year (inside, beyond) _____ the regular total.
6. Millions of illegal aliens have entered the United States from _____ .

Knowledge Objective: To examine constitutional protections of property
7. The Supreme Court (has, has not) _____ held that contracts between individuals could be modified by state law.
8. The due process of law clause is contained in both the _____ and _____ Amendments.
9. There are two kinds of due process, _____ and _____ .
10. Procedural due process (does, does not) _____ apply to many methods of law enforcement.
11. The unrestricted right of women to have an abortion during the first trimester of pregnancy is an example of _____ due process.
12. The Supreme Court (has, has not) _____ ruled that state employees are entitled to due process hearings before being fired.
13. Faculty members in public institutions are not entitled to due process before being denied tenure because they have no _____ right to teaching jobs.
14. State laws that prohibit homosexual acts in private homes have been (upheld, struck down) _____ by the Supreme Court.
15. _____ due process places limits on how governmental power may be exercised.
16. _____ due process places limits on why governmental power may be exercised.
17. Substantive due process deals with the _____ of the law.

Knowledge Objective To inquire into arbitrary arrest, questioning, and imprisonment
18. Police (have, do not have) _____ the right to administer drug tests on railroad workers involved in accidents.
19. Officers (may, may not) _____ stop and search suspects if they have reason to believe they are armed and dangerous.
20. A search warrant must describe what places are to be _____ and the things that are to be_____ .
21. In Mapp v. Ohio, the Supreme Court ruled that evidence obtained unconstitutionally (can, cannot) _____ be used in a criminal trial.

22. Witnesses before a Congressional committee may not refuse to testify if they have been granted _____ .

23. Critics of the exclusionary rule argue that the solution is to punish the (police, suspect) _____ .

24. In <u>Miranda</u> v. <u>Arizona</u>, the Supreme Court held that a conviction (could, could not) _____ stand if evidence introduced at the trial was a result of "custodial interrogation."

25. A retroactive criminal law that works to the disadvantage of an individual is called an _____ _____ _____ law.

26. A legislative act inflicting punishment without judicial trial is called a _____ _____ _____ .

Knowledge Objective: To examine the nationalization of civil rights

27. Double jeopardy prevents two criminal trials by the _____ government for the same _____ offense.

28. An accused person may not be held in custody without being charged because of his rights of _____ _____ .

Knowledge Objective: To evaluate our system of justice

29. Critics who claim our justice system is unreliable often point to trial by _____ as the chief source of trouble.

30. Critics charge that the grand jury has become a tool of the _____ .

31. Many members of minorities (do, do not) _____ believe that they have equal protection under the law.

32. In the United States, our emphasis on judicial protection of civil liberties focuses attention on the _____ _____ .

PART V — POST-TEST

1. To become a citizen of the United States, aliens have to do all of the following things except
    a. renounce allegiance to their native country.
    b. swear that they will bear arms for the U.S.
    c. swear to defend the Constitution.
    d. own property worth at least $2,000.

2. Naturalized citizens are not required to demonstrate that they
    a. are of good moral character.
    b. are able to speak and write English.
    c. know the principles of U.S. government.
    d. have a sponsoring family.

3. In its efforts to block the entry of illegal aliens, the Naturalization Service has been
    a. moderately successful.
    b. unsuccessful.
    c. extremely successful.
    d. uninvolved.

4. Under <u>Roe</u> v. <u>Wade</u> the Court held that a woman in her first three months of pregnancy had a(n) _____ right to abortion.
    a. no
    b. limited
    c. court approved
    d. unrestricted

5. Police do not have an unrestricted right to use
   a. trained dogs.   c. recording devices.
   b. secret cameras.   d. tapped telephones.

6. A criminal who pleads guilty to an offense that is lesser than the one with which he had been charged is said to have engaged in
   a. the exclusionary process.   c. plea bargaining.
   b. self-incrimination.   d. double jeopardy.

7. The "exclusionary rule" provides that certain evidence cannot be used to convict a person in a criminal trial.
   a. employees against employers
   b. children against parents
   c. illegal police searches
   d. testimony given in exchange for immunity

8. As a result of the Miranda decision, all persons accused of a crime have the following rights except
   a. to remain silent.
   b. have a lawyer represent them.
   c. freedom on bail.
   d. halt their interrogation any point.

9. All of the following legal procedures are constitutional except
   a. *habeas corpus.*   c. injunctions.
   b. subpoenas.   d. bills of attainder.

10. The Privacy Act placed restrictions *on all* of the following *except*
    a. university records.   c. federal agency files.
    b. censorship of letters.   d. student grades.

PART VI — POLITICAL DIALOGUE:
THE CLASH OF ISSUES AND IDEAS

1. In our concern of privacy we are destroying a practice that supplemented laws for hundreds of years — local traditions and customs. Discuss.

2. Is it true that "one thousand guilty should go free rather than one innocent be convicted"?

3. "The law in its magnificent equality forbids the rich as well as the poor to sleep under bridges, to beg in the streets, and to steal bread." Anatole France.

4. "Employers should not be penalized because the government is not stopping illegal immigration."

5. "If the crime rate continues to go up, would you favor giving the police any of the following powers?" (National responses indicated.)
   a. Require all adults to be fingerprinted. (Approve - 73%)
   b. Stop and search anybody on suspicion. (Approve - 50%)
   c. Wiretap telephone lines of anyone they suspect. (Approve - 44%)
   d. Hold someone on suspicion 24 hours without bail. (Approve - 42%)
   e. Search a house without a warrant. (Approve - 27%)
   f. None of them. (Approve - 20%)

6. Comment on the following statements:
    a. "Anyone who takes the "Fifth" must be guilty"
    b. "If you have nothing to hide, why not submit to a lie detector test."

7. The State of Texarkana passed a law prohibiting people over 75 from voting (a retirement law for voters). Mr. Newborne, age 76, contested the law in the federal courts, saying that he was being denied equal protection of law (14th Amendment). What would the Supreme Court, which would finally hear the case, say? Why?

8. A prominent attorney in many civil rights cases states that telephone tapping and electronic eavesdropping by police should be outlawed. It might be easier, he admits, to catch spies and hoodlums, but in doing so "we would be trying to protect democracy with the tools of totalitarianism."

   Another constitutional scholar regrets the loss of privacy in court-supervised telephone taps by police officers but views it as a result of advancing technology and the problems of a complex society. He goes on to say, "If we wish the government to protect us against quacks, frauds, swindlers, maniacs, and criminals, we must give it powers of prosecution, punishment, and licensing."

   Which position do you favor? Why? Is physical entry with a search warrant less of a threat to privacy than a wire tap under a court order?

9. Frustrated by the inability of the Border Patrol to stop illegal Mexican immigration, one commentator has suggested that we build a twelve foot wall along the entire length of the U.S. - Mexican border and man it with sharp shooters. In front of this we would create a barren stretch of two miles.

   Does this defensive barrier differ from the Berlin Wall? How? What would be the impact of an alternate proposal in which we would negotiate a treaty with Mexico that would raise wages in Mexico twenty percent annually for five years?

PART VII — POLITICAL SCIENCE TODAY

1. Imagine that an interstate highway is being built as a joint project between the federal government and the states. Assume also that in several cases, a considerable number of historic homes have now become earmarked for destruction because they are located in a manner designed to add thousands, perhaps millions of dollars to the overall cost of the highway's construction if they are not removed. Will the right of eminent domain force the homeowners to sell their property and move elsewhere? Or, as the text chapter points out, would a court decide in favor of the homeowners if a proper case can be developed and argued effectively? How would you rule if you were a judge in this eminent domain case? What factors might influence your decision one way or the other? Debate the issue in class if at all possible.

2. The "right to life" and the "right to die" may eventually be linked under a future Supreme Court ruling regarding the constitutional right to privacy. In a *New York Times* article of July 25, 1989 entitled "Does Right to Privacy Include Right to Die? Court to Decide" by Linda Greenhouse (pp. 1, 8), it was noted that "the Court agreed to decide whether a state can require an unconscious person to be maintained indefinitely by medical technology against the wishes of family members who believe the patient would prefer to die." Greenhouse goes on to explain this "rights dilemma" in further detail:

The case is an appeal by the parents of a 31-year old Missouri woman, seeking removal of the feeding tube that has kept their daughter alive despite devastating brain injuries from an automobile accident more than six years ago. The woman, Nancy Beth Cruzan, has no chance for recovery, but with the tube in place she could live another 30 years.

The Court's future decision in the "constitutional privacy doctrine" area would hopefully resolve previous state court decisions which tried to balance two interests —"the state's interest in preserving life against the individual's interest in being free of the intrusion of unwanted medical treatment." (p. 8) Previous cases in New Jersey and Missouri had resulted in one favoring the individual's interest, the other the state's interest. The Missouri view of the state protecting human beings from conception until natural death is a minority one, since courts in nine other states would authorize a halt to the "artificial feeding" of a patient who had no hope of recovery. Furthermore, "guidelines adopted in the last three years by both the American Medical Association and the American Association of Neurological Surgeons would both have permitted withdrawal of the feeding tube in cases like this." Finally, Miss Cruzan had never signed a "living will" (a prior declaration that one does not wish to be subjected to a death-prolonging procedure) but she had told friends "that she would not want to be kept alive with a serious injury or illness unless she could live 'halfway normally.'" Greenhouse summarizes the issue thusly:

An issue before the Justices is therefore what quality of evidence courts can require in deciding whether to carry out an incompetent person's presumed wish not to be kept alive. New York State's highest court, in a decision last year, said the evidence must be "clear and convincing," the highest evidentiary standard in civil law. M. Rose Gasner, a lawyer for the Society for the Right to Die, said the standard was "totally unworkable" because it could almost never be met. (p. 8)

Imagine you were a Supreme Court justice hearing this privacy case from the state of Missouri. How would you vote and why? A brief essay on the hypothetical ruling might help you to organize your thoughts on the case. As another approach to the "right to die - privacy" principle, you may wish to research how the Supreme Court actually did rule during the 1989-1990 session.

3. A heated debate over immigration occurred in California during the 1994 election year. California voters were asked to approve or reject Proposition 187, a proposal to deny illegal or undocumented aliens a variety of government services such as schooling and non-emergency health care. In addition, teachers and physicians would be mandated to give immigration authorities the names of suspected aliens they taught or treated. Pete Wilson, the governor of California, insisted that the state could not afford to provide such expensive services to these aliens. Ethnic minorities in California charged that prejudice was the real motivation behind Proposition 187. Whether the Proposition would pass in November remained an open question.

What happened to the Proposition? Find an article or two written after the November election that explained the outcome. Also, would you have voted for or against this Proposition? Explain why.

PART VIII — DATA ANALYSIS

1. Suppose you are riding in your car when suddenly you see a highway patrol car in your rear-view mirror. The officer motions for you to pull over to the side of the road. You do so. The officer indicates that you were driving in a suspicious manner (he does not specify what he means by "suspicious"), that the particular road you are on has been frequently used by drug traffickers, and that your car resembles the make and model year of one known as a carrier of drugs (from an all-points bulletin of the previous day).

Consequently, the officer asks you to move away from the car. He intends to search your automobile thoroughly for drugs, even though he does not have a search warrant. Does the officer have the right to do so? Does his action not violate the constitutional prohibition toward unreasonable searches and seizures? What do you think? Before consulting the answer key, try to think about the issues involved in this situation, write your thoughts down, and then see if you were correct or not.

2. The death penalty or capital punishment remains a controversial issue in American politics. To its detractors, the death penalty represents cruel and unusual punishment, a barbaric throwback to earlier, primitive societies. Furthermore, opponents argue that the death penalty really does not prevent or deter murder, so why use it? Also, there is always the possibility of executing an innocent man/woman. Proponents argue that the public supports the death penalty and that the penalty is a proper instrument of justice and social retribution. As of June, 1989, there were roughly 2100 death row convicts in the United States awaiting execution.
With that brief introduction, look at the collection of capital punishment data presented in *The New York Times* of June 19, 1989, p. 11. What basic conclusions can you draw about the *reality* of executions in America regarding frequency and the types of people actually executed? "By comparison, there were over 2500 death row inmates awaiting execution in mid-1994."

PART IX — TEST ANSWERS

Pretest

1. a	6. a
2. a	7. d
3. d	8. c
4. b	9. d
5. d	10. c

Programmed Review

1. Fourteenth	17. content
2. *jus soli*	18. have
3. *jus sanguinis*	19. may
4. undocumented	20. searched; seized
5. beyond	21. cannot
6. Mexico	22. immunity
7. has	23. police
8. Fifth; Fourteenth	24. could not
9. procedural; substantive	25. *ex post facto*
10. does	26. bill of attainder
11. substantive	27. same; criminal
12. has	28. *habeas corpus*
13. constitutional	29. jury
14. upheld	30. prosecutor
15. Procedural	31. do not
16. Substantive	32. Supreme Court

Post-test

1. d	6. c
2. d	7. c
3. b	8. c
4. d	9. d
5. d	10. b

Data Analysis

1. This case boils down to the principle of "probable cause," i.e., did the officer have a legitimate suspicion that you and your car were possibly involved in criminal activity? Under the most recent Supreme Court ruling, a policeman can search an automobile without a search warrant provided the criterion of probable cause is met.

2. One obvious conclusion is that despite the many death row prisoners awaiting execution, comparatively few are being actually executed. Consider the fact that 37 states do allow the death penalty and intend to implement it (note that only 13 states have actually held executions since 1976). Another conclusion might be that prisoners belonging to racial/ethnic minorities seem to stand a better chance of execution, especially in proportion to their numbers in general population.

CHAPTER 7
POLITICAL CULTURE AND IDEOLOGY

Our basic constitution sought to define and guarantee our existing rights in the agricultural society in which we lived. It was a society in which wealth and income were relatively equal (slavery excepted) and social classes were not distinct. Our evolution into an industrial and post industrial society has shifted many parts of that original arrangement and caused some to be questioned. Yet to an amazing degree our original values remain.

Today our ideologies are so complex that the older divisions between Democrats and Republicans are practically meaningless. More descriptive are terms like classical liberal, New Deal liberal, neoliberal, traditional conservative, New Right, libertarian. This chapter is dedicated to drawing the distinctions between these opposing ideologies.

PART I — GUIDEPOSTS

1. American Beliefs and Behavior Patterns
   a. What attitudes do Americans share?
   b. What basic beliefs do they hold in common?
   c. What kinds of conflict exist within our ideology and culture?
   d. As compared with other Western democracies, in which political virtues do we seem to excel?

2. The Quest For Additional Rights
   a. How did original agrarian roots give support to the idea of equality?
   b. How was that concept challenged by the rise of corporations?
   c. What contradiction apparently exists between unregulated capitalism and democracy?
   d. What new rights did FDR sponsor for Americans?
   e. What is the American Dream?

3. Liberalism, Conservatism and Public Policy
   a. In trying to define liberal and conservative attitudes what tests apply?
   b. Why are clear-cut labels hard to define?
   c. How are today's liberals different from earlier ones? Contrast their attitudes toward the role of government.
   d. What attitudes do liberals have toward the possibility of progress?
   e. Contrast their views with those of conservatives. What is a neoconservative? Radical Rightist? Neoliberal?

4. A Central Tension: Political Equality Versus Capitalism
   a. How do the central values of political equality and a free market system conflict?
   b. Why should the American system be described as "mixed?"
   c. What do Americans believe about rewarding people of ability? Private property? Inheritance?
   d. What trend seems to be developing in the way American wealth is distributed between the wealthy and the poor?
   e. What tensions does this create in a society that believes in political equality?

5. Ideology and Tolerance
   a. What clear-cut differences separate conservatives and liberals on the issue of tolerance?
   b. How do they differ on civil rights and liberties?
   c. Identify three issues on which liberals display intolerance.
   d. What are the issues that bring a demand for conservative government restrictions?

PART II — GLOSSARY

IDEOLOGY - A person's basic beliefs in economics, politics, and religion.

POLITICAL CULTURE - Widely shared beliefs, values and norms in a society.

RECALL - Removal of a public official before the end of a term by popular vote.

LIBERALS - In the contemporary world they believe government should play a major role in bringing about progress.

NEOLIBERALS - Are those who are skeptical of government's ability to bring about many of the changes that old fashioned liberals advocated.

CONSERVATIVES - Believe in limited government and emphasize individual achievement under stable conditions.

RADICAL RIGHT - Believe in a return to traditional values and a strong military force through the support of government.

NEOCONSERVATIVES - Those who believe that liberals have depended too heavily on government to solve many national problems, yet favor military strength and wars on crime and drugs.

SOCIALISM - A belief that favors public ownership of production and distribution.

LIBERTARIANISM - A belief that favors very limited government and great personal freedom.

PART III — PRETEST

1. Most Americans share *all but one* of the following values:
   a. religion   c. big business
   b. free enterprise   d. free press

2. Americans for the most part *do not believe* in
   a. pragmatism.
   b. free speech.
   c. active political participation.
   d. passive government.

3. Americans do believe in
   a. self help.   c. a common dream.
   b. government regulation.   d. a class system.

4. Americans believe that _____ is necessary to make the system work.
   a. unemployment   c. education
   b. discrimination   d. uniformity of belief

5. According to most Americans, we are not a land of
   a. cooperative endeavors.   c. common sense.
   b. opportunity.   d. rugged individualism.

6. For the most part, Americans are
    a. nonideological.
    b. theorists.
    c. selfish.
    d. careful spenders.

7. Although some beliefs conflict with others, Americans in large numbers believe in *all but one* of these slogans.
    a. root hog or die
    b. Everybody help somebody
    c. survival of the fittest
    d. Don't fence me in

8. In regard to their past experience, most Americans feel they should regard it
    a. with apology.
    b. as unique.
    c. part of world evolution.
    d. no special destiny.

9. Supply side economics is also called
    a. Democratic dogma.
    b. liberal lunacy.
    c. Reaganomics.
    d. witch doctor illusions.

10. The Moral Majority represents a group with a _____ base.
    a. rural
    b. economic
    c. mystical
    d. religious

PART IV — PROGRAMMED REVIEW

Knowledge Objective: What are the basic features of American culture and ideology
    1. Classical liberalism stresses the importance of the _____ .
    2. Liberal political philosophers claimed individuals have certain _____ _____ and the state must be limited.
    3. The Constitution, like the American Revolution, defines our nation and its _____ .
    4. The idea that every individual has a right to equal protection and voting power is called _____ _____ .
    5. Americans are optimistic about _____, but not about our government.
    6. Widely shared beliefs and values are called our political _____ .
    7. Perhaps our most commonly held belief is that of _____ .
    8. In the American system of values, the role of government is to _____ _____ _____ .
    9. Americans believe that (more, less) _____ direct political power should be in the hands of the people.
    10. In a broad sense America (does, does not) _____ have an official philosophy.

Knowledge Objective: To trace the demand for additional rights in American experience: the American Dream
    11. One of the first rights to be won in America was the right to _____ .
    12. Inequality of _____ was the result of the growth of corporations.
    13. The unregulated growth of American capitalism was challenged by the _____ _____ .
    14. Huge _____ do not fit into our basic democratic theory.
    15. Franklin Roosevelt declared that all Americans had the right to adequate _____ care.

16. Roosevelt also said that every American had the right to a useful _____ .
17. The gap between rich and poor in the United States has _____ in recent years.
18. Americans dream of acquiring _____ .
19. The American Dream includes (inequality, equality) _____ of income.
20. The American Dream does not believe in stringent _____ taxes.

Knowledge Objective: To distinguish between liberal and conservative public policies

21. Modern _____ political leaders favor greater government activity.
22. _____ leaders believe that national progress is possible.
23. Liberals who have lost faith in welfare programs and bureaucracy are called _____ .
24. Private property rights and free enterprise are basic beliefs of _____ .
25. _____ believe that most people who fail are personally responsible for their failure.
26. A brand of conservatism that is more radical, the New _____ has emerged in recent years.
27. Many former Democrats, who have rejected recent Democratic leadership, call themselves _____ .
28. _____ favor an expanded government that would own the means of production and distribution.
29. _____ favor a severely curbed role for government in domestic and foreign affairs.

Knowledge Objective: To define the basic political tension in modern America

30. Our national political life is based on a (carefully defined, vague) _____ theory.
31. American political parties are (more, less) _____ ideological than European parties.
32. Tolerance is most prevalent among _____ (liberals/conservatives).
33. Conservatives show more concern for the rights of _____ _____ _____ while liberals show more concern for the rights of the _____ .
34. Conservatives prize the private sector over the _____ sector.
35. Conservatives believe that America has become too _____ .

PART V — POST-TEST

1. Which one of the following groups want the least government?
   - a. Libertarians
   - b. Conservatives
   - c. Liberals
   - d. Socialists

2. Which group demands the most government?
   - a. Socialists
   - b. Neoliberals
   - c. Libertarians
   - d. Neoconservatives

3. Equality of opportunity is least frequently denied today on the basis of
   - a. religion.
   - b. sex.
   - c. race.
   - d. ethnic background.

4. A major barrier to equality of opportunity today is
   - a. failure to vote.
   - b. lack of education.
   - c. unequal start.
   - d. high taxes.

5. When the Great Depression began we had
   - a. unemployment compensation.
   - b. bank deposit guarantees.
   - c. regulation of security exchanges.
   - d. the vote for women.

6. The American president most responsible for greatly expanding the rights of all Americans was
    a. Truman.
    b. Eisenhower.
    c. Hoover.
    d. F.D. Roosevelt.

7. Those who favor expansion of government control over drinking, drugs, abortion, prayer and life style are
    a. Conservatives.
    b. Radical Right.
    c. Neoconservatives.
    d. Libertarians.

8. The conservative cause in the United States was advanced most by President
    a. Bush.
    b. Reagan.
    c. Kennedy.
    d. Truman.

9. The political group who today advocates the withdrawal of our forces from Europe and the decriminalization of drug possession is
    a. Conservatives.
    b. Liberals.
    c. Libertarians.
    d. Socialists.

10. In today's world the greatest conflict is between the free market enterprise system and
    a. socialism.
    b. equality of opportunity.
    c. private property.
    d. voting rights.

PART VI — POLITICAL DIALOGUE: THE CLASH OF ISSUES AND IDEAS

1. "The mixed economy under which the United States operates today is the great success story of the modern world. We as a nation have a high living standard and yet we retain a great degree of personal liberty. We walk a fine line between unrestricted capitalism and socialism-communism while permitting freedom of enterprise and equality of opportunity." An old New England motto was: "If it ain't broke, don't fix it." We should leave well enough alone, and not tinker with our existing political-economic system. Comment.

2. "The gap between rich and poor is steadily widening in the United States. Unless we reverse this trend we will end up with a society of a few 'haves' and majority of 'have nots,' just as President John Adams predicted long ago. Our wealth is steadily being concentrated in enormous corporations controlled by no one. At the bottom of the pile are the landless and propertyless poor, jammed into vast ghettos. Not only can it happen here. It is happening." Comment.

3. "The American Dream is a reality that no one can disprove. It assumes that ultimate wisdom lies with the common man. He, rather than the expert, is better equipped to judge what is best for him and the nation. If given a chance he will rise above his heritage to succeed on his own. And he will share his blessings with less fortunate people everywhere. Only in America could we have invented the Peace Corps, the Marshall Plan, and the United Nations." What does the historical record show regarding this assertion?

4. "Fortunately, most Americans are not very active politically. At best half of those eligible to vote do not cast ballots. Hence, by a kind of self selection, the more intelligent and politically aware people select our leaders and monitor their performance. It may upset some of our cherished illusions, but American democracy works because most Americans are only marginally involved in politics." Comment.

PART VII — POLITICAL SCIENCE TODAY

1. Ask members of the class to list what they see as the main components of the "American Ideology." Which values/concepts appear to be named most frequently and why? Do any of these values/concepts represent "myths" from an objective standpoint?

2. Review FDR's delineation of a "Second Bill of Rights" as covered in the chapter. Is it still relevant to contemporary America? For example, "the right to earn enough" was a recurrent policy controversy as Congress and the president periodically tussled over proposed increases in the minimum wage or the issue of tax cuts. In addition, the "right of every family to have a home" was becoming more difficult for many Americans, especially young wage-earners. Even the "right to a good education" suffered according to experts who pointed out the reduction in student loans during the cost-cutting Reagan era. Farmers continued to lose their land, businessmen complained about unfair trade practices by other nations (Japan, Europe, etc.), and the issue of high medical costs and continued Social Security benefits for Americans (especially the elderly) were all recurrent social and political issues.

 As a possible research project take one or two of the rights contained in FDR's 1944 speech and propose ways (either your own or previous proposals by policy-makers) that these rights might be established and perfected for the affected segments of society. What obstacles have existed in the past to the full implementation of these rights? Can these obstacles be removed in the future - why or why not? Some of your findings could be shared with fellow classmates.

3. Do you believe most members of your class in American Government are political "liberals" or "conservatives"? As part of a modest survey project, construct perhaps five to ten questions tapping the liberal or conservative component and administer it to the class. (Your instructor may be of some assistance in developing and implementing the survey). The questions should involve the preferred degree of governmental intervention in the economy, the equality of opportunity vs. liberty dilemma (see text for help in this area), crime and punishment, the environment, national defense, prayer in the public school, civil liberties/rights, welfare, taxes, abortion, pornography, and attitude toward communism, among others. You may also wish to compare your findings with national surveys which also pose similar questions, especially among Americans who fall within the 18-26 age category and who possess college degrees.

4. Closely examine the chapter section on the ideology of libertarianism. Do any of the ideology's policies make sense to you? In your own mind spell out the consequences for the nation if, as the libertarians suggest, (a) American troops from overseas missions were completely withdrawn or (b) the FBI and CIA were abolished or (c) all welfare programs were abolished or (d) marijuana and prostitution were legalized. A paper covering the pros and cons of each of the four policies could prove interesting. If not a paper, then some discussion in class with classmates and the instructor would sharpen critical thinking skills.

5. Imagine you were listening to a debate on whether government should take greater pains to control big business, especially the large corporation. One speaker, a corporate president, defends the concept of laissez-faire and very minimal federal interference in business practices, argues for lower corporate taxes in order to spur investment and research, and reminds the audience that the overall economic success of corporations is closely linked to high employment figures and overall prosperity. The corporate chief also asserts that corporations care about the consumer and their employees, in that corporate profits and success are inseparably linked to contented employees and satisfied customers in the marketplace. Summing up, the corporate president argues for less federal support of labor unions and supervision of workplace safety by federal agencies. After all, it is in the corporation's best interest to handle such matters.

The opposing speaker heads a consumer group. He argues that big business has been guilty of a number of abuses in the past and that the only institution capable of controlling the corporation's excesses is the federal government. She ticks off a number of examples to prove her point: (a) The Firestone Tire Company took its Radial 500 tire off the market six years after it became aware of the tire's defects (a number of drivers were seriously injured due to blow-outs and tread failure); (b) The Beech Nut Corporation continued to advertise its juice for babies as 100 percent apple juice even though there was no real juice in the product; (c) Until Ralph Nader, auto companies refused to fix defects involving safety considerations in their cars; (d) Corporations commonly pollute the environment, and have only been constrained by the power of government to levy fines.

There are many other issues which could be covered in the above-hypothetical debate. But even this brief sketch might force you to consider the general merits and demerits of controlling un-bridled capitalism. Further research and/or discussion might help you to resolve this issue in your own mind.

PART VIII — DATA ANALYSIS

1. To test your understanding of the ideological precepts of liberalism, conservatism, socialism, and libertarianism, place the name of the ideology (which most closely corresponds to the principle stated below) in the blank line provided after each "principle-statement."

    a. Big Business and big labor require big government as a balancing force in the economy. _____

    b. Criminals commit their crimes due to defects in their personality and/or minds. _____

    c. The unity and interest of the community is important. _____

    d. A gradual rather than rapid pace of change is preferable. _____

    e. Public ownership of certain forms of property is necessary if inequities in property ownership are to be eliminated. _____

    f. Tax policies should have the effect of redistributing income from the rich to the poor. _____

    g. All subsidies to corporations from the federal government should be eliminated. _____

    h. Government has created social and economic policies which cannot solve the problems they originally addressed. _____

2. Review Table 7.1, "It Depends on What You Mean by Rights and Freedoms." Then ask members of the class whether they would "agree" or "disagree" with the four assertions. Probe as to the reasons behind their opinions. Also, do you find that class "liberals" or "conservatives" differ considerably in their responses?

PART IX — TEST ANSWERS

Pretest

1. c
2. d
3. a
4. c
5. a

6. a
7. b
8. b
9. c
10. d

Programmed Review

1. individual
2. natural rights
3. values
4. political equality
5. people
6. culture
7. liberty
8. serve the people
9. more
10. does not
11. vote
12. wealth
13. Great Depression
14. corporations
15. medical
16. job
17. grown
18. property

19. inequality
20. inheritance
21. liberal
22. Liberal
23. neoliberals
24. conservatives
25. Conservatives
26. Right
27. neoconservatives
28. Socialists
29. Libertarians
30. vague
31. less
32. liberals
33. victims of crime; accused
34. public
35. permissive

Post-test

1. a
2. a
3. a
4. c
5. d

6. d
7. b
8. b
9. c
10. b

Data Analysis

1. a. liberalism
    b. conservatism
    c. conservatism
    d. conservatism
    e. socialism
    f. socialism
    g. libertarianism
    h. conservatism and libertarianism

2. The student's research results will vary depending upon the particular configuration in his or her class.

CHAPTER 8
THE AMERICAN POLITICAL LANDSCAPE

The broadest description of a nation's pattern of behavior is its special culture. The set of beliefs upon which that culture is based is called its ideology. Anyone attempting to describe the patterns of culture and ideology for a complex nation of 250 million people with all their individual differences and conflicting beliefs faces a tremendous challenge, especially when immigration adds nearly a million people each year.

Yet we know that despite all of these differences there are similarities that override these distinctions. Such phrases as "American Dream", "democracy" and "equality" are commonly agreed upon as factors that set our nation apart from all others. These unique characteristics are the components that bind this chapter together.

PART I — GUIDEPOSTS

1. Where Are We From?
    a. How does geography explain our diversity?
    b. Why is the South the most distinct district in the United States?
    c. How have the South's voting patterns changed in recent years?
    d. What makes California distinctive?
    e. What has "white flight" done to the modern day city?
    f. How has the growth of metropolitan areas rearranged black-white relationships?

2. A Land of Diversity
    a. How has immigration made us so diverse?
    b. How does diversity promote tension?

3. Race and Ethnicity
    a. Who are the major racial groups in the United States?
    b. What percentage of the population does each group compose?
    c. Trace black migration patterns within the United States.
    d. What are the major areas of disagreement between blacks and whites?
    e. How have African Americans increased their political power? Which party do most African Americans favor? Why?
    f. Why have Asian-Americans been the most successful racial group economically and educationally?
    g. Under what legal handicaps do Native Americans operate?
    h. Why are the Hispanics considered an ethnic group?

4. Gender
    a. How has the political power of women changed in the last two decades?
    b. Why is income a major issue on the women's political agenda?
    c. What policy issues divide men and women?

5. Other Institutional Differences
    a. What role does religion play in the United States?
    b. What shifts in wealth and income have occurred since 1980?
    c. What distinctions exist between an industrial society and a post-industrial society?
    d. Why has social class been relatively unimportant in the United States? Could this change?
    e. Why have the elderly been such a political success?
    f. How important is education to a diverse society?

6. Unity in a Land of Diversity
    a. What factors unify our diverse population?

PART II — GLOSSARY

ETHNOCENTRISM - Values and attitudes based on individual experience.

MANIFEST DESTINY - A belief that the United States had been foreordained to occupy a position of world power and influence.

WHITE FLIGHT - The white desertion of central cities to the suburbs after World War II.

POLITICAL SOCIALIZATION - Values and attitudes that are conveyed to children by their parents.

DEMOGRAPHICS - Characteristics of the population.

REINFORCING CLEAVAGES - Situations in which personal, social and economic experiences coincide.

CROSSCUTTING CLEAVAGES - Situations in which personal, cultural and economic experiences are in conflict.

ETHNICITY - A group's background based on nationality or religion.

GENDER GAP - The difference that generally exists between men and women on opinions and voting.

POST INDUSTRIAL SOCIETY - A society (like the United States) that stresses technical ability.

SOCIAL CLASS - Division of society based on objective data on occupation, income and education.

PART III — PRETEST

1. The tendency of every person to make sweeping judgments based on their limited personal experience is called
    a. ethnocentricism.
    b. wisdom.
    c. experience.
    d. selfishness.

2. The most distinct geographical region in the United States is the
    a. midwest.   c. south.
    b. southwest.   d. west.

3. Only one of these cities *does not* have a majority black population.
    a. Phoenix
    b. Baltimore
    c. Richmond
    d. New Orleans

4. Which of these groups has the smallest proportion of college graduates?
   a. African Americans
   b. Hispanic
   c. Asiatics
   d. Native Americans

5. The most politically underrepresented group has been
   a. Asians.
   b. African Americans.
   c. Hispanic.
   d. women.

6. The most potent politically active group has been
   a. college students.
   b. the elderly.
   c. the poor.
   d. the common man.

7. A popular theory that explains the unity achieved by Americans is the
   a. salad bowl.
   b. melting pot.
   c. welding.
   d. ethnicity.

8. Compared to most industrialized countries, the United States does not have a high degree of
   _____ awareness.
   a. social class
   b. religious intolerance
   c. personal achievement
   d. acceptance of a leisure class

9. In recent years the South has given its vote for president to
   a. Republicans.
   b. Democrats.
   c. no decisive pattern.
   d. varied.

10. Black migration from the South occurred chiefly after
    a. 1865.
    b. 1950.
    c. 1970.
    d. 1900.

PART IV — PROGRAMMED REVIEW

Knowledge Objective: To trace the roots of the American people

1. During the 1980s a number of states voted legislation to make _____ the official language.
2. The tendency to generalize from our own experience is called _____ .
3. The belief that we have a foreordained role to become a world power is called _____ .
4. The most distinct section of the United States is the _____ .
5. After the Civil War the South normally supported the _____ party.
6. The West has developed a strong sense of _____ .
7. Although the nation's rural population has greatly diminished, its values are held by (few, many) _____ Americans.

8. The migration of white Americans to the suburbs after World War II is known as the _____ _____ .

9. Migration of the whites from the cities has resulted in a _____ tax base.

Knowledge Objective: To distinguish the various elements in our diverse society

10. Children normally learn their political values within the _____ .
11. When cultural values are in conflict the result is called _____ _____ cleavages.
12. Politically the United States compared to Ireland has less emphasis on _____ .
13. In the 1990 census _____ out of five Americans are white.
14. The mass migration of blacks to the city gave them greater _____ power but left them with limited _____ power.
15. Nearly _____ of the blacks fall below the poverty level.
16. Native American families are _____ as likely to be poor as blacks or whites.
17. Hispanics can be of any _____ .
18. Generally speaking older ethnic groups have greater _____ power than newer ethnic groups.
19. Compared to the women in other countries, American women vote _____ (more, less).
20. The largest segment of Americans are _____ .
21. Women for the most part (do, do not) _____ support female candidates.
22. As women age, the earnings gap _____ .
23. Significant political difference between men and women is called the _____ _____ .
24. A defining characteristic of religion in America is the variety of _____ .

Knowledge Objective: To investigate social and economic differences

25. Compared to most other countries, Americans have _____ incomes.
26. Widespread income distribution results in political _____ .
27. One of the most important means for Americans to achieve economic and social mobility is _____ .
28. Originally most Americans worked as _____ .
29. Today America is known as a _____ _____ society.
30. In terms of social class most Americans believe that they are _____ class.
31. In recent years the American Dream has been challenged by foreign _____ .

PART V — POST-TEST

1. Democratic strengths in the South have been greatest in elections for
    a. president.
    b. U.S. Senate.
    c. representative.
    d. no pattern.

2. The state with the largest population is
    a. New York.
    b. Pennsylvania.
    c. California.
    d. Texas.

3. *All but one* of these states lost representation as a result of the 1990 census.
    a. California
    b. Montana
    c. New York
    d. Pennsylvania

4. The population of American cities has *all but one* of the following characteristics.
    a. poor   c. independent
    b. black   d. democratic

5. Black unemployment is a result of *all but one* of the following.
    a. limited education
    b. youth
    c. depressed urban areas
    d. limited political power

6. Most Asian Americans live in *all but one* of the following states.
    a. Michigan
    b. Hawaii
    c. Washington
    d. California

7. Recent Asian American migration has been from *all but one* of the following.
    a. Korea
    b. Japan
    c. Philippines
    d. Southeast Asia

8. The fastest growing ethnic group in the United States is
    a. Hispanics.
    b. African Americans.
    c. Asians.
    d. Native Americans.

9. The gray lobby has *all but one* of these political assets.
    a. mostly male
    b. disposable income
    c. discretionary time
    d. focused issues

10. American unity is strengthened by *all but one* of the following.
    a. the American dream
    b. work ethic
    c. economic opportunity
    d. foreign investment

PART VI — POLITICAL DIALOGUE: THE CLASH OF ISSUES AND IDEAS

1. "Alexander Solzhenitsyn had it right when he declared that America had no soul nor sense of direction. We wallow in a moral-spiritual vacuum that encourages crime, violence, pornography and a lack of taste. Although this is bitter medicine, it happens to be true. Check it out any time of the day by turning on your TV set." Discuss.

2. Arthur Schlesinger in a recent book, *The Disuniting of America*, declares that in promoting cultural diversity current educators are destroying American unity. He says that in an effort to give American blacks pride and a sense of worth, we have greatly distorted European history and

Western values. The current collapse of the Soviet Union, Czechoslovakia and Yugoslavia into mutually warring groups is the end result of an American educated in multiculturalism. Is multiculturalism in conflict with truth and unity?

3. In his recent "best-seller," *Bonfire of the Vanities*, Tom Wolfe describes contemporary New York City as a tiny white island surrounded by a turbulent sea of racial minorities potentially ready at all times to wipe out the affluent white survivors. These survivors vaguely know of the threat, but ignore it, encased in their little world of furs, posh restaurants, and lavishly decorated apartments. The other New York is one of violence, drugs, prisons, and overcrowding. Without raising the question, Wolfe's portrait poses this issue: Can such a stark disparities of wealth and poverty continue to coexist? What do you think? Is Los Angeles becoming another such city?

PART VII — POLITICAL SCIENCE TODAY

1. Are your church or synagogue religious leaders active in local, state, or even national politics? If so, do you believe that such activities violate the church-state separation principle in American politics? If so, why? If not, why not?

2. Debate and/or analyze the merits of the "salad bowl" analogy. Is it relatively accurate or not? Try to explain why or why not.

3. Based upon the chapter material, do you believe the rich-poor gap is widening in America? Second, do you believe it is a problem? Third, do you believe that the federal government is capable of eliminating or seriously reducing the number of poor people in America today? Cite your reasons.

4. Discuss with your instructor how America's "diversity" has strengthened the nation's development. Conversely, how does this "diversity" weaken the nation?

5. What obstacles do you believe female candidates have in running for political office, either at the federal or state/local levels? Also, do you believe that you will see a woman elected President of the United States in your lifetime—why or why not?

PART VIII — DATA ANALYSIS

1. Increasingly, there have been acts of discrimination directed at some of America's recent immigrants, such as the Vietnamese or Koreans. For example, in the LA riots of 1992, which followed the not-guilty verdict in the Rodney King case, many Korean-owned businesses were burned to the ground. Research the reasons behind such acts. Does your research indicate Black-Korean race conflicts not only in LA, but in other larger metropolitan areas across the nation? What types of public policies could resolve these conflicts?

2. The chapter notes that despite Americans becoming "more and more educated, roughly two-thirds of Americans have never gone to college" and that the "experience of higher education has not been uniformly shared" (blacks and Hispanics have been short-changed). Therefore, would American society benefit if the federal government assured a college education for every American who wished to attend a college or university? Imagine that the college-educated percentage of the population would double (at least)? How would this affect the political process or the nation's capacity to compete with the other industrialized nations of the world? Are there other social and economic implications which would follow? Speculate on these and other consequences.

3. The chapter asserts that senior citizens vote more regularly and have become a potent political

force in America. Research the impact of the senior citizen vote in the 1994 congressional elections by perusing relevant articles in newspapers, magazines, or journals. In which states were senior citizens particularly influential?

PART IX — TEST ANSWERS

Pretest

1. a
2. c
3. a
4. d
5. d

6. b
7. b
8. a
9. a
10. b

Programmed Review

1. English
2. Ethnocentricism
3. Manifest destiny
4. South
5. Democratic
6. Individualism
7. Many
8. White flight
9. Declining
10. Family
11. Cross-cutting
12. Religion
13. Four
14. Political; economic
15. One third
16. Twice

17. Race
18. Economic
19. Less
20. Women
21. Do not
22. Widens
23. Gender gap
24. Denominations
25. High
26. Stability
27. Education
28. Farmers
29. Post industrial
30. Middle
31. Competition

Post-test

1. c
2. c
3. a
4. c
5. d

6. a
7. b
8. a
9. a
10. d

Data Analysis

Answers to both exercises 1, 2, and 3 will vary depending upon the individual student's research and approach.

CHAPTER 9
INTEREST GROUPS: THE POLITICS OF INFLUENCE

One permanent feature of our political landscape is the division of Americans into contending factions. Much of our political history can be captured in the rise and fall of these groups, their conflicts, and their compromises. Beyond their families, most Americans owe their top loyalty to an economic group, a professional group, an ideological group, and any one of hundreds of other causes that have their own groups. James Madison foresaw and accepted this organization of society two centuries ago. Today interest groups seem to dominate the political scene far more than do political parties.

The modern twist in interest group politics is the growth of PAC's. By 1990 they had become a major financial factor in Congressional elections and since most of their money goes to influential incumbents, they have thus become a powerful voice in all legislation.

An important question constantly echoed is: "Are interest groups becoming too strong"?

One opinion: By organizing and using the political process, individuals can be more effective. Further, groups are competitive, and in politics they generally cancel each other.

Dissenting opinion: Interest groups are using money and the mass media to influence and persuade so effectively that older concepts of power are out of date. So are our techniques of control.

Another point of view: The problem is not so much the growing number of interest groups as it is a problem of how they distort the general interest of the nation.

PART I — GUIDEPOSTS

1. The Maze of Interest Groups
    a. Madison foresaw "factions" as an inevitable development of popular government. How did he propose to control this problem in *Federalist, No. 51*?
    b. What is an interest group?
    c. Why are they organized?
    d. What makes public interest groups distinctive?
    e. How do movements differ from interest groups?

2. Major Interest Groups: Size and Scope
    a. What are the "big three" economic interest groups?
    b. What are the major professional interest groups?
    c. Name three non-occupational interest groups.
    d. What groups are organized to influence foreign policy?
    e. Why do single cause interest groups offer a challenge to democracy?

3. Weapons of Group Power
    a. What advantages do large interest groups have? What weaknesses?
    b. How is overlapping membership a limiting factor?
    c. What factors contribute to an effective interest group?

  d. How do interest groups attract members and get financial support?
  e. How do interest groups use each of the following techniques in lobbying: persuasion; elections; litigation; mass mailing; rule making?
  f. What is cooperative lobbying?

4. Lobbying: Old and New Approaches
  a. How does modern lobbying differ from that of the 1800s?
  b. What are the rules for successful lobbying?
  c. What skills does a lobbyist need?

5. PAC's: Interest Groups in Combat
  a. What is a PAC?
  b. How do PAC's allocate their contributions?
  c. Why has PAC money become so important in Congressional races?
  d. How much influence does PAC money have on elections and legislation?

6. Controlling Factions
  a. How would Madison react to the modern lobbying scene?
  b. What constitutional issue is raised when we try to control interest groups?
  c. Why is Congress reluctant to reform PAC's?
  d. Is lobbying a good or evil force in the United States?

PART II — GLOSSARY

PAC - Political Action Committee organized to influence elections and legislation.
FEDERALIST NO. 10 - An essay, written by Madison, that describes the inevitability of factions in a democratic government.
FEDERALIST NO. 51 - An essay by Madison, suggesting that the power of interest groups could be curbed by the system of checks and balances.
OVERLAPPING MEMBERSHIP - The theory that an interest group's power can be diluted by the multiple affiliations of its members.
SINGLE INTEREST GROUP - A group whose power and concern is concentrated in a single issue.
PUBLIC INTEREST GROUP - A group that claims to be interested only in the general welfare, rather than a narrower, selfish cause. Example: Common Cause.
INTEREST GROUP - A political group whose members share certain attitudes which exerts influence to achieve its objectives.
LOBBYING - Activities aimed at influencing legislative or administrative decision-making.
NONPARTISAN GROUP - A group not affiliated with a political party.
ELECTIONEERING - Campaigning for a candidate, party or issue in an election.
LITIGATION - Pursuing a case or claim through the judicial process.
AMICUS CURIAE - Translated as "friend of the court". Such an individual or group cannot initiate a suit, but may give testimony in a pending case. For example, the court might permit the American Civil Liberties Union to file briefs showing the larger applications.

PART III — PRETEST

 1. The loyalty of interest group members is often diminished by their
  a. overlapping allegiances.
  c. limited time.
  b. inability to pay dues.
  d. religious convictions.

2. Nearly all adult Americans belong to an _____ interest group.
    a. social   c. ideological
    b. religious   d. occupational

3. In recent years the great expansion of PACs has been in the _____ sector.
    a. labor   c. business
    b. professional   d. farming

4. The chief influence of PACs in election campaigns has been their
    a. contributions.   c. door-bell ringing.
    b. advice.   d. professional aid.

5. In its efforts to control factions and interest groups, the United States has rejected
    a. their prohibition.
    b. publicizing their activity.
    c. regulating their activity.
    d. lobbying.

6. The commonly accepted doctrine with respect to women's rights in colonial America was
    a. women had no rights before marriage.
    b. a wife is dead in law.
    c. spinsters are outside the law.
    d. better an in-law than an out-law.

7. Which one of the following interest groups cuts across religious, ethnic, and economic groups?
    a. American Medical Association
    b. American Soybean Association
    c. Knights of Columbus
    d. Young Americans for Freedom

8. The interest group that has advocated an open political process and electoral reform is
    a. the National Rifle Association.
    b. Nuclear Freeze.
    c. the Trilateral Commission.
    d. Common Cause.

9. Efforts to represent the general welfare are thwarted by _____ groups.
    a. public interest   c. occupational
    b. single cause   d. organized

10. Labor's political clout is concentrated in a major PAC called
    a. CIO.   c. NIP.
    b. COPE.   d. POL.

PART IV — PROGRAMMED REVIEW

Knowledge Objective: To examine factions as a force in politics
    1. James Madison's famous essay on the role of factions is called _____ _____
    _____ .
    2. Madison believed that popular government normally resulted in instability, injustice, and confusion because it encouraged the growth of _____ .
    3. Any group whose members share attitudes and try to achieve certain aims and objectives is called an _____ group.

4. Movements normally arise when segments of the population find that the dominant political culture does not share their _____ .
5. Movement politics normally is successful in raising the political _____ of their followers.
6. In early American History women had no _____ rights.
7. The Nineteenth Amendment was a milestone in the women's movement that gave them the right to _____ .

Knowledge Objective: To describe the various kinds of interest groups

8. Nearly every employed person belongs to an _____ interest group.
9. The major farm interest group is _____ _____ _____ ; labor's largest group is _____ ; and the largest business group is_____ _____ _____ _____ .
10. Common Cause is an example of a _____ _____ group.
11. The highly articulate spokesman for a conglomerate of consumer interest groups is _____ _____ .
12. The ACLU is an example of an _____ interest group.
13. _____ _____ groups focus on highly specialized political issues.

Knowledge Objective: To investigate the techniques of interest group politics

14. Central tests of a group's power are its _____ and _____ .
15. The cohesiveness of any interest group is weakened by _____ memberships.
16. The AARP uses _____ to combat the free-rider problem.
17. Civil liberties, environmental, and black groups have used _____ as a weapon to achieve their goals.
18. The Food Group is an example of _____ lobbying.
19. The employee of an interest group who presents its point of view to legislators is called a _____ .
20. The employment cycle from government to interest group is known as the _____ .
21. Lobbyists have the _____ _____ needed by legislators for policy making.

Knowledge Objective: To examine the scope of PACs

22. The newest form of interest groups that back candidates and raise money are _____ .
23. The great expansion of PACs during the 1980s was among _____ interest groups.
24. Contributors to PACs normally (do, do not) _____ demand immediate payoffs if their candidate wins.
25. Big labor's political arm is called _____ .
26. Today it is not uncommon for U.S. House candidates to spend a _____ dollars.
27. _____ is not a major criterion used by big corporations in financing the campaigns of Congressional candidates.
28. Most PAC funds go to _____ Congressmen.

Knowledge Objective: To survey the proposals for controlling factions

29. Strengthening _____ _____ would be one way to reduce the power of special interest groups.
30. The impact of the 1971 Federal Election Campaign Law bas been to (increase, decrease) _____ political activity of interest groups.
31. Interest groups provide _____ representation.

PART V — POST-TEST

1. James Madison urged the control of contending factions under the new constitution in an essay called
    a. *Failing Factions.*
    b. *Letters of the Federal Farmer.*
    c. *Downing #9.*
    d. *Federalist #10.*

2. Many of the strongest "unions" in terms of their political effectiveness are _____ organizations.
    a. recreational
    b. racial
    c. feminine
    d. professional

3. Those organizations that insist that they are solely devoted to the public welfare are called
    a. ideological.
    b. professional.
    c. public interest.
    d. political.

4. One of the following factors is normally not critical in determining a group's political strength.
    a. strong leadership
    b. size of membership
    c. unity of membership
    d. geographical distribution

5. Ralph Nader, the American Civil Liberties Union, and the NAACP have depended heavily upon _____ to influence public policy.
    a. litigation
    b. direct action
    c. persuasion
    d. campaign spending

6. The political arm of a business-labor-professional interest group is called a
    a. LEG.
    b. GYP.
    c. CON.
    d. PAC.

7. The least important factor in determining the support of candidates by business PACs is their
    a. voting record.
    b. incumbency.
    c. winability.
    d. party affiliation.

8. An interest group that "targets" political candidates on the basis of ideology is
    a. Victory Action Committee.
    b. National Education Association.
    c. AFL-CIO.
    d. COPE.

9. When a group finds the normal political processes closed, they are apt to turn to
    a. propaganda.
    b. rule-making.
    c. litigation.
    d. persuasion.

10. From a Congressional point of view, the most useful service provided by lobbyists is
    a. public opinion polls.
    b. specialized information.
    c. influence.
    d. speech writing.

PART VI — POLITICAL DIALOGUE:
THE CLASH OF ISSUES AND IDEAS

1. Special interest PAC "investments" in incumbents are rigging our elections and corrupting the political system. Comment.

2. The present PAC-rigged system is creating a challenger-proof Congress. Only seven House incumbents lost during the 1988 elections. A record 98 percent of members of Congress seeking reelection won. Would you join Common Cause to reform the present system.

3. In Congressman Otis Pike's "Farewell Address," he declared that he was constantly being badgered by shrill constituents (as many as 300 a day) demanding specific legislation favorable to themselves. These people, Pike said, concentrated only on their own narrow issues, with no concern for the broad voting record of their Congressman or the general welfare. How should a Congressman react when confronted by a single interest group in his district that flourished hundred-dollar bills and a substantial voting bloc to a candidate?

4. James Madison thought that "factions" were bound to emerge in a democratic society. Why? What antidote did he rely on?

5. Madison was concerned about religious, political and economic factions. What are the key issues and groups today?

6. Recent events may have diminished or destroyed the alleged "hammerlock" that incumbents had on Congressional seats. States in growing numbers are placing limits on the number of terms that a person may serve in Congress. Even without these limits Congressional scandals such as Congressional cheque overdrafts on the House bank appear to be the reason why long-term Congressional members are failing to file for reelection, or, if they run, are defeated. Clearly the next Congress is going to see many new faces and probably an erosion of power since the new members owe leaders nothing. Comment.

7. "Movement Politics is a defensive tactic, used only by those who are politically weak. When any movement gets political clout it becomes even more Establishment-oriented than the existing political Establishment and quite prone to ignore minority rights." Do you agree or disagree with the foregoing statement? Apply your analysis to the Women's movement.

8. The political socialization of persons in movements tends to be more intense than that of persons in run-of-the-mill interest groups. What is meant by consciousness-raising? Why does the feeling that one is an outsider, that direct action is needed, or that no compromise can be accepted help to achieve a political socialization that may be in opposition to one's family or social background?

PART VII — POLITICAL SCIENCE TODAY

1. One powerful interest group in America is the NRA—the National Rifle Association. The NRA has always maintained that the right to bear arms is guaranteed by the second Amendment to the Constitution and that individuals, in order to protect their lives, liberties, and property, should confront few restrictions on gun ownership or acquisition. Traditionally, the NRA has been able to influence members of Congress to oppose gun control legislation or to punish those members who support such legislation.

However, during the Clinton Administration, NRA lobbying failed to stop the passage of the Brady bill (imposed a waiting period for the purchase of handguns) and a crime bill that banned the sale and manufacture of 19 assault weapons. Increasingly, politicians viewed the NRA as extremist. Also, the American public was deeply worried about crime. The NRA responded by targeting anti-NRA House and Senate members in the 1994 elections and funneling millions of dollars to pro-NRA challengers.

How effective was the NRA in these elections? See if you can find any evidence of the organization's success or failure through a perusal of newspaper or journal sources.

2. It should be remembered that the clash of interests does not occur solely between or among groups or individuals who are outside of governmental service. A good example of this interaction between a business interest group and a government official occurred in 1989 when the Grumman Corporation fought to save the F-14 fighter from being cut out of the defense budget.

The account of the clash can be found in *The New York Times* article of July 14, 1989 entitled "F-14; Test of Cheney's Power Against Long Island Lobby" (p. 9) by writer Richard Halloran. Halloran described how Defense Secretary Dick Cheney wished to stop producing the F-14 in order to reduce the military budget. Conversely, Grumman and congressmen from Long Island (the location of the company) argued that continued production of the plane was "vital to the company's survival and to 5,100 jobs on the Island." While the House Armed Services Committee voted to continue production, the Senate Armed Services Committee voted not to continue building the plane. Fierce lobbying continued to try and affect the floor votes of each house.

Grumman lobbyists were able to enlist the support of two important Senators, John Glenn of Ohio and John McCain of Arizona. Both Senators insisted that the security of the nation would be jeopardized if new production were halted. Cheney insisted that at some point in time, production of old weapons must stop and new ones must begin. Cheney, through Pentagon aides, lobbied a large number of congressmen and senators in anticipation of a final decision later in the month.

What happened to the F-14? Check back in *The New York Times* (use the *Index*) and find the outcome. Was Grumman or Cheney successful? What reasons can you uncover for the final policy decision rendered by Congress?

3. In the 1990s, anti-smoking interest groups and members of Congress weakened the tobacco lobby. Proposed smoking bans in public buildings (the Pentagon had banned smoking in most military workplaces) and advertising restrictions were considered as the evidence of health damage from secondary cigarette smoke mounted. Legislators asserted that the tobacco industry had been unyielding in its assertion that smoking was not harmful (an EPA report had shown a connection between second-hand smoke and cancer) or addictive (the media charged that tobacco companies had "spiked" nicotine levels in cigarettes to make them more addictive). The tobacco companies responded by asserting that the personal freedom of smokers was being threatened and that tobacco sales were important to the economy.

Imagine that you were a member of Congress. Would you favor or oppose legislation proposing (a) a total, national ban on smoking in all public places, including restaurants; (b) a total ban on all cigarette ads; (c) a $2.00 additional excise tax on each pack of cigarettes where this tax would go to alleviate the costs of national health care? Explain your reasoning in each of the three proposals.

PART VIII — DATA ANALYSIS

1. Frequently, one interest group will make demands that conflict with another interest group's wishes. For example, suppose a federal highway is proposed through a picturesque site. The building of a new highway will be favored by construction firms and related labor unions but may be opposed by groups dedicated to preserving the environment.

   In a similar fashion, suppose that the government agency responsible for promoting highway safety announces that it is considering the adoption of a new regulation. The proposed regulation would compel automobile manufacturers to include air bags for both the driver and front-seat passenger (air bags would inflate in a head-on collision within milli-seconds, thus saving lives) in all new cars and trucks. Which of the following interest groups do you think would be for and against the regulation? Write your thoughts in the space provided after each group; then check the answer key.

   a. automobile manufacturers

   b. UAW - United Autoworkers Union

   c. consumer rights groups

   d. a safety engineers association

   e. an association of independent truck drivers

2. There are a number of factors that determine the political power and effectiveness of each interest group. Some of these factors are size, prestige, financial strength, leadership skills, internal cohesion, and the dedication of opposing interest groups. Think about these and other factors mentioned in the chapter and explain the following situation.

   The AFL-CIO is certainly one of the largest interest groups in America and also one of the best financed. It maintains a significant number of lobbyists at all levels of government. However, the AFL-CIO has never been able to persuade the Congress to pass a comprehensive national health insurance program which it has supported for over a decade. Why has the AFL-CIO not been successful in this effort? Jot down some possible reasons in the space below and then consult the Answer Key.

PART IX — TEST ANSWERS

Pretest

1. a
2. d
3. c
4. a
5. a

6. b
7. d
8. d
9. b
10. b

Programmed Review

1. *Federalist* # 10
2. factions
3. interest
4. values
5. conscience
6. legal
7. vote
8. occupational
9. American Farm Bureau; AFL-CIO; US Chamber of Commerce
10. public interest
11. Ralph Nadar
12. ideological
13. single interest
14. size, involvement
15. overlapping
16. incentives

17. litigation
18. cooperative
19. lobbyist
20. revolving door
21. specialized knowledge
22. PACs
23. business
24. do not
25. COPE
26. million
27. party
28. incumbent
29. political parties
30. increase
31. functional

Post-test

1. d
2. d
3. c
4. b
5. a

6. d
7. d
8. a
9. c
10. b

Data Analysis

1. Auto manufacturers are going to increase the price of their cars since the two air bags will add at least $1000 to each car's cost. Hence, their cars may suffer from price competition. The UAW would probably support the law, provided management would not try to cut jobs in order to shave costs. Consumer rights groups and the safety engineers association would probably be supportive of the law, especially the latter. Truck drivers would have mixed feelings, since the danger of head-on collisions might appear less probable to them. The cost of air-bag equipped trucks could also be a factor to them.

2. The AFL-CI0 has encountered opposition from other interest groups who oppose the cost of such a program. Also, organized labor has lost some of its political clout and membership over the past decade.

CHAPTER 10
POLITICAL PARTIES

I t is difficult to imagine a modern democratic government without political parties. Parties have become so much a part of our concept of a free society that we cannot understand why many of the Founding Fathers were suspicious and even hostile to them. There is no mention of political parties in the Constitution, and George Washington devoted a good portion of his Farewell Address warning against parties and factions.

Parties, therefore, have earned a high place in the list of fundamental democratic institutions. The basic question, then, is not whether we should have political parties or whether we should have the two-party system. Both of these questions have been answered. The problem is, rather, "Are political parties strong enough to raise the pertinent issues, to pose honest alternatives, and, after the elections are over, to translate campaign promises into legislative realities?"

One view: The moderate character of American political parties represents the genius of the American system. Our parties do raise issues but, perhaps, what is even more important, they help us arrive at consensus.

Another view: We need a thorough going revision of the party system. Today's political parties do not raise the big problems but rather take evasive stands on issues which they cannot avoid.

One development of the last forty years has been the cleavage between presidential party politics (Republicans have won the Presidency in seven out of the last eleven elections). On the other hand, Democrats have held a majority in both houses of Congress with few exceptions since the 1930s. The latest exception is the 1994 mid-term elections. Also, during most of this period Democrats have held a majority of the governorships and state legislatures. The confusing picture demonstrates that on the national political scene party loyalty has been, until the 1994 mid-term elections, at best a scrambled pattern. In fact, each party has lost membership to those who regard themselves as "independents," without any deep-seated loyalty to either party.

Yet the political parties remain an integral part of our political process. They serve as a bonding agent that offers voters a choice of policies and candidates at every level of government. Reports of their decline and disappearance are premature. Although scarred by conflict and unrealized goals, they are nevertheless living institutions, deeply rooted in the American democratic process.

Proposals for reform and rehabilitation abound. Democrats have tried to reach out to minorities while keeping the loyalty of middle and upper class voters. To give the party an up-to-the-minute look they tried and then abandoned midterm conventions. Republicans have been at least partially successful in winning elections in the long-time Democratic "Solid South". They have also been in the vanguard with modern campaign techniques, public opinion polling, and professional help for candidates. Each party dreams of a massive political realignment that will give it a permanent majority.

So the old political parties are not dead nor dormant. Each tries to reach out for attractive issues and candidates. Losers in every election lick their wounds and vow to do better next time. Each winner analyzes mistakes and hopes for a greater victory in the next encounter.

PART I — GUIDEPOSTS

1. What Parties Do for Democracy
    a. What are the major functions of parties? Evaluate their performance in each category.
    b. What three methods have been used by parties to select candidates? Which method is the most common today?
    c. Are political parties an appropriate vehicle for social reform?
    d. What is the role of third parties?
    e. What contributions to American government have third parties made?
    f. Why do third parties usually fail?

2. Parties: Their Rise and Role
    a. What was the attitude of the Founding Fathers toward parties? Why?
    b. What were the original names of the Democratic party?
    c. What party emerged to replace the Federalists?
    d. How was the spoils system used by political parties?
    e. What were the origins of the GOP?
    f. How did reforms of the Progressive Era affect political parties?
    g. What groups were brought together in FDR's New Deal?
    h. In what sense were attempts of Reagan to make Republicans the dominant party thwarted?

3. American Parties Today
    a. What characteristics do both major parties share today?
    b. How do Americans view political parties today?
    c. How are parties organized at the national level? Describe the role of the presidential convention; the national committee; the national party chairperson.
    d. What is the role of congressional and senatorial campaign committees?
    e. How are parties organized at the state, county and local level?
    f. How do political parties operate in the Congress; Executive Branch; Judicial Branch, State and Local Governments?

4. Parties in the Electorate
    a. What distinctions have existed historically between Democrats and Republicans? How do they differ today?
    b. What are the different ways citizens view party partisanship?
    c. How important is party identification?
    d. What is meant by party realignment? What prospects confront each party in the 1990s?

5. Saving the Parties
    a. Are parties dying?
    b. What procedural reforms have been adopted by Democrats? Republicans?
    c. What prospects for renewal have been adopted by each party?

PART II — GLOSSARY

SPLIT TICKET - Casting a ballot for candidates of different parties in an election.
SUPERDELEGATE - A Democratic policy that gives party leaders an automatic seat at the national convention.
PATRONAGE - Awarding government jobs to political supporters.
DIRECT PRIMARY - An election in which party members select their candidates for the general election.

THIRD PARTY - A political party that challenges the two traditional parties.
GRASS ROOTS - The ordinary voters.
REALIGNMENT - A shift of voters from one party to the other.
TWO-PARTY SYSTEM - A political system in which there are only two major parties — one in power, one in opposition.
PARTY CONVENTION - A meeting of party delegates to pass on matters of policy and party matters, and in some cases to select party candidates for public office. Conventions are held on county, state, and national levels.
CAUCUS - A closed meeting of party leaders.
RANK AND FILE - The regular, ordinary party members.
GRAND OLD PARTY (GOP) - The Republican party.
OFFICEHOLDER OR CANDIDATE POLITICS - Description of our political system perhaps more apt than *party politics:* Political activity revolves around people seeking or holding office rather than around an integrated, hierarchical party system.
COALITION - An alliance of distinct factions or parties to form a stronger group for mutual action.
UNIT RULE - Formerly used in the national nominating conventions of both parties; under this system the vote of the entire delegation was cast as a unit on a majority vote basis.
GRAND COALITION - An alliance of diverse factions, groups, or voting alignments which support a particular party for an extended period of time.

PART III — PRETEST

1. The Republican coalition put together by Ronald Reagan did not include
    a. born-again Christians.
    b. African Americans.
    c. white Southerners.
    d. conservatives.

2. Managing the presidential campaign is the job of
    a. the national committee.
    b. the national chairman.
    c. the attorney general.
    d. the presidential press secretary.

3. The first Republican party was led by
    a. Jefferson.
    b. Hamilton.
    c. Washington.
    d. Adams.

4. Candidates are selected by their parties because of
    a. party loyalty.
    b. personal appeal.
    c. endorsement by party leaders.
    d. ideological correctness.

5. When voters may choose what ballot they will vote in a primary, it is called
    a. closed.
    b. open.
    c. realignment.
    d. dealiagnment.

6. The purpose of a political party is
    a. to recruit potential officeholders.
    b. to simplify alternatives.
    c. to unite the electorate.
    d. all of the above.

7. A striking characteristic of third parties is that they
    a. advance controversial issues and ideas.
    b. are always radical.
    c. are always conservative.
    d. have no place in the American system.

8. The most significant factor influencing the character of American political parties is
    a. the federal system.   c. the party senority system.
    b. the national convention.   d. the presidential primary.

9. Which of the following is *not* a present-day function of political parties?
    a. distribution of welfare handouts
    b. stimulation of interest in public affairs
    c. recruitment of political leadership
    d. linkage between the mass public and government

10. A major cause for the persistence of the two-party system in the United States is that
    a. the major parties have become disciplined and issue-oriented.
    b. election districts have a single incumbent.
    c. third parties have failed to point up issues.
    d. major party ideas and platform are too much like religious dogma.

PART IV — PROGRAMMED REVIEW

Knowledge objective: To analyze what parties do for democracy
    1. Parties organize the _____ by choosing candidates to run under their label.
    2. Lacking organized party support in seeking nomination, a candidate builds a _____ organization.
    3. Parties failed to unify the electorate in the 1860s over the issue of _____ .
    4. The outcomes of American elections (do, do not) _____ make a difference in public policy.
    5. Party _____ include simplifying issues, stimulating interest, uniting different segments of society, and recruiting political leadership.
    6. Political parties formerly served as a kind of employment agency through their control of _____ .
    7. As a method of choosing candidates, the caucus was replaced by party _____ which on the state level were replaced by the _____ .
    8. The American two-party system is maintained because in our single election districts only _____ candidate wins.

Knowledge Objective: To review the long history of American political parties
    9. The second U.S. constitution (unwritten) shifted power from the established branches of government to _____ _____ .
    10. The Federalist party was challenged by the first _____ party, headed by Jefferson.
    11. Today's _____ party (Grand Old Party) arose out of the Civil War.
    12. _____ created a party coalition of Southerners, labor, farmers, the unemployed and suburbanites.
    13. Until the 1994 mid-term elections, Republicans have been more successful in winning _____ elections than congressional elections.

Knowledge Objective: To review the present state of our parties
    14. Modern political parties have (more, less) _____ voice in choosing presidential candidates.

15. Both parties today are (moderate, sharply different) _____ in policies and leadership.
16. Political parties in the United States are primarily organized to win political _____ .
17. The reason why political parties are so decentralized is the _____ basis of our government.
18. American political parties are basically loose _____ of state and local committees.
19. The supreme authority in both political parties is the national _____ convention.
20. A national_____ heads each of the two major parties.
21. In the US Congress, the committee chairs of all the standing committees come from the _____ party.
22. Party platforms try to _____ differences in order to appeal to as many voters as possible.
23. Democrats are (more/less) _____ likely than Republicans to give government a large role in social-economic programs.
24. Democrats, as a rule, are ideologically (more/less) _____ diverse than Republicans.
25. A _____ primary is one in which voters are restricted to a single party in the primary election.
26. Party _____ is the single best predictor of the voter.
27. Efforts to reshuffle existing political coalitions is called _____ .
28. Pure _____ are the least apt to vote.
29. The main charges against political parties is failure to take meaningful stands on _____ and weak _____ .
30. The technology that has had the most impact on elections is the _____ .

Knowledge Objective: To look at the question, "Can parties be saved?"

31. _____ have followed a middle path in their efforts at party reform.
32. Republican efforts at party renewal have concentrated on more effective _____ techniques.
33. Both Republicans and Democrats are more interested in party _____ than party reforms.

PART V — POST-TEST

1. The person least likely to vote is a
   a. strong Democrat.
   b. weak Republican.
   c. pure Independent.
   d. middle-of-road Democrat.

2. The _____ party evolved out of the crisis over slavery.
   a. Whig
   b. Democratic
   c. Modern Republican
   d. Second Federalist

3. Third-party leaders have included all of the following *except*
   a. John Anderson.
   b. Ross Perot.
   c. George Wallace.
   d. Governor Jerry Brown.

4. In both major parties, the supreme authority is the
   a. candidate.
   b. party chairman.
   c. national presidential convention.
   d. primaries.

5. The grass roots of each party is
    a. in the deep south.
    b. in the western states.
    c. at the city, town, ward, and precinct level.
    d. at the family, church, and school level.

6. The party that put together a grand coalition lasting from the Civil War until 1932 was
    a. Democratic.   c. Whigs.
    b. Republican.   d. none of the above.

7. Under the dealignment theory, people have
    a. become Reagan Democrats.
    b. become presidential Democrats.
    c. abandoned both parties to become Independents.
    d. returned to liberal Democrats.

8. When a voter must be registered in a party to vote in the primary, it is called
    a. closed.
    b. open.
    c. direct.
    d. crossover.

9. Republicans in the past decade have not emphasized one of the following reforms
    a. membership recruitment.   c. grassroots organization.
    b. racial and sex quotas.   d. candidate training programs.

10. Both major political parties today are
    a. relatively weak.   c. class-oriented.
    b. strong coalitions.   d. tightly disciplined.

PART VI — POLITICAL DIALOGUE:
THE CLASH OF ISSUES AND IDEAS

1. In our most hotly contested Presidential elections nearly half of Americans do not vote. This proves the political parties are ineffective. Comment.

2. Interest groups and PACs have for all practical purposes replaced political parties. It is futile to try to revive them. Discuss.

3. George Washington warned against "the baneful effects of the spirit of party" and Jefferson said "If I could not go to heaven but with a party, I would not go there at all." Were these comments justified, given our 200 years experience with parties.

4. Third parties are living proof that the major parties have failed. Comment.

5. In 1992 Ross Perot demonstrated great popular appeal by campaigning as an independent outside the political party system. Was his campaign an aberration or did it represent a permanent shift in the time-honored political party system? What advantages did Perot have?

6. Neither major political party is today willing to solve the problem of the national debt. Do you agree or disagree? Why?

7. Today's pace of social change makes parties useless. They should be scrapped and some other political device substituted. Discuss.

8. "The Republican Party's reforms have made it more responsive to America's true needs than have party reforms by Democrats." Discuss.

PART VII — POLITICAL SCIENCE TODAY

1. The American political party system has traditionally revolved around two major parties, both committed to our constitutional and economic values. Accordingly, both the Democratic and Republican parties are centrist institutions, i.e., they make their appeals to the broad mainstream of American society. The party which best captures the broad center of the political spectrum is the party likely to achieve victory. Thus, when a presidential candidate representing a major party is perceived as too far removed from the center, the electoral result is disaster. This happened to the Republican Barry Goldwater in 1964 (too far to the right), Democrat George McGovern in 1972 (too far to the left), and, to a lesser extent, Democrat Michael Dukakis in the 1988 presidential election who was portrayed as too liberal by challenger George Bush.

The plight of Michael Dukakis centered around the "L" word's connotations in 1988 - the association of liberalism with the breakdown of the family, immoral behavior, overall permissiveness, high crime rates, protests from minorities, and generalized anti-Americanism. Unfortunately for Dukakis, voters saw the Dukakis-style liberalism as being on the wrong side of the key campaign issues. Irving Kristol, in an October 30, 1988 (p. E 23) *New York Times* article entitled "The Conservatives Have Better Ideas," explained as follows:

Foreign policy: "It is obvious to every American, as well as to foreign observers, that George Bush will favor larger military expenditures than will Michael Dukakis. It is also obvious that his foreign policy will be closer to President Reagan's than will Mr. Dukakis', whose foreign policy statements evoke echoes of Jimmy Carter.

Even the flap over the Pledge of Allegiance — dismissed by so many commentators as pointless and demeaning — has a bearing on perceived differences in foreign policy. Mr. Bush has aligned himself with the nationalist temper so visible among Americans, while Mr. Dukakis' attitude suggests a more familiar liberal-internationalist perspective."

Kristol argued that on social policy, many Americans favored the death penalty, were very worried about crime, and were anxious that the rights of criminals had been given precedence over the safety of their victims. In Kristol's words, "Mr. Dukakis is a liberal Democrat who has understandably aligned himself with what is accurately regarded as a liberal-permissive approach to crime." In addition, "Mr. Dukakis' failure to disengage himself unequivocally from the ultra-liberal (and somewhat bizarre) views of the American Civil Liberties Union has been costly."

Although Mr. Kristol is a conservative, it is true that in the mind of many voters Dukakis was identified with ideas and policies not acceptable to the mainstream of American thinking in 1988. This signified a major defeat for the Democratic Party, at least on the presidential level. However, the Democrats did maintain their control of both houses of Congress.

Speculate on how Dukakis could have avoided this unpopular label. Should he have stressed liberalism's concern for the poor, minorities, etc. even more than he did? Or should he have deliberately adopted the view of George Bush on the key issues of the day? Finally, given the experience of Dukakis in 1988, how did Governor Bill Clinton of Arkansas challenge President Bush's allegation of "radical liberalism" in the 1992 election? In order to help you, read the following recommendation by famed scholar Seymour Martin Lipset which appeared in the October 28, 1988 issue of *The New York Times*: "What can liberals and Democrats do? For one, they can try to change their ideological label as Tip O'Neill suggested early in the campaign, when he said that Michael Dukakis is not a liberal but a 'progressive.' When the progressive label had its greatest currency in American politics, from the turn of the century to the Great Depression, it was linked to fights against big business and for environmental and nationalist concerns. It meant something close to New Dealism and is still popular." In November, 1985, *The New York Times*/CBS News Poll asked whether respondents would 'feel more favorable or less favorable' to a public figure described as 'conservative,' 'liberal,' 'populist,' or 'progressive.' The most popular was progressive (37 percent to 7 percent) followed by conservative (27-13), liberal (15-17) and, worst of all, populist (6-21). In your research, did Clinton follow Lipset's advice in the 1992 campaign?

2. Periodically, the Gallup Poll asks the public what their images are of each major party in terms of each party's ability to handle the crucial issues and problems of the day. Check the most recent Gallup poll available as to which party is held by the American people to be best able to handle the questions of war or peace abroad and the promotion of economic prosperity at home. Can you detect any trends? Jot down your findings and consider the political implications of those findings.

3. Is it possible that a third political party can ever challenge the dominance of the two major parties in a presidential or even congressional race? First, after consulting appropriate sources and reading Chapter 10, speculate as to what specific institutional and social patterns would have to be modified or eliminated to allow a third party to be successful? Second, polls in late 1994 indicated a growing public disenchantment with both major parties. A poll in *The New York Times* (September 21, 1994, p. A12) revealed that 53% of the American people agreed that a third major political party was needed. The poll showed a cynical public that was turned off by traditional politicians of both parties as well as the "Ross Perot" (third party) phenomenon being firmly ingrained in the public's thinking. Would you personally vote for a third party candidate in future presidential or congressional elections? Why or why not? Also, do you believe that a third party presidential candidate will be elected, perhaps in 1996, 2000, or 2004? Explain your reasoning.

PART VIII — DATA ANALYSIS

1. Look at the "party scorecard" data that follows (*New York Times*, August 28, 1988, p. 17). This data was compiled *before* the 1988 presidential election. Since that time, have Republicans made progress in state legislatures *and* party identification? Using appropriate research sources (*New York Times Index, Gallup Poll*, Council of State Governments, etc.), complete the data to the *present*. Are the Democrats in danger of becoming a minority party not only at the presidential level, but at the state level as well? Or has there been little change overall in the party balance, excluding presidential politics? You should reflect upon the Republican sweep in the 1994 elections when the GOP gained control of both houses of Congress for the first time since 1954.

2. Look at the election data derived from *The New York Times*/CBS Poll of November 13, 1988. What appears to be the salient regional and racial patterns emerging from the data? After appropriate research, extend the data to the present, i.e., the 1994 year (include the results of the 1994 election). Have trends in the data changed substantially? If so, how? If not, why not?

A Party Scorecard

Republicans lead in Presidential elections. . .

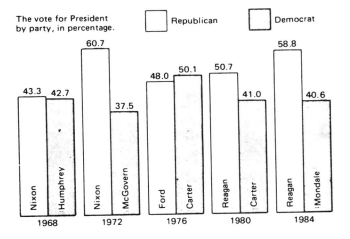

. . .but not in state legislatures. . .

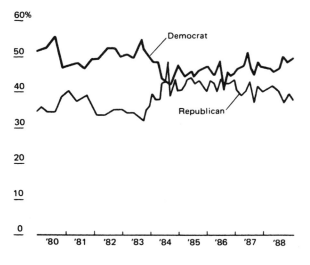

**. . .and they are still behind
in party identification**

Percentage of people who identify themselves with each party.
Independents who said they leaned to a party included. Based
on New York Times/CBS News Polls; February and September
1985 from New York Times Polls. August and October 1980
based on registered voters only.

3. Prior to the 1994 mid-term elections (October), more than 300 Republican candidates for the House of Representatives assembled on the steps of the Capital to sign what they called a "Contract With America." This "Contract" contained 10 measures that the Republicans promised to bring to a vote if they controlled the next Congress. These measures contained tax breaks designed to help middle and upper-income taxpayers, cuts in welfare payments, a balanced budget amendment by the year 2002, a legislative line-item veto, and so forth. These tax cuts would be partially offset by spending reductions over a five year period. When the GOP swept into power after the elections, the new House Speaker, Newt Gingrich (Ga.), promised to implement this contract when the new Republican-controlled 104th Congress convened in January of 1995.

How successful were the Republicans in making good on their contractual promises? How many of the ten measures were eventually enacted into law? Finally, what was the extent of Democratic cooperation or obstruction. Research these questions. The material you find could form the basis of an interesting term paper or oral report.

PART IX — TEST ANSWERS

Pretest

1. b
2. b
3. a
4. b
5. b

6. d
7. a
8. a
9. a
10. b

Programmed Review

1. competition
2. personal
3. slavery
4. do
5. function
6. patronage
7. conventions; primaries
8. one
9. necessity
10. Republican
11. Republican
12. FDR
13. presidential
14. less
15. moderate
16. power
17. federal

18. coalitions
19. presidential
20. committee
21. majority
22. conceal
23. more
24. more
25. closed
26. identification
27. realignment
28. independents
29. issues; organization
30. television
31. Republican
32. campaign
33. renewal

Post-test

1. c
2. c
3. d
4. c
5. c

6. b
7. c
8. a
9. b
10. a

Data Analysis

1. Findings will depend upon the point in time post-1988 data is consulted.

2. The "solid South" seems to have become a Republican stronghold. Also, black voters remain overwhelmingly loyal to the Democratic Party. It could be argued that if the South is no longer part of the Democratic coalition, then the Republicans should continue to dominate national elections.

3. At the time of publication, the January-March of 1995 congressional actions had not occurred. However, the outcomes of the GOP contract can be easily traced by consulting *The New York Times*, *Time* or *Newsweek* magazines, the *Congressional Quarterly* or *Digest*, or other appropriate reference sources published during that time frame.

CHAPTER 11
PUBLIC OPINION, POLITICAL PARTICIPATION AND VOTING

Public opinion lies beneath all voting patterns. That opinion rests upon family and community attitudes, together with mass media exposure, personal experience and religious-ethnic background. In measuring public opinion we talk about such factors as intensity, latency, and salience. Our ability to measure public opinion (polling) has grown over the past thirty years to be a highly sophisticated, accurate science. To an amazing degree, pollsters can now tell us what the American people think and feel before any election or at any specific point between elections. But, as all Americans know, no election is the final word. Not only do we argue over the true meaning of any specific election, we also believe that existing public opinion and voting patterns are subject to shifts in the public mood. No public opinion is set in concrete. No vote is the final answer, forever locked in place.

The ballot box lies at the very heart of the democratic political process. It is here that public opinion, interest group, political parties, and movement culminate in decision-making. But voting itself remains something of a mystery, although we now know more about it, thanks to recent research. Why do a thin majority of Americans cast ballots on election day? Why do nearly half of potential voters stay home? How do voters reach their political decisions? What, if any, long range patterns of voting are occurring in the 1990s?

PART I — GUIDEPOSTS

1. Public Opinion
    a. What is public opinion?
    b. What is meant by intensity, latency and salience as applied to public opinion?
    c. Name an issue about which there is general consensus. One issue which the public is polarized.

2. Political Socialization
    a. How influential is your family in shaping your political attitudes?
    b. What institution ranks next to the family?
    c. What part does ideology play?
    d. Why is the mass media (especially TV) important?
    e. Why are religion and ethnic background important?
    f. Why do adults sometimes shift their childhood attitudes?
    h. Name an issue about which there is general consensus. One about which the public is polarized.

3. Voters: Who and Why
    a. How can a citizen participate in government other than voting?
    b. Trace the expansion of suffrage in the United States.
    c. In which election is voter turnout the greatest? the lowest?
    d. How can voting laws affect voting rates?

4. Nonvoting: Who and Why?
>   a. What are the causes of low turnout?
>   b. Is nonvoting a serious problem?
>   c. What are the characteristics of nonvoters?
>   d. How can the barriers to nonvoting be reduced?
>   e. What are the characteristics of those who vote?
>   f. How does social status impact on voting behavior?

5. Voting Behavior in the United States
>   a. How does partisanship identification differ from party registration?
>   b. Who are the independents? How do they differ from partisans?
>   c. What is a realignment election?
>   d. What are the positive aspects of candidate appeal? Give examples of candidates with positive appeal, negative appeal.
>   e. How important are issues in determining how a person votes?

PART II — GLOSSARY

PARTISAN - One who is a member of or is identified with a political party. Strong partisans are more likely to vote than nonpartisans or independents.

REALIGNING ELECTION - An election in which the basic commitments of a significant segment of the electorate change.

PUBLIC OPINION - A cluster of views and attitudes held by a public on a significant issue. Since any complex society has many groups, it is more precise to talk about publics, subpublics, and public opinions than about a single public opinion.

ATTENTIVE PUBLIC - The informed and knowledgeable segment of the population.

SALIENCY - The significance and pertinency of an event or issue.

LATENT OPINION - An opinion or public attitude that is silent or not widely articulated but that can be converted into action by an event or shift in opinion.

MASS MEDIA - Channels or vehicles of communication that reach large numbers of people: the press, radio, television, and movies.

INTENSITY - The depth of feeling a voter has.

SOCIAL ENVIRONMENT - The total social and economic institutions that affect a person's attitudes.

CROSS-PRESSURE - A pressure that pulls an individual in different directions.

STRAW-POLLS - Informal, unscientific surveys.

CHRONIC POLITICAL KNOW-NOTHINGS - Those individuals who neither know or care about political activity.

POLITICAL SOCIALIZATION - Process by which we develop our political attitudes and values.

POLARIZATION - Issue about which opposing groups have deeply-held opinions.

PART III — PRETEST

1. Nonvoters do *not* have one of the following characteristics.
   - a. poor
   - b. less educated
   - c. less religious
   - d. less white

2. Public opinion is best thought of as
   - a. the will of the people.
   - b. a diversity of opinion within a particular population.
   - c. media reflection of public attitudes.
   - d. voter attitudes.

3. An institutional barrier that blocks people from voting is
   - a. distant voting booths.
   - b. registration.
   - c. unattractive candidates.
   - d. lack of party competition.

4. The group least apt to vote is
   - a. 18-24 year olds.
   - b. Gray Panthers.
   - c. blue collar workers.
   - d. women.

5. The most homogeneous of all groups in molding political opinion is
   - a. school.
   - b. work.
   - c. church membership.
   - d. family.

6. Which of the following was most apt to vote Democratic in recent elections?
   - a. Jews
   - b. Blacks
   - c. White Protestants
   - d. Catholics

7. The major force in the early socialization of children is
   - a. television.
   - b. family.
   - c. school.
   - d. playmates.

8. The most influential factor in forming the attitudes of children is
   - a. intelligence.
   - b. psychological and genetic traits.
   - c. class and race.
   - d. family and school.

9. The most conservative economic attitudes are to be found in _____ homes.
   - a. Catholic
   - b. Jewish
   - c. atheist
   - d. Protestant

10. Younger voters with above-average incomes and college educations tend to be
    - a. partisan.
    - b. reluctant to vote.
    - c. independent.
    - d. Democrats.

PART IV — PROGRAMMED REVIEW

Knowledge Objective: To consider the complexity of public opinion
   1. The people speak with many voices. There is no one set _____ _____ .
   2. The characteristic of public opinion that measures how strongly people feel on an issue is called _____ .

3. _____ attitudes are dormant but may be evoked into action.
4. Opinions which are closely associated with the lives of the individuals are called _____ .
5. When a large majority of voters agree on an issue, we have reached _____ .
6. When strong opinions are nearly equally divided on an issue, the result is _____ .

Knowledge Objective: To examine how we acquire our political attitudes
7. The _____ unit instills the basic attitudes that shape future opinions.
8. The process by which we develop our political attitudes is called political _____ .
9. The attitudes of children are shaped by their family and their political-social _____ .
10. When a person's family background and peer group disagree, they experience _____ .
11. Evangelicals tend to be (more, less) _____ socially conservative than nonevangelicals.

Knowledge Objective: To examine the practice of "taking the pulse of the people"
12. An accurate poll must be based on a _____ sample of the total universe.
13. A poll used to predict in advance how an election will turn out is called _____ .

Knowledge Objective: To identify those who vote and those who do not
14. The type of political activity most Americans engage in is _____ .
15. A subset of the public that has a high level of political interest and awareness is the _____ public
16. In recent presidential elections, slightly more than (half, three-quarters) _____ of potential voters cast ballots.
17. Compared to other nations, voting participation by Americans is (low, high) _____ .
18. Millions of Americans fail to vote because they feel there is no real _____ .
19. The key factor that determines the degree of voting participation is _____ .
20. Persons in the 18-24 age group have the (highest, lowest) _____ voting participation record.
21. Highly educated people are (more, less) _____ apt to vote.
22. The major institutional block to voting is _____ .

Knowledge Objective: To determine the patterns of American voting
23. Nonvoting on the part of the _____ is a part of a larger political-psychological environment that discourages their political activity.
24. Our national elections are frequently unpredictable because of the millions of _____ voters.
25. The _____ has the greatest influence in determining a person's voting patterns and party allegiance.
26. The best indicator of how a person will vote is _____ identification.
27. More than a third of the voters can be called _____ .
28. Blacks today are the strongest supporters of the _____ party.
29. Low income voters tend to judge a candidate (more/less) on the basis of their own personal financial condition.
30. A person's subjective sense of political identification is called _____ .
31. Outranking issues or political ideology is _____ identification.
32. Most presidential candidates (do, do not) _____ clearly define their attitudes on issues.

PART V — POST-TEST

1. The most important factor underlying low Black voter turnout in the South is
    a. apathy.   c. lack of organization.
    b. literacy tests.   d. physical threats.

2. One of the following *is not* a reason why low-income people vote in fewer numbers.
    a. They have less sense of involvement and confidence.
    b. They feel at a disadvantage in social contacts.
    c. Their social norms tend to deemphasize politics.
    d. They can't afford registration fees.

3. All of the following are true about voter statistics *except*
    a. men out-vote women by a large majority.
    b. middle-aged people are more likely to vote than younger people.
    c. college-educated persons vote more than high school graduates.
    d. persons who are active in organized groups are more likely to vote.

4. An off year election is one in which
    a. the president is running for reelection.
    b. governors are selected.
    c. senators are selected.
    d. local officials are selected.

5. Candidates with positive appeal include *all but*
    a. Eisenhower.   c. Carter.
    b. Kennedy.   d. Reagan.

6. Voters tend to vote against an incumbent if
    a. the budget is out of balance.
    b. there is an issue conflict.
    c. their personal fortunes are declining.
    d. they have not implemented their campaign promises.

7. Which of the following groups is the most conservative?
    a. Catholics   c. Protestants
    b. Jews   d. Evangelicals

8. Voter registration procedures have been eased by connecting registration to
    a. college registration.
    b. E-mail.
    c. a driver's license.
    d. W-4 forms.

9. A good public opinion poll *does not* require
    a. qualified interviewers.
    b. carefully phrased questions.
    c. a 25% sample of the universe.
    d. a representative sample of the universe.

10. Pollsters get the most accurate measure of public opinion through a _____ sample.
    a. representative   c. quota
    b. random   d. demographic

PART VI — POLITICAL DIALOGUE:
THE CLASH OF ISSUES AND IDEAS

1. "The Democratic Party is no longer the majority party in presidential elections but then neither is the Republican Party."

2. Suppose we were to enact a law on compulsory voting and fined every voter $25 if he failed to cast a ballot. Would such a system strengthen or weaken democracy? Who does not vote at the present time? Are there any ways of expanding the percentage of voters without using penalties? Is there a case for nonvoting? Should we expand the electorate to the point where over 90 percent of all eligible voters vote on election day?

3. In the 1980 Presidential election all TV networks announced the winner before polling places had closed on the West Coast. Allegedly, some potential West Coast voters reacted to this news by staying home, thereby causing the defeat of many Democratic candidates. Should TV networks be prohibited from making such announcements in future elections? If a ban is imposed, is freedom of speech being restricted?

4. Present several controversial issues raised in this chapter in a debate format:

   a. **Resolved**: Public opinion polls should be eliminated or at least restrained because they tend to abort discussion on public issues and public candidates and because they tend to induce in public officials an attitude of fellowship rather than leadership.
   b. **Resolved**: That government should establish a national public opinion research center which will survey the public on all significant issues relating to national policy.

5. As an innocent bystander you become involved in a discussion centered around the topic, "better brains for better politics." A speaker in the group complains that the average person votes his prejudices, his private interests, his ignorance. "Look at the absurdity of the present situation," he says, "You spend four years in college and your vote is not worth any more than that of the butcher, the baker, the candlestick maker." To correct this, the speaker proposes a system of weighted voting which would reward the diligent and the informed citizen. His plan calls for a program of multi-voting in which:

   a. Every qualified citizen would have one vote.
   b. Every qualified citizen would receive an additional vote for higher education; one vote for each of the following degrees: associate of arts (junior college); bachelor's degree; master's degree; doctor's degree.
   c. Every qualified citizen would receive an additional vote for distinguished citations — starred scientist; Pulitzer prize winner; Nobel prize winner; Who's Who listing, etc.
   d. Every qualified citizen would receive an additional vote for each creative achievement such as writing a significant book or making an important invention. A national board would determine whether the achievement could be classified as "creative".

How would you respond to the speaker's proposal?
What fallacies or errors do you see in his assumptions?

PART VII — POLITICAL SCIENCE TODAY

1. As the chapter suggests, the role of the family is quite important to the overall political socialization process. Try to think about your own childhood and the kind of political environment to which you were exposed. Did your parents talk about politics often around the dinner table or on numerous family occasions? Or were political events and personalities hardly mentioned? Did your parents disagree about politics? Were they members of different political parties? Do you currently identify with the party of your parents (assuming they both belonged to one party)? Finally, what specific political values and/or assumptions do you think were learned from your family? It might prove interesting to talk with other classmates about their early political socialization experiences.

2. Do you classify yourself as a political liberal or conservative? Assuming you are in your first year or second year of college, do you believe your ideological views will change by the time you graduate — why or why not? As a possible research project, the preparation of a survey for graduating seniors asking whether the college experience has moved them in a liberal or conservative direction (and why) might prove valuable.

3. Could one argue that non-voting is actually beneficial for American democracy? After all, non-voters are usually less interested in politics and probably less-informed. People who do take the time to vote believe in the system and are likely to be moderates. An influx of large numbers of citizens who never voted before might disrupt the stability of the political system.

   Does this argument make sense to you — why or why not? Isn't a democracy supposed to rest upon active and extensive political participation from as many citizens as possible? Debate the question either in paper or oral report form.

4. As a corollary point of #3, do you believe citizens should be fined (actually pay a penalty to government) for refusing to vote on election day? Would these fines increase participation across the nation or would they be counterproductive? After all, isn't the choice of non-voting a form of voting? Again, debate the question.

5. *Exit polls* have become a useful survey technique in recent years. They are often used by television networks on election night to ascertain trends in the voting. With appropriate research find out how exit polls work and whether they are usually accurate (if so, why). Also, discover why TV networks use exit polls so frequently to broadcast predictions. Are there any problems associated with these types of polls?

6. Toward which political issues of the day do you feel the public would have high levels of *salience* and *intensity*? If you contrasted your age bracket with the age category of your parents or even grandparents, how would the list of issues change (or would they?)? As an experiment, compile a list relevant to you and your classmates, then ask your parents and/or grandparents which issues would be viewed as important by them. You may find that age differences are frequently linked to different sets of opinions or even what issues are worth thinking about.

7. The voters of America were in an especially disgusted and cynical mood prior to the November, 1994 elections. This mood resulted in an historic GOP sweep of both houses of Congress and major gains in state governorships for the Republicans. Public opinion polls revealed that only about one-third of voters were satisfied with political life in America. Other polls demonstrated that substantial majorities of voters believed that (a) the government in Washington was untrustworthy, (b) the lives of the next generation of Americans would worsen, (c) their opinions had little impact upon government policies, (d) government was inefficient and wasteful, and (e) that it was time for politicians in Washington to make room for new leaders (See the *Atlanta Constitution*, November 9, 1994, p. C1 and *The New York Times*, November 3, 1994, p. A1, A10.)

Class Division

Percentage of people who say abortion
should be legal:

by household income

$0 - 20,000

52%

$20,000 - 50,000

68%

$50,000 +

74%

by education level

Less than high school diploma

47%

High school diploma

65%

College

72%

Postgrad

79%

Reprinted by permission of The Wall Street Journal.
© Dow Jones & Company, Inc. 1989.
All Rights Reserved Worldwide.

Abortion Attitudes: Case by Case

Please tell me whether or not you think it should be possible for a
pregnant woman to obtain a legal abortion. . .

. . .if the woman's health is seriously endangered by the pregnancy?

| Yes 87% | 7% No |

. . .if there is a strong chance of serious defect in the baby?

| 69 | 21 |

. . .if the samily has a very low income and cannot afford any more
children?

| 43 | 49 |

. . .if she is not married and does not want to marry the man?

| 42 | 50 |

. . .if the pregnancy interfered with work or education?

| 26 | 65 |

. . .and a Spectrum of Acceptance

Those who say abortion should be possible:

In all five circum-stances	In four of the five circum-stances	In three of the five circum-stances	In two of the five circum-stances	In one of the five circum-stances	None of the five
21%	15%	12%	26%	17%	10%

From your own knowledge of politics and current events, why do you think the voters were in this deeply "disgusted and cynical mood"? Was life in America and its politicians really so bad? What roles did issues such as crime, health care, taxes, social security, welfare, defense spending, and foreign policy play in creating such a mood? Finally, do you detect any changes in the most recent polls available to suggest a degree of greater optimism since the November, 1994 opinion climate? If not, why? If so, why?

PART VIII — DATA ANALYSIS

1. Look at the two polls on abortion taken from the April 26, 1989 editions of *The Wall Street Journal* (p. 10) and *The New York Times* (p. 1). What conclusions can you draw from the poll data?

Second, find two polls on abortion from 1994 or later that contain similar questions and/or demographic breakdowns. Has public opinion on the abortion issues changed dramatically in the five or more years since the 1989 polls? If so, speculate as to why? If not, cite reasons as well.

2. Look at Table ll-2 on p. 274 of the text. In which presidential elections from 1944-1992 were the pollsters most accurate or least accurate in predicting the presidential winner? Based upon your knowledge of those elections, which specific campaign and voting factors probably create the greatest accuracy problems for polling organizations?

Part IX — Test Answers

Pretest

1. c
2. b
3. b
4. a
5. d

6. b
7. b
8. d
9. d
10. c

Programmed Review

1. public opinion
2. intensity
3. Latent
4. salient
5. consensus
6. polarization
7. family
8. socialization
9. environment
10. cross-pressure
11. more
12. representative
13. election forecasting
14. voting
15. attentive
16. half

17. low
18. choice
19. education
20. lowest
21. more
22. registration
23. poor
24. independent
25. family
26. party
27. independent
28. Democratic
29. more
30. partisanship
31. partisan
32. do not

Post-test

1. c
2. d
3. a
4. d
5. c

6. c
7. d
8. c
9. c
10. a

Data Analysis

1. First, it is obvious that Americans are deeply ambivalent and divided over the abortion issue. In *The New York Times*, it would appear that a majority would accept abortion in at least two of the five circumstances delineated in the poll. However, the "none," "one," and "two" options, if all added together, would also constitute a majority. In short, the nation is truly polarized. Yet, the base of support does consist of allowing abortion if the woman's health is endangered and if there is a serious defect in the baby. *The Wall Street Journal* poll clearly reveals that the better-educated, higher income individual will be more likely to favor the legal availability of abortion. Education tends to be a liberalizing experience. Whether these observations held true in 1994 or in later years will probably depend upon the polls selected by the student.

2. Most accurate - 1944, 1956, 1964; least accurate - 1948, 1980. The rise of the independent voter and the tendency of voters to make up their minds late in the campaign have contributed to poll volatility and a greater degree of imprecision.

CHAPTER 12
CAMPAIGNS AND ELECTIONS: DEMOCRACY IN ACTION

Members of Congress are elected directly by voters, first in primaries and then in general elections. In the House of Representatives before the election of 1992 incumbents were virtually assured of reelection regardless of their party. Although the odds still favored incumbents, increasingly states were passing laws placing an upper limit on the terms a Representative might serve (two-four-six were typical) and a general revulsion over scandal associated with cheque overdrafts and special perquisites for Congressmen threatened to disrupt normal voting patterns.

To a limited extent this voter disenchantment with existing office holders extended to the Senate. In the traditional sense there were many fewer "safe" Senate seats.

All Congressional races are financed by the candidates. Currently much of this funding comes from PACs, which may leave the Congressional recipients indebted to these contributors.

In the 1992 Presidential election there were originally five Democratic contenders (Tsongis, Brown, Harkin, Kerry, Clinton) and only two Republicans (Bush and Buchanan). By mid-summer of 1992— two months before the convention, the winners were known, Clinton and Bush. But 1992 was unusual because an independent, Ross Perot, led each of these candidates in popular polls. For a short period it seemed entirely possible that the final selection of a President would be the choice of the Electoral College or the House of Representatives. Such an eventuality would have prompted a revival of all latent proposals for changing our Presidential election procedures.

PART I — GUIDEPOSTS

1. The Rules of the Game
    a. Who determines the rules for US elections?
    b. When are elections held in the United States?
    c. Explain: fixed term; staggered term and term limitation.
    d. What effect does the winner-take-all rule have on our elections?
    e. What is the Electoral College? How important is it?

2. Running for Office
    a. Why do campaigns for Congress vary so widely?
    b. What are some similarities between campaigns for the House and the Senate?
    c. How is the election process distorted today?
    d. How does an emphasis on personality and negative campaigning detract from the true issues?
    e. What is the recent success rate of Representatives who run for reelection? Why do critics say we are electing "representatives for life"?
    f. Why must most Representatives build a personal rather than a party organization?
    g. What advantages do incumbents have in running for reelection?
    h. Does a big budget assure election to the House?
    i. How much does an average Senate race cost?
    j. Why are Senate races more difficult to win?

k. Why are Senate races of the future less apt to favor incumbents?

l. Does negative campaigning seem to be effective?

3. Running for the President

a. How are most delegates to the national convention selected?

b. Why do Iowa and New Hampshire loom so large in the delegate selection process?

c. How have recent conventions been decided in advance?

d. Of what value is the party platform?

e. How is the candidate for vice-president selected?

f. Why do parties continue to have conventions?

g. How do you run for president of the United States without political party backing?

h. What factors are considered by candidates in planning their fall campaigns?

i. How do campaigns resemble marathons?

j. What is the impact of Presidential Debates?

4. Improving Elections

a. What advantages are claimed for the party primary system?

b. What are the alleged disadvantages?

c. Why might a national primary be better?

d. Might national caucuses be better?

e. Should direct election of the president be substituted for the electoral college?

f. Is reform of the electoral college likely?

5. Campaign Money

a. Cite the major scandals involving campaign money.

b. Why do the costs of campaigns continue to rise?

c. Why is PAC money so controversial?

d. How do we now finance presidential campaigns?

e. What provisions have been made to publicize spending in Congressional races?

f. Has the regulation of campaign spending reduced campaign costs?

g. Why have restrictions on campaign spending not been extended to Congressional races?

h. What are some criticisms of the FECA?

i. How did Ross Perot bypass campaign finance reform?

j. Why is bipartisan campaign finance reform so difficult to achieve?

6. Interpreting the 1992 Election and the 1994 Election

a. What were the outstanding characteristics of the 1992 and the 1994 elections?

PART II — GLOSSARY

COATTAIL EFFECT - The effect that a strong candidate has in aiding other candidates of the same party.

CAUCUS - A meeting of party members.

SUPER TUESDAY - The arrangement used in the 1988 election, when a bloc of Southern states held their primaries on the same day.

CONVENTION DELEGATE - A party representative selected to attend the national Presidential Convention.

DIRECT PRIMARY - Voter participation in the nominating process by means of voting for candidates in primary elections.

CAMPAIGN REFORM BILL OF 1974 - Provides for both disclosures and limitations on campaign spending. Also provides for some public funding.

INCUMBENT - An individual already occupying an elective office. Incumbents, especially in national offices, usually have special advantages in running for reelection.

PRESIDENTIAL PRIMARY - A method of choosing delegates to the national convention. The results of a presidential primary may be binding on the delegates or purely advisory.

ELECTORAL COLLEGE - A group of presidential electors from each state chosen by the people to elect a President and Vice-President. Each state is allotted as many electors as it has senators and representatives in Congress.

NATIONAL PRESIDENTIAL PRIMARY - A plan frequently proposed which would abolish the convention and nominate candidates in a national primary held simultaneously in every state.

PART III — PRETEST

1. The most important factor in winning a congressional race is
   a. personal contact.
   b. TV time.
   c. press coverage.
   d. money.

2. Recent presidential conventions have been noteworthy because
   a. the winner was known in advance.
   b. major rivals made a down-to-the-wire finish.
   c. excitement ran high.
   d. philosophical differences were deep.

3. The political strength of congressional incumbents has made modern elections
   a. highly competitive.
   b. political party contests.
   c. uncompetitive.
   d. strictly rational contests.

4. The campaign reform law of 1974 was chiefly concerned with
   a. campaign finance.
   b. media coverage.
   c. nomination procedures.
   d. delegate selection.

5. To attain the presidency, a candidate must achieve two goals. These are
   a. have the largest number of delegates prior to coming to the national convention, and then obtain a majority of the popular vote.
   b. be nominated at the party convention, and obtain a majority of the electoral votes.
   c. be nominated at the party's convention, and obtain both a majority of the popular vote and the electoral vote.
   d. be nominated at the party convention, and win a majority of the popular vote.

6. A recent movement for change in the electoral system has pushed for
   a. fixed terms.
   b. staggered terms.
   c. term limitations.
   d. uniform terms.

7. A general criticism of the 1988 Presidential campaign was that it had
   a. erotic symbols.
   b. no debates.
   c. negative advertising.
   d. ethnic slurs.

8. In the event that no presidential candidate receives a majority of the electoral vote, the president is chosen by
   a. Congress.
   b. Supreme Court.
   c. House of Representatives.
   d. Senate.

9. Money not subject to disclosure rules used by political parties at election time is called
    a. tight.
    c. hard.
    b. easy.
    d. soft.

10. The largest item in recent congressional campaigns has been for
    a. TV-radio advertising.
    c. polls.
    b. consultants.
    d. printing and mailing.

PART IV — PROGRAMMED REVIEW

Knowledge objective: To review the rules for elections

1. Most electoral rules are still matters of _____ law.
2. Federal general elections are the first Tuesday after the first _____ in November of _____ numbered years.
3. Politicians can plan for the next election because we have _____ terms.
4. A recent movement wants to _____ terms of office.
5. Politicians who announce they will not run again are called _____ _____ .
6. With our winner take all system a winner does not necessarily need to have a _____ of the vote.
7. Proportional representation rewards _____ parties.
8. To win the presidency, the candidate must have a majority vote of the _____ _____ .
9. Under the electoral college system, a candidate either wins _____ or _____ of a state's electoral votes.
10. Most states provide for the selection of electors on a (state, district) _____ basis.
11. If no presidential candidate secures a majority of the electoral votes the _____ _____ _____ decides.

Knowledge Objective: To examine the process of running for Congress

12. Competitiveness in congressional elections (has, has not) _____ increased slightly over the past twenty years.
13. Senate elections are like to be (more, less) _____ competitive than House elections.
14. Congressional candidates whose vote is increased by a strong presidential candidate are said to benefit from the _____ influence.
15. New campaign technology tends to emphasize _____ over issues.
16. Keeping a House seat is (easier, harder) _____ than gaining one.
17. In midterm elections support for the party in power almost always _____ .
18. Candidates for Congress secure most of their campaign funds from (the party, personal contributions) _____ .
19. Focusing on an opponent's failings is _____ campaigning.

Knowledge Objective: To trace the steps in nominating and electing a president

20. Presidential candidates are now selected by their parties chiefly through the use of _____ .
21. When voters in a presidential primary indicate their preference from a list of candidates, the election is commonly referred to as a _____ contest.
22. National conventions normally select a party candidate for president and vice president and write a _____ .
23. The party platform is (binding, non-binding) _____ on the candidate.
24. Nominating conventions provide a time to build party _____ .
25. Mistakes made during a presidential debate may damage the candidate's _____ .

Knowledge Objective: To study proposed reforms of the electoral college and presidential primaries

26. In caucus states, candidates are less dependent on the _____ and more dependent on their abilities to reach _____ activists.
27. Reform of presidential primaries concentrates on _____ or a _____ primary.
28. The main argument for presidential primaries is that they open up the nomination process to _____ voters.
29. Critics contend the primaries test the candidate for the ability to play the _____ _____ .
30. A _____ will most likely cause electoral reform.

Knowledge Objective: To analyze the sources and uses of money in national campaigns

31. The Keating 5 is an example of the undue influence that comes with large _____ .
32. All congressional candidates (are, are not)_____ required to report their campaign contributions and expenditures.
33. Federal financing of presidential elections has made it (easier, harder) _____ for rich candidates to win.
34. The key to congressional campaigns are_____ .
35. Organizations and individuals (do, do not)_____ have limitations placed on the amount they may spend independently of a campaign organization.
36. Congressional candidates (do, do not) _____ receive federal campaign funds.
37. Reform of political money has pursued three basic strategies: limitations, disclosure, and government _____ for campaigns.
38. The 1974 campaign reform law achieved a breakthrough by providing for public _____ of presidential campaigns.
39. The Court has held that, if a party or candidate takes public funds, they can be required to _____ what they spend in the campaign.
40. Most money for the presidential election now comes from _____ sources.

PART V — POST-TEST

1. Only one of the following presidential candidates was elected, although each received more popular votes than his opponent.
   a. Jackson (1824)
   b. Cleveland (1888)
   c. Tilden (1876)
   d. Truman (1948)

2. The bias of the electoral college favors
   a. one-party states.
   b. rural areas.
   c. populous urban states.
   d. modified one-party states.

3. A state's electoral vote is determined by
   a. population.
   b. previous voting patterns in presidential elections.
   c. a complicated formula devised by Congress.
   d. the number of its representatives and senators.

4. The Supreme Court voided which of the following provisions of the 1974 campaign reform law?
   a. limitations on spending
   b. limitations on giving
   c. public funding of presidential elections
   d. election-day registration

5. To be elected president, a candidate must receive
    a. a plurality of electoral votes.
    b. a majority of electoral votes.
    c. a majority of states as well as electoral votes.
    d. a majority of the popular vote.

6. Most delegates to the national nominating convention are chosen by
    a. popular votes.   c. state conventions.
    b. primary elections.   d. state committees.

7. Presidential candidates are nominated by
    a. party caucus.
    b. national party conventions.
    c. national party committee.
    d. presidential primary.

8. New candidates for the House of Representatives are normally concerned with
    a. timing.   c. recognition.
    b. financial support.   d. all of the above

9. The 1974 campaign expense law placed a limit on the contributions that could be made by
    a. individuals.   c. political parties.
    b. organizations.   d. all of the above

10. A "permanent Congress" is a result of
    a. advantages held by incumbents.
    b. direct mail.
    c. redistricting.
    d. direct primaries.

PART VI — POLITICAL DIALOGUE
THE CLASH OF ISSUES AND IDEAS

1. Evaluate each of the following proposals as to their impact on the presidential election process:
    a. Restrict state primaries to a time framework (5-10 months) before the election.
    b. A single national primary four months before the final election.
    c. A mini-convention 2 months before the November election dedicated only to writing party platforms.
    d. A general election in November with the winner being determined by the national popular vote.
    e. A general election in November with a winner in each Congressional district receiving one vote (plus two votes for carrying the state).

2. Describe the strategies you would use to win a congressional seat.

3. Debate whether the debates staged between presidential contenders have been useful to voters.

4. Explain why Congress has refused to provide federal financing for congressional elections.

5. Analyze criticisms of the electoral college system and the alleged advantages and disadvantages of various reform proposals.

6. Comment on the following observations:
   a. A defeated nominee for the Presidency rarely has a second chance.
   b. A mid-term election brings out Presidential timber.
   c. An incumbent always wins in periods of prosperity.
   d. A party in power loses 20 to 40 House seats in mid-term election.
   e. Technology has made image more important than issues.

PART VII — POLITICAL SCIENCE TODAY

1. Imagine you were considering running against an incumbent congressman who had been in office for five full terms (10 years in all). The incumbent from your district is immensely popular, has trounced his last four opponents, and has a strong funding base from groups and individuals. However, during the past two years, the incumbent has voted on a few issues of concern to the district which have met with opposition from newspapers and a few influential civic groups. You, as the challenger, are also promised by your party that they are going to support you fully with volunteer staff, consultants, and funds to run your campaign. However, party leaders do admit that unseating this incumbent (for that matter, any incumbent) will not be easy.

   Do you decide to throw your "hat in the ring" or not? If you do, what steps and strategies must you undertake in order to enhance your election chances? Even if you lose, do you plan to run again in two more years? In other words, are you setting the stage for eventual victory at some point in the future? Finally, what would be your personal reasons for wanting to enter politics by running for Congress?

   Outline steps/strategies and a few reasons why you might decide to run. Conversely, if you chose not to run, outline reasons for that decision as well.

2. Admittedly, money plays an important role in modern political campaigning. But does the campaigner who always spends the most money necessarily win? Try to find examples of campaigns from recent political history, preferably at the congressional or senatorial level, where the candidate who was actually outspent emerged victorious anyway. In those races where this phenomena occurred, analyze why money, by itself, was not enough to insure victory.

3. Note that with the current structure and operation of the Electoral College, it would be possible for a presidential candidate to receive a majority of the national popular vote but not a majority of the electoral vote. Consequently, should the Electoral College be changed or even abolished in order to prevent this outcome? Why not merely abolish the Electoral College and simply elect the man and woman who receives the most popular votes—period? A provision could be inserted that no candidate could be elected (assume a third party candidate was running) unless he or she received at least forty percent of the popular vote. If this did not happen, then there would be a national runoff between the top two vote-getters.

   Would you favor or oppose this plan? Try to cite your reasons for your viewpoint. Reviewing appropriate text sections will help you.

4. What political, economic, and social factors influenced the outcome of the 1992 presidential election? Find one or two articles written in November of 1992 that attempted to explain the outcome of the election. Similarly, which specific factors influenced the 1994 midterm elections? Research newspaper or magazine articles in November of 1994 that explained the GOP victories in Congress and even in gubernatorial races.

PART VIII — DATA ANALYSIS

1. As soon as possible, acquire the pertinent voting data from the 1994 midterm election. Based upon those voting patterns, what lessons should both the Democratic and Republican party leaders learn regarding the next presidential election?

2. After the dramatic GOP victory in the midterm elections of 1994, Republicans set their sights on the 1996 presidential election. Their hope was that they would control both the executive and legislative branches after 1996. Consequently, GOP politicians began traveling to Iowa in late 1994 and a few even announced they were running for President. Some of the presidential hopefuls were as follows: (a) Lamar Alexander, former Governor of Tennessee; (b) James A. Baker, White House Chief of Staff and Treasury Secretary under President Reagan; (c) Senator Bob Dole from Kansas: (d) Colin L. Powell, former Chairman of the Joint Chiefs of Staff; (e) Senator Arlen Specter from Pennsylvania and (f) Senator Phil Gramm from Texas.

Which of these candidates officially declared that they were a candidate for President in 1996? Of those that did announce, which ones were able to launch successful pre-primary efforts and why? Conversely, which individuals failed to do so and why? Track their moves during the late 1994 period until 1995. What campaign "lessons" can you discern from your data?

PART IX — TEST ANSWERS

Pretest

1. a
2. a
3. c
4. a
5. b
6. c
7. c
8. c
9. d
10. a

Programmed Review

1. state
2. Monday; even
3. fixed
4. limit
5. lame duck
6. majority
7. minority
8. electoral college
9. all; none
10. state
11. House of Representatives
12. has not
13. more
14. coattail
15. personality
16. easier
17. declines
18. personal contributions
19. negative
20. primaries
21. beauty
22. platform
23. non-binding
24. unity
25. credibility
26. media; political
27. national; regional
28. more
29. media game
30. crisis
31. contributions
32. are
33. easier
34. PACs
35. do not
36. do not
37. subsidies
38. financing
39. limit
40. government

Post-test

1. d
2. c
3. d
4. a
5. b
6. b
7. b
8. d
9. d
10. a

Data Analysis

1. Analysis will naturally depend upon the actual data, which was not available at the time of publication.

2. This information can be discerned from newspaper and magazine accounts that will become available as campaign events unfold in the future.

CHAPTER 13
THE MEDIA AND AMERICAN POLITICS

Much of today's politics is played out before television cameras and watched nightly by millions of TV viewers as part of the six-o'clock news. The President is the focal point of this news, and anchor persons are the stars in what seems to be an adversary relationship. Critics see the mass media as having almost unlimited power over public opinion, replacing the family, the community and political parties. This charge seems to be an overstatement, but the media does seem to be a central force in setting the national political agenda (the problems in the forefront of public discussion).

That agenda seems to be set in competitive fashion, with no media source wanting to be left out. Newspapers across the United States are apt to have the same national-international headlines, varying only in their coverage of local stories. News magazines and television news sources generally agree on the day's top stories. As a nation we end up concentrating on this agenda, set forth by the media. The end result may be good, but it is fixed at the top. Rather than the concerns of the people, the concerns of the media are established as the topics of the day. In our society developments in science, technology, the arts, and religion are displaced by political and disaster stories.

Most significantly, media dominance has greatly altered political campaigns. The great cost of recent contests is directly related to per minute charge for air time; voters seem increasingly to back candidates who have TV presence and charm.

PART I — GUIDEPOSTS

1. The Influence of the Mass Media
   a. How did the media handle the reporting in the Persian Gulf?
   b. What is the media's major role in American politics?
   c. How is our culture affected by the mass media?
   d. What new technological changes in the media are emerging?
   e. How are new competitors affecting the established media?
   f. Why is the media the primary linking mechanism in American politics?

2. The Rise of an Autonomous Press
   a. How is the role of today's press different from the press of Thomas Jefferson's day?
   b. What is objective journalism?
   c. How did FDR use radio as a political tool?
   d. Where do Americans get most of their news?
   e. Is the mass media a business or a public service industry?
   f. What do journalists believe is their function in elections?

3. The Media and Public Opinions
   a. How have the media changed American politics? Why did early studies tend to minimize media power?
   b. What factors determine how a person interprets media messages?
   c. Why do both liberals and conservatives feel the media is biased?
   d. Why is the media's role in setting the national agenda so important?
   e. Who favors greater regulations of the media? Why is media regulation difficult?

4. The Media and Elections
   a. How has modern media changed political campaigns?
   b. How do media consultants differ from political party advisers?
   c. Why does the media often picture campaigns as a game rather than a serious contest over issues?
   d. Do voters make their decisions on the basis of media reporting?
   e. How does the reporting of election results influence elections?

5. Media and Governance
   a. What is the media's role in the policy process?
   b. What has been the relationship of recent presidents with the press?
   c. Why has Congress suffered at the hands of the press?
   d. Why is the Supreme Court the least dependent upon the press?
   e. Is the claim the media is the fourth branch of the government exaggerated?

PART II — GLOSSARY

MASS MEDIA - The large, privately owned companies that dispense information through newspapers, radio, television, movies, and magazines to great segments of the general public.

MASS CULTURE - The beliefs and attitudes held by a majority of people in any society.

SELECTIVE PERCEPTION - The process whereby viewers, listeners and readers filter information to conform to their existing prejudices.

ADVOCACY JOURNALISM - Journalists who side with those less powerful citizens who are unable to speak for themselves.

ADVERSARIAL JOURNALISM - Practice of challenging government and serving as opposition to elected officials.

SELECTIVE EXPOSURE - Screening out those messages that do not conform to personal biases.

ELITE JOURNALISTS - Those who work for national news groups and tend to share a cosmopolitan, urban, upper-class background.

AGENDA FUNCTION - The ability of the media to determine the topics that dominate national concern.

CONSERVATIVE MEDIA BIAS - The thesis that the media generally support conservative attitudes, using evidence of newspapers' editorial endorsements and owner attitudes.

LIBERAL MEDIA BIAS - The thesis that the media generally support liberal attitudes, using as evidence the results of polls that show reporters and anchor persons to be more liberal than a cross-section of voters.

POLITICAL CONSULTANT - A specialized campaign adviser, who is concerned with the candidate's image, and use of television-newspaper reporting.

C-SPAN - Nonprofit, cable satellite that covers public affairs and Congress.

PART III — PRETEST

1. Freedom of the press is guaranteed by
   a. American tradition.
   b. common law.
   c. Congress.
   d. a constitutional amendment.

2. One of the following media powers is normally *not* included in the top national ranking.
   a. *Reader's Digest*   c. *The Wall Street Journal*
   b. ABC.   d. *USA Today*

3. The media's new form of a town meeting is
   a. 60 Minutes.
   b. computer voting.
   c. the talk show.
   d. soundbites.

4. The network semi-monopoly over television has been _____ by C-SPAN and CNN.
   a. reinforced
   b. diminished
   c. untouched
   d. overshadowed

5. The media during a presidential election tends not to stress
   a. issues.
   b. personalities.
   c. strategy.
   d. the race.

6. Recent studies of the media's political reporting tend to be critical of their
   a. partisan bias.
   b. skimpy political coverage.
   c. repetitive coverage of issues.
   d. treatment of the election as a contest.

7. Which of the following has not become a national newspaper?
   a. *Washington Post*
   b. *USA Today*
   c. *The Wall Street Journal*
   d. *The New York Times*

8. The most trusted source of news is
   a. newspapers.
   b. news magazines.
   c. radio.
   d. television.

9. The President who has been most successful in using television to further his goals has been
   a. John Kennedy.
   b. Dwight Eisenhower.
   c. Franklin Roosevelt.
   d. Ronald Reagan.

10. The mass media's impact on most Americans is modified by their
    a. regionalism.
    b. viewing habits.
    c. lack of background.
    d. selective perception.

PART IV — PROGRAMMED REVIEW

Knowledge Objective: To evaluate the power of the mass media

1. In modern America the mass media is so powerful that it is sometimes called the _____ _____ of government.
2. Recent expansion of news sources has resulted in more competition for _____ .
3. The media have become the primary _____ mechanism in American politics.
4. The early American press served as a political _____ for political leaders.
5. Professional journalists believe the journalists should be _____ of partisan politics.
6. FDR effectively used the radio to _____ the editorial screening of the press.
7. Today _____ is the most important source of news for most Americans.
8. Media conglomerates now dominate the media business and have contributed to the _____ of news.

9. Critics charge that information today is more diluted and moderated because local TV and newspapers are not owned by _____ firms.
10. The _____ , not political parties, are now judging candidates in terms of character.

Knowledge Objective: To examine the relationship of the media and public opinion

11. For a long time political scientists have tended to (stress, play down) _____ the mass media's political influence.
12. Defense mechanisms such as _____ perception modify the influence of the mass media.
13. A powerful check on media as an opinion-making force is _____ _____ .
14. Much of the media's opinion-making role is (direct, indirect) _____ .
15. The final decision in determining the public agenda (is, is not) _____ made by the media.
16. _____ complain that the media are too liberal, and the liberals claim the media are too _____ .
17. David Broder has expressed concern about the _____ of journalists who previously were in government service.
18. Modern presidents have turned away from the press and to _____ and _____ to communicate with the public.
19. In recent decades, newspaper publishers tended to support _____ presidential candidates.
20. Generally, reporters are _____ , while publishers take _____ positions.
21. Critics of presidential use of television have called TV a _____ .
22. Critics hesitate to propose sweeping regulations for the media because it threatens _____ _____ rights.
23. A recent study indicates that the liberal bias of reporters (is, is not) _____ reflected in their on-the-job performance.

Knowledge Objective: To evaluate the role of the media in elections

24. The media tend to portray the presidential election as a _____ .
25. Public relations experts attached to campaigns tend to stress the candidate's _____ .
26. Election experts tend to determine their campaign strategy on the basis of _____ .
27. Old-time party leaders have been replaced in presidential campaigns by experts and _____ .
28. Newspapers and television seem to have (more/less) effect in determining the outcome of primaries than of general elections.

Knowledge Objective: To evaluate media power in American politics

29. Walt Lippmann likened media's influence on public affairs to a _____ of a searchlight.
30. In evaluating media power, the media scholars (agree, disagree) _____ .
31. The news media's greatest role as a participant is probably at the _____ level of government.
32. Most media coverage of Congress is its reaction to initiatives of the _____ .
33. Most Americans believe that the media (is, is not) _____ a valuable watchdog over government.

PART V — POST-TEST

1. In most national elections a majority of newspapers endorse _____ candidates.
   a. conservative
   b. liberal
   c. independent
   d. no

2. Critics of media employees charge that an overwhelming majority are
   a. conservative.
   b. liberal.
   c. independent.
   d. apolitical.

3. The most influential component of today's mass media is
   a. newspapers.
   b. television.
   c. radio.
   d. news magazines.

4. In addition to their public service role in providing information, the media also
   a. are privately owned.
   b. are big business.
   c. stress profits.
   d. all of the above

5. The modern President who has held the fewest news conferences has been
   a. Carter.
   b. Reagan.
   c. Ford.
   d. Johnson.

6. A member of Congress will be most concerned about news coverage by
   a. local TV news.
   b. national networks.
   c. C-SPAN.
   d. Washington Post.

7. Ownership of media outlets is
   a. widely dispersed.
   b. concentrated.
   c. unprofitable.
   d. family-oriented.

8. Journalists who side with those who are less powerful in society practice:
   a. selective perception.
   b. elite objectivity.
   c. advocacy journalism.
   d. adversarial journalism.

9. How citizens interpret information from politicians depends upon *all but one* of the following:
   a. recall ability.
   b. political socialization.
   c. hours spent watching TV.
   d. selectivity.

10. The institution least dependent on the press is
    a. the Supreme Court
    b. the presidency
    c. the bureaucracy
    d. the Congress

PART VI — POLITICAL DIALOGUE
THE CLASH OF ISSUES AND IDEAS

1. Shortly before his death, the veteran political reporter, Theodore H. White had this to say about television and politics. "American politics and television are now so completely locked together that it is impossible to tell the story of the one without the other. Television in modern politics has been as revolutionary as the development of printing in the time of old Gutenberg."
Is White correct?

2. Why has the media had great success in setting the national agenda?

3. Concentration of media ownership tends to destroy the original justification for protection of a free press.

4. Government-owned media would provide the public with more and better information. Evaluate.

5. The media were an effective force in challenging government policy in Vietnam and Watergate.

6. TV anchorpersons are a political wild card - unelected, irresponsible and powerful.

7. Charges are made that television emphasizes personalities and the "horse race" aspect of elections over issues. Defend or refute this criticism.

8. New stars of the television world are the talk show hosts. Larry King, Ted Koppel and Jay Leno are the people who have replaced Tom Brokaw, Dan Rather and Peter Jennings by giving in-depth treatment to presidential candidates. Is this change an improvement?

PART VII — POLITICAL SCIENCE TODAY

1. Recall your reaction to the selection of Dan Quayle as George Bush's running mate in 1988. Were you affected by the newspaper and television reports about Senator Quayle's service in the national guard (instead of in Vietnam), college record, etc.? From the perspective of Quayle's record as vice-president in the Bush Administration, do you think the media distorted Quayle's real capabilities or not? Finally, did media treatment of Vice President Quayle change during the 1988 to 1995 period, including the 1992 presidential campaign and Quayle's subsequent interest in pursuing the presidency in 1996?

2. Watch an evening television news broadcast on one of the major networks. How much time is devoted to each of the major stories covered? Make a list of each story by topic and allotted time. What conclusions can you reach about television's ability to inform the viewing public fully? Conversely, find the same story, if possible, covered by a major newspaper, preferably *The New York Times, Washington Post, Wall Street Journal,* or *Christian Science Monitor.* What differences in approach can you discern between the two media forms? Finally, if more people watch television than read newspaper editorials or features, then what is the ultimate impact upon levels of political information possessed by the mass public?

3. Obviously, television has played a very important role in presidential elections. An especially significant impact has been created from presidential debates in 1960, 1976, 1980, 1984, and 1988. For example, in 1960, the first debate between Senator John F. Kennedy and then Vice President Richard M. Nixon was a truly historic one. As Theodore White explains in his book *Making of the President-1960,* television's emphasis upon appearance as opposed to substance

cost Nixon politically. While people listening to the radio thought Nixon had "won" the debate with better responses to reporter questions, individuals watching the debate on TV gave Kennedy the overwhelming victory simply because Nixon looked so bad that evening (Nixon had lost weight, was given a poor make-up job for his heavy beard, and so forth).

Physical appearance is important on television. But television amplifies a mistake or the "communication" image made/projected by a candidate. Thus, in 1976, President Gerald Ford persisted in arguing that Eastern Europe was not under the domination of the Soviet Union, allowing Jimmy Carter to seize the campaign initiative. However, in 1980, Carter's serious distant communication image contrasted sharply with candidate Ronald Reagan's warm, personable imagery. Reagan's telling "are you better off today than you were four years ago" encapsulated the main theme of the campaign. In 1988, challenger Dukakis lost valuable ground when he failed to respond emotionally to a question posing a hypothetical case involving the rape and murder of his wife. In 1992, incumbent George Bush had a difficult time defending his administration's record and the status of the national economy in several three way debates involving Democrat Bill Clinton and independent candidate Ross Perot. Look back in newspapers and/or magazines as to what the reaction was to any of the above-mentioned debates. What do the reactions tell you about the media's role in influencing voter images of each presidential candidate?

4. Did your hometown newspaper endorse a Republican or Democratic candidate for president in the last election? Is that newspaper consistent in endorsing one party over the other in other federal and state/local elections? If so, why? If not, why not? As a possible research paper, you might investigate the political values and opinions of the newspaper's editorial staff and/or ownership.

5. Would you agree with the oft-quoted assertion that the news media favors the status quo? Can you find any news stories which propose radical new solutions for long-standing policy problems, particularly in the "establishment press"?

6. Try to obtain a copy of the motion-picture POWER, now on videocassette. The movie portrays how a media consultant (Richard Gere) tries to sell political candidates through skillful and at times cynical packaging in TV commercials. After viewing the tape, see if you can find material on how the various media consultants tried to package both Bush and Dukakis in the 1988 presidential election. Can you uncover any deliberate distortions which were effective in influencing the voter?

PART VIII — DATA ANALYSIS

1. Imagine that the federal government were to sponsor an official television channel, nation-wide, that would be devoted to the objective presentation of debate and policy options on some of the most important issues facing the country — abortion, capital punishment, the deficit, ecological crisis, drugs, education, poverty programs, and so forth. Debates would be true debates with careful summaries provided the viewer by commentators. Policy solutions would also be offered in some detail, with each solution's costs and benefits being delineated carefully and completely. This presentation of information would not be constrained by time. A particular problem might be debated for several hours each day, and last several weeks. In short, would such a channel be a useful tool in educating the public - why or why not? Jot down your thoughts below.

2. As a corollary of Exercise #2 in the Political Science Today section, were you able to find any particular evidence of liberal or conservative bias in commentaries by journalists on TV or in the newspapers? If so, cite some specifics.

PART IX — TEST ANSWERS

Pretest

1. d
2. a
3. c
4. b
5. a

6. d
7. a
8. d
9. d
10. d

Programmed Review

1. fourth branch
2. network news
3. linkage
4. mouthpiece
5. independent
6. bypass
7. television
8. centralization
9. local
10. press
11. play down
12. selective
13. group affiliation
14. indirect
15. is not
16. Conservatives;
    pro-establishment
17. objectivity
18. radio, television

19. Republican
20. liberal; conservative
21. throne
22. First Amendment
23. is not
24. race
25. image
26. polls
27. consultants
28. more
29. beam
30. disagree
31. local
32. President
33. is

Post-test

1. a
2. b
3. b
4. d
5. b

6. a
7. b
8. c
9. c
10. a

Data Analysis

1. The question is whether enough citizens would watch this national public-service channel. Would the average viewer really prefer a prolonged policy debate lasting for hours or days to his/her favorite soap opera, sporting event, or quiz show? Conversely, would the popularity of this channel increase over time if public schools used it to educate a new generation of Americans? These questions might be considered in your analysis.

2. This answer will vary depending upon the particular news broadcast selected.

CHAPTER 14
CONGRESS: THE PEOPLE'S BRANCH

C ongress is complicated. Its rules are intricate; its organization is centralized; its major areas of control surprisingly dispersed; its principal functions are not clearly defined; its critics are too numerous to mention; its internal reform proposals endless; its turnover of bills staggering — and yet, it is the greatest legislative body in the world.

To graft an old phrase on a new word: Congress is all things to all people. It is a deliberative body and has been likened to a court of appeals; it is a mediating body resolving conflicts among minority groups and special interests; it is an investigative body probing misconduct and corruption; it is a political body where politicians form party blocs to defeat or promote policy, and oftentimes frustrate one another by filibustering; it is a rival to the President seeking greater involvement in domestic, budgetary and foreign policies; and, perhaps most important of all, it is the principal source in our country where authoritative law is made.

Its committee system is like an octopus with chairmen barely astride the many legs of committees and subcommittees. Yet, these committees are miniature powerhouses. Its chairmen are often selected on the basis of seniority which many contend is unfair; yet, seniority bespeaks years of experience.

Its legislators are under great political and collegial pressures and influences; yet, they are listeners to their colleagues, to the President, and to their constituents back home, in gathering information for their decisionmaking.

Its labyrinth of bill passage channels would often make the most intelligent mouse give up in a similarly constructed maze; yet bills are passed and the rigorous pathway confirms their legitimacy.

Moreover, Congress has changed as much as any other political institution.

Yet this powerful body is often held up to ridicule and treated with contempt or worse. In recent years it has been racked by scandal, partisan infighting, and charges of influence peddling, bribery, and corruption. Individual Congressmen are often viewed as helpful allies by all kinds of constituents. But the general impression remains that of a body out of control, requiring drastic reform. With the risks that any prediction entails, the time seems ripe for Congress to regain public esteem by a thorough-going "House Cleaning."

PART I — GUIDEPOSTS

1. Congressional Elections
   a. What is meant by a "safe seat"? "Competitive seat"?
   b. How does gerrymandering play a role in Congressional elections? What triggers the periodic redistricting? Under what restrictions are Congressional district lines drawn?
   c. Why is incumbency an advantage?
   d. What overriding factor determines voter decisions?
   e. What are general characteristics of legislators with respect to sex, education, economic background, political background, race and religion?
   f. What profession tends to dominate legislative backgrounds?

2. Powers of Congress
   a. What general powers were given to Congress by the Constitution?
   b. What special powers was it given?
   c. In the national contest for power why has the President gained more than Congress?

3. The Houses of Congress
   a. Why was the legislative branch originally divided into two parts?
   b. How has the House of Representatives made its procedures more efficient?
   c. What special powers does the Speaker have?
   d. What other officers supplement the Speaker's leadership?
   e. What key role is played by the Rules Committee?
   f. What official dominates Senate procedure?
   g. How have Senate minorities used the filibuster? How can cloture be used to end filibusters?
   h. Why have confirmations by the Senate become more political?

4. The Job of Legislator
   a. What is the *delegate* theory of representation? The *trustee* theory? Who is apt to hold each view?
   b. What role do each of the following play in a Congressman's voting record: ideology? voter opinion? colleagues? staff? party? President? other influences?
   c. How do PACs influence the legislative process?

5. The Legislative Obstacle Course
   a. How is power dispersed in Congress?
   b. What is a rider? Why are they used?
   c. What is meant by authorization and appropriation?
   d. Why is compromise so important in Congress?

6. Committees: The Little Legislatures?
   a. Why is Congress sometimes called a collection of committees?
   b. How are committee members selected?
   c. How important are the chairs of committees and subcommittees?
   d. What role does seniority play in committees?
   e. How valuable are committee investigations?
   f. How important are conference committees?

7. Is Congress Effective? Congressional Reform?
   a. What are the most frequent criticisms of Congress?
   b. Evaluate each criticism.
   c. How is Congress fragmented?
   d. In what sense is Congress acting as the Founders anticipated?

PART II — GLOSSARY

SENIORITY - Length of time in office. Used as determining factor in appointing Congressional committees.

PRESIDENT PRO TEMPORE - Official Chairperson in Senate when Vice President is absent.

HOUSE RULES COMMITTEE - Committee that schedules House calendar of business.

FILIBUSTER - Device employing long-drawn-out speeches that prevent Senate vote on a controversial issue.

CLOTURE - A procedure for halting Senate debate (filibuster).

SPEAKER - Presiding officer of the House, formally elected by whole House, but actually by
   majority party.
POCKET VETO - A special veto occurring only when Congress adjourns with ten days, requiring
   no formal presidential action.
WHIPS - Important House members who serve as "go-betweens" in the process involving general
   members and leaders.
CONFERENCE COMMITTEE - A committee composed of appointed members of both Houses to
   compromise different versions of a bill.
DISCHARGE PETITION - A petition signed by a majority of House members to pry a bill from a
   committee.
MINORITY FLOOR LEADER - Party leader elected by the minority in each House to serve as an
   opposition spokesperson.
CAUCUS OR CONFERENCE - A meeting of the members of each party to select leaders and
   determine policy.
DELEGATE ROLE - The concept that a Congressperson should reflect the prevailing sentiment of
   the district.
TRUSTEE ROLE - The concept that an elected representative should reflect independent judgment,
   rather than the current attitude of the district.

PART III — PRETEST

1. All of the following are true about senators and representatives *except*
   a. they come from upper and middle-class families.
   b. nearly half the members of Congress are lawyers.
   c. they are disproportionately from rural areas.
   d. a third come from blue collar occupations.

2. Gerrymandering occurs when the majority party
   a. supports benefits for blue collar workers.
   b. promises to promote legislation for certain districts.
   c. draws district lines to win as many districts as possible.
   d. draws district lines to maximize its popular vote.

3. Which factor is most important in winning a congressional seat?
   a. candidate appeal
   b. campaign strategy
   c. safe seat
   d. local issue

4. The chief responsibility of congressional staff is to
   a. handle constituent mail.
   b. serve as receptionists.
   c. schedule office appointments.
   d. advise on legislation.

5. Congress *does not* perform one of these functions.
   a. policy clarification
   b. consensus building
   c. foreign policy initiatives
   d. lawmaking

6. The Speaker of the House of Representatives does all of the following *except*
   a. grants recognition to a member.
   b. appoints select and conference committees.
   c. controls committee assignments.
   d. directs general business on the floor.

7. In the Senate, the committee responsible for each party's overall legislative program is called the _____ committee.
   a. policy   c. strategy
   b. direction   d. ways-and-means

8. Legislators who base their votes on their analysis of the long-run welfare of the nation are playing a _____ role.
   a. delegate   c. pragmatic
   b. trustee   d. pollster's

9. The seniority system as it now operates favors
   a. southerners.   c. northerners.
   b. women.   d. Republicans.

10. Critics of Congress do not commonly complain that it is
   a. inefficient.   c. dominated by the President.
   b. unrepresentative.   d. independent of lobbyists.

PART IV — PROGRAMMED REVIEW

Knowledge objective: To review the system for election to Congress and to profile those elected
1. Redrawing the district lines of U.S. Representatives after each census is the responsibility of _____ _____ .
2. _____ is the process of drawing electoral boundaries to maximize the majority party's house majority.
3. Being an incumbent is an _____ for a member of Congress seeking reelection.
4. Redistricting occurs after each national _____ .
5. The overwhelming number of national legislators are from _____ to _____ income backgrounds.
6. Nearly half of the legislators are _____ by profession.

Knowledge Objective: To analyze the structure and powers of the houses of Congress
7. The framers designed the _____ to reflect the popular will and the _____ to provide stability.
8. The _____ holds the place in government the framers intended for Congress.
9. By sitting as the Committee of the _____ , the House is able to operate more informally and expeditiously than under regular rules.
10. The Speaker of the House chairs the influential _____ and _____ Committee that was created in 1973.
11. Assisting each floor leader are the party _____ who serve as liaisons between the House leadership and the rank-and-file members.
12. In the Senate, each party has a _____ _____ which is in theory responsible for the party's overall legislative program.
13. The practice of the President consulting with a Senator before naming a presidential nominee is called _____ _____ .
14. Debate in the Senate can be shut off only by a _____ vote.
15. The Senate has the power to _____ presidential nominations.

Knowledge Objective: To consider the job of the legislator

16. Members of Congress who see their role as _____ believe they should serve the "folks back home."
17. Members of Congress who see their role as _____ are free-thinking legislators who vote their conscience.
18. The main influence on legislators is their perception of how their _____ feel about the matters brought before Congress.
19. Most members of Congress are now highly dependent on their _____ .
20. Roughly ninety percent of the bills introduced every two years _____ in a subcommittee.
21. Senators use _____ to force the president to accept unwanted legislation.

Knowledge Objective: To trace the lawmaking process

22. From the very beginning, Congress has been a system of multiple_____ .
23. To follow a bill through the congressional labyrinth is to see the _____ of power in Congress.
24. Proponents of new legislation must win at every step; _____ need win only once.

Knowledge Objective: To examine the committee system

25. All bills introduced in the House are sent to _____ committees.
26. As the power of Congressional subcommittees has expanded, the importance of _____ has diminished.
27. _____ are still usually named on the basis of seniority.
28. If neither house will accept the other's bills, a _____ _____ settles the difference.
29. Critics judge that Congress is _____ because the committee system responds too much to organized regional interests.
30. Congress lacks collective _____ .
31. Congress (has, has not) _____ created Ethics Committees to monitor the behavior of members.
32. There is a constant tendency for Congress to delegate authority to _____ agencies.

PART V — POST-TEST

1. The profile of a typical senator or representative would tend to bear out the charge that they
   a. are elitist.
   b. are ill-educated.
   c. are lower middle-class.
   d. over-represent minorities.

2. Members of Congress from competitive districts are apt to make _____ their first priority.
   a. serving the home folks
   b. foreign policy
   c. national issues
   d. supporting the president

3. Special responsibilities of the Senate do *not* include two of the following.
   a. ratification of treaties
   b. confirmation of presidential nominees
   c. a final veto on appropriations
   d. nomination of ambassadors to foreign countries

4. In terms of the general makeup of Congress, which of the following people would be most typical?
      a. a millionaire Jewish stockbroker
      b. a Catholic steel worker
      c. a Protestant female elementary teacher
      d. a middle-income male lawyer

5. Today, the Rules Committee can be characterized as
      a. an arm of the leadership.
      b. a block to legislation.
      c. a coalition of Republicans and conservative Democrats.
      d. ultra liberal.

6. Free-thinking and independent legislators see their role as
      a. national figures.   c. diplomats.
      b. trustees.   d. ambassadors from localities.

7. The role of the president has become enhanced at the expense of the Congress, especially _____ policy.
      a. domestic   c. economic
      b. foreign   d. social

8. The vast majority of the 15,000 or so bills introduced every two years in both chambers are
      a. passed.   c. killed.
      b. still under debate.   d. withdrawn.

9. The majority floor leader is an officer
      a. only of his party.
      b. in charge of both parties in standing and conference committees.
      c. in charge of both parties on the floor.
      d. who presides over the Senate.

10. House party whips do all of the following *except*
      a. serve as liaison between leadership and the rank-and-file.
      b. inform members when important bills will be voted.
      c. lobby strongly for support of the majority leader.
      d. try to ensure maximum attendance for critical votes.

PART VI — POLITICAL DIALOGUE:
THE CLASH OF ISSUES AND IDEAS

1. "Any examination of Congressional backgrounds confirms the charge that they are an elitist group that is elected and kept in office by the "well-fed, well-bred, well-wed" segment of American society that controls things, rather than a cross-section of all Americans. Elitist blocs elect Congress: Congress in turn does what these elites want. It's all very cozy and unrepresentative." Discuss.

2. Recent election figures seem to confirm that we elect Congressmen for *life* rather than for two or six year terms. Of those Representatives who ran for reelection in 1988, ninety-eight percent were elected. Can we claim that we continue to have representative government when incumbents have such a hammerlock on Congressional seats? Comment.

3. The House Banking scandal proves that Congress has become too pampered and has set up a way of life far beyond the wildest dreams of the average voters who elect them. Cheap haircuts, a gymnasium, free medical care are only the beginning of a list that seems to stretch endlessly. No sane person would believe that these people could or would reform themselves. Comment.

4. The distinguished Senator, Sam Ervin, who sat on the Watergate Committee once said on the issue of trustee versus delegate, "My home state voters sent me to the Senate because they trusted my good judgment. I don't have to go back to them for guidance every time I vote. They don't have the time or inclination to sort out every issue. That's what they sent me to Washington for." Is this a valid position?

5. Congress has been so fragmented in the name of reform that it is an impotent octopus, without a central nervous system to give it coordination or direction. What we need to do is toss out thirty years of "reform" and recreate authority and leadership. Discuss.

6. The frustrations of Congressmen who hope to achieve any goal are enormous. What we have lost by way of potential leadership is unmeasurable. Who can replace the wisdom and legislative skills of such men as Barber Conable, Thomas O'Neill, Otis Pike, William Proxmire, Howard Baker? How can we restore the dignity and honor once accorded to Congress and Congressmen?

PART VII — POLITICAL SCIENCE TODAY

1. Congressmen, particularly members of the House of Representatives who have two year terms as opposed to six year terms for U.S. Senators, must constantly work at reelection, especially if they contemplate serious opposition in the near future. Consequently, a great deal of a congressman's time is spent in communicating with constituents back home in the district and performing political "fence-mending" actions.

One typical information device is the "newsletter" whereby a congressmen reports on important bills, highlights activities that he or she has participated in the district, and perhaps most importantly, suggests what he or she is specifically doing to promote the interests and well-being of the district. For example, before his retirement from Congress in 1992, Congressman J. Roy Rowland of the Eighth Congressional District in Georgia typically sent out two newsletters per year. Typical was a newsletter sent out in mid-year (1989) where the congressman talked about his co-sponsorship of a bill to reduce infant mortality ("I am playing a key role in steering the bill before Congress"), his efforts to delay a surtax imposed on the elderly in their Medicare benefits, co-sponsorship of a financial package to assist rural hospitals, and his request to the House Appropriations Committee to consider additional funding for counties in his district where federal wildlife refuges were located. Information was also included covering the Eighth District's Congressional Arts Competition (Rowland was pictured with the high school student who was the grand prize winner), how to obtain a medical information directory from the federal National Library of Medicine, and how copies of the high school National Debate Topic Book could be obtained by teachers, youth organizations and interested citizens.

To see how a newsletter or comparable-mailing from your congressman compares to the above description, call a local or the Washington, D.C. office of your representative. Ask for the most recent newsletter (or its equivalent) available and see how long it takes to get to you. This may be a good indication of how efficient your congressman's staff is and perhaps also some sign as to the degree of reelection pressure he or she is facing in the next election.

Incidentally, these information newsletters or other similar mailings are mailed postage-free by the representative under the franking privilege. The franking privilege is a system which entitles members of Congress to send mail to constituents without charge by putting their frank, or mark, on the envelope. The law prohibits this privilege for soliciting campaign money or votes, or for mass mailings 60 days before an election. However, is a newsletter detailing a congressman's accomplishments or proposals not inherently political? Does the franking privilege not give an obvious and clear advantage to incumbents? Should the system be changed? On the other hand, how could a congressman afford to send out mail of a non-political nature to hundreds of thousands of constituents without a break on postage? Debate the issue with fellow classmates and/or your instructor.

2. In a *Los Angeles Times* reprint on "Congress — Too Many Free Agents" by staff writer Sara Fritz (January 24,1988), the various problems with Congress were examined closely. Ms. Fritz asserted the following in her analysis.

(a) Americans of all political persuasions regard Congress with a "combination of contempt and disgust." This public distaste apparently stems from the fact that Congress has been unable, structurally, to respond to the rapid pace of change and the international realities of the contemporary era. Partisan bickering, the breakdown of the lawmaking process, and the diffusion of power have all characterized the institution.

(b) In a survey of congressmen, nearly 95% of those questioned said changes are required such as improved legislative scheduling, higher pay, improved campaign financing and fewer subcommittees. But many experts on Congress argued that reforms of the post-Watergate era have worsened the situation (party leaders and committee chairmen lost much of their authority).

(c) Instead of reaching a broad consensus on major problems, most congressmen react to the needs of their constituencies and the special lobbying interests in their respective districts. Congressmen become champions of specialized causes and pressure groups.

(d) The level of trust and cooperation between the President and Congress has declined. Further contributing to this tendency is the voter tendency to elect Democratic congresses and Republican presidents.

(e) Debate in the Senate has largely become meaningless. Many senators openly declare their positions on a bill even before debate has begun. Also, the filibuster has become "trivialized" in that some senators threaten to filibuster on issues that are relatively minor. Thus, according to one survey, 77% of senators favor limiting the use of the filibuster. Another 62% favor limiting the right of senators to offer amendments to any bill, where appropriate or not.

(f) Some reforms may be forthcoming and a few have been realized, such as extending the Senate working week from Monday through Friday periodically. There may also be momentum building for a degree of greater centralized leadership in both houses in order to bring some order out of recurrent chaos.

Reviewing the above material and correlative content in the chapter, it appears that many of the assertions made by author Sara Fritz still ring true for the 104th Congress that convened in 1995. For example, in late 1994, it appeared well over 70% of the American people disapproved of Congress, a percentage consistent with the notation made in (a) However, note that (d) was no longer true. The voter tendency to "elect Democratic congresses" was dramatically reversed when the Republicans gained control of both Houses of Congress after the 1994 midterm elections. The new Congress consisted of 230 Republicans, 204 Democrats, 1 independent in the House and 53

Republicans and 47 Democrats in the U.S. Senate. Democratic President Bill Clinton therefore faced a major political dilemma, i.e., would "the level of trust and cooperation between the President and Congress further decline" during his two remaining years in the White House?

In addition, what other problems do you perceive as the most significant regarding congressional operations? What are some potential reforms you would like to see introduced? The answers to such questions could form the basis of a research paper and/or oral report.

PART VIII — DATA ANALYSIS

1. Many members of Congress wrestle with the potential conflict between the national interest and their district's needs. In order to examine the nature of this conflict further, how do you think the following hypothetical member of Congress would vote in this situation:

In order to cut spending, the president and Department of Defense intend to close a number of military bases around the country. One base, employing some 5000 civilians and crucial to the district's economic growth, is on this "hit list." the President calls the congressman and asks for his support in this national effort to cut federal spending. How is this congressman likely to respond when the base closing bill comes up for a vote (the bill will be voted on roughly six months before the next congressional election)?

2. Review the text material on "A Profile of Members of Congress." What salient conclusions can you draw from the description regarding the composition of Congress and possible policy concerns or results?

PART IX — TEST ANSWERS

Pretest

1. d	6. c
2. c	7. a
3. d	8. b
4. d	9. d
5. c	10. c

Programmed Review

1. state legislatures	16. delegate
2. Gerrymandering	17. Trustee
3. advantage	18. constituents
4. census	19. staff
5. middle; upper-middle	20. die
6. lawyers	21. riders
7. House; Senate	22. vetoes
8. President	23. dispersion
9. Whole	24. opponents
10. Steering; Policy	25. standing
11. whips	26. seniority
12. policy committee	27. Chairpersons
13. senatorial courtesy	28. conference committee
14. cloture	29. unrepresentative
15. confirm	30. responsibility
	31. has
	32. administrative

Post-test

1. a	6. b
2. a	7. b
3. c, d	8. c
4. d	9. a
5. a	10. c

Data Analysis

1. It would seem obvious that this is one issue which will be politically sensitive to the "folks back home." A congressman who willingly voted to put 5000 constituents out of work would not be very popular. Also the economic loss of the base would have a strong ripple effect among district businessmen, labor unions, educators, politicians, and so forth. This is the kind of bread and butter vote that most congressmen will cast in favor of unambiguous district preferences.

2. As the text chapter states (please review if necessary), the very small number of blacks and women in both houses of Congress could lead to the charge of congressional insensitivity to the issues of civil rights, women's rights, and poverty issues. However, Congress's upper-class and male-dominated profile has not prevented landmark legislation from helping both women and blacks in the past. The large number of lawyers in Congress does make sense given the fundamental nature of the legislative process, procedurally and substantively.

CHAPTER 15
THE PRESIDENCY: THE LEADERSHIP BRANCH

For the past fifty years, domestic and foreign crises have increased presidential power and responsibility. Additionally, there have been rising public expectations regarding strong presidential leadership. The result has been the emergence of the presidency as the leadership branch.

But this enormous strength, enthroned in secrecy, emergency powers, and manipulation, has often had behind it in recent years anyone but Abraham Lincoln. In other words, the great Oz machine with its wheels of power and secrecy, when uncovered has frequently revealed a person defensively attempting to compensate for his sense of inadequacy. Curiously, in a somewhat similar fashion the swelling of the presidency has also covered up institutional shortcomings and weaknesses.

Today executive power is far-reaching. Congress has delegated many emergency powers to the president, and the president has almost total control in national security matters. Television and the televised press conference have extended the speech-making powers of the presidency. The office of the president is indeed enormous. It is the heart of policy formulation in both domestic and foreign affairs. It is the office to which we look in time of emergency and crisis.

The president is no longer one person but an institution of people gathered about the president to aid him in the decision-making process. Although ultimate power still rests in the hands of one person, modern presidents have created a staff to cope with national and international affairs. This extension is The Executive Office with components that separately manage domestic policy, economic policy, national security (foreign affairs), congressional relations and public relations.

The chapter presents a number of vexing questions. Do the qualities of personality and style which serve a candidate so well become stumbling blocks when the individual reaches the White House? Is the presidency equal to the jobs imposed upon the office? How can we make the office of the presidency safe for democracy?

PART I — GUIDEPOSTS

1. What can we look for in a president?
    a. What are the mixed reactions Americans have to presidential power?
    b. What qualities do we demand of our presidents?
    c. Whom do we rate as our five best presidents?
    d. In defining desirable presidential characteristics, how do Americans rank policy preferences, eloquence, and character?

2. Roots of Divided Government
    a. Why did the framers design a government that almost from the outset was in internal conflict?
    b. How have the following factors led to divided government: different constituencies; varying office terms; divided party control of the branches; weak political parties; fluctuating power?
    c. What are a president's sources of influence in Congress?
    d. What is the ultimate weapon that Congress can use against the president?

3. The Job of the President
    a. What built-in checks apply to presidential power?
    b. Why did the framers outline the powers of the president in such broad terms?

4. Presidents as Policy Managers
    a. Is a president's military power practically limitless?
    b. What types of domestic crises bring a popular demand for presidential action?
    c. In what ways is public attention focused on the presidency?
    d. How can this attention be used to his advantage? Can this attention turn against him?
    e. How does a president's role as ceremonial leader conflict with his partisan political image?
    f. Why can a president's appointments have long-range consequences?
    g. What voice do presidents have in setting national priorities?
    h. Why does the president play a central role in foreign policy?
    i. How does the president's help determine national economic policy?
    j. How do presidents enlist the direct support of the people?
    k. Of what use are State of the Union addresses?
    l. Why are effective presidents also adroit politicians?
    m. In what ways is the veto useful to presidents? What forms can it take?
    n. What is an item veto? Why does the president want this power? What is the probability that he will get it?

5. Presidents as Administrators
    a. Why do presidents face potential damage by restricting their advisors to a small circle of "yes" men?
    b. What is meant by the executive office of the president? Who composes it?
    c. Why does the Cabinet not replace the president's executive office?
    d. Do vice-presidents generally perform important functions?
    e. How influential are presidents' spouses?

6. Does the President Have Too Much or Too Little Power?
    a. How does the Congress serve as a check on presidential power?
    b. Why is media coverage of the president normally adversarial?
    c. In what ways is our political culture hierarchical? individualistic? equalitarian?
    d. Why does Paul Kennedy believe that the United States will be limited in its future international relations?

7. The President and Congress: A Continuing Struggle
    a. Can Congress replace the president in leadership?
    b. Who is imperial — the president or Congress?
    c. Can the continuing struggle between Congress and the president ever be resolved?

8. Making the Presidency Effective
    a. What American experiences suggest the dangers of presidential power?
    b. What qualities do successful presidents share?
    c. What paradox do Americans have to wrestle with if the presidency is to thrive?

PART II — GLOSSARY

INTERMINGLING OF POWERS - The sharing of decision-making between Congress and the President.

EXECUTIVE AGREEMENT - A Presidential international understanding with the force of a treaty, that does not require Senate approval.

CURTISS-WRIGHT CASE - Supreme Court decision of 1936 that give the President extensive, undefined powers in foreign affairs.

EXECUTIVE OFFICE OF THE PRESIDENT - A cluster of staff agencies that assist the President.

OFFICE OF MANAGEMENT AND BUDGET - Presidential staff agency concerned with budget and management.

NATIONAL SECURITY COUNCIL - Presidential agency concerned with national security.

KENNEDY THEORY - Analysis by historian Paul Kennedy who declares that the United States has passed its zenith as a world power and that its future will be determined by its ability to adjust to this fact.

PRESIDENTIAL VETO - A formal action by the president, returning a bill unsigned to Congress, stating his objections.

POCKET VETO - A special veto occurring only when Congress adjourns within ten days, requiring no formal presidential action.

ITEM VETO - A specialized veto power of governors to veto only selected portions of a bill. Requested by Reagan and Bush of Congress without success.

WAR POWERS ACT - Restrictions on the president's power to wage war without Congressional approval.

PART III — PRETEST

1. Critics of the presidency seldom charge that it is a(n) _____ institution.
   - a. remote, aristocratic
   - b. weak, flabby
   - c. status quo
   - d. Establishment

2. Only one of the following presidents is likely to appear on a list of "greats."
   - a. Buchanan
   - b. Grant
   - c. Truman
   - d. Harding

3. The framers of the Constitution did not fully anticipate presidential
   - a. symbolic functions.
   - b. abuses of power.
   - c. magisterial functions.
   - d. legislative role.

4. The Supreme Court decision in Curtiss-Wright (1936) upheld strong presidential authority over
   - a. foreign policy.
   - b. domestic policy.
   - c. budget.
   - d. appointments.

5. The president's influence over his party includes selecting
   - a. the party chairman.
   - b. congressional candidates.
   - c. state officials.
   - d. precinct workers.

6. The central presidential staff agency that advises the president about hundreds of government agencies is the
   - a. Office of Oversight and Investigation.
   - b. Central Intelligence Agency.
   - c. Office of Management and Budget.
   - d. GAO.

7. The vice president has not been used by modern presidents to
    a. chair advisory councils.
    b. execute day-to-day policy.
    c. undertake good will missions.
    d. serve as a senior advisor.

8. The following persisting paradoxes of the American presidency are true *except* that a president should be
    a. programmatic, but a pragmatic and flexible leader.
    b. a common person who can give an uncommon performance.
    c. a person who delivers more than he or she promises.
    d. above politics, yet a skilled political coalition builder.

9. In comparing constitutional powers granted to the president and to Congress, the following generalization is true.
    a. Both are described in vague terms.
    b. Congressional powers are detailed; presidential powers are vague.
    c. Presidential power is detailed; congressional power is vague.
    d. Both are described in detail.

10. In one of the following instances, the War Powers Act does *not* authorize the president to commit the armed forces.
    a. a congressional declaration of war
    b. specific statutory authorization
    c. a national majority vote
    d. certain national emergencies

PART IV — PROGRAMMED REVIEW

Knowledge Objective: To analyze the characteristics that Americans expect of their president
    1. The framers of the Constitution wanted a strong leader but feared _____ of power.
    2. The central characteristic that Americans demand of their president is the quality of _____.
    3. In judging presidents, voters rate _____ and _____ over policy decisions.
    4. President Johnson lost his effectiveness because of the war in _____ .

Knowledge Objective: To examine the president's constitutional position
    5. Rather than having a complete separation of powers, we actually have an _____ of powers.
    6. The president's power is limited by a system of _____ and _____ .
    7. The dimensions of presidential power at any given moment are a consequence of the incumbent's _____ and _____ .
    8. During the past two centuries in democracies, power has shifted from legislators to _____ .

Knowledge Objective: To examine the role of Congress and the president within a system of checks and balances
    9. The Constitution (does, does not) _____ confer policy-making powers on both Congress and the president.
    10. Framers of the Constitution expected the president to be dominant in _____ policy.
    11. Congress and the president usually (do, do not) _____ work together.
    12. Congress and the president are answerable to (the same, different) _____ constituencies.

13. Most members of Congress (are, are not) _____ dependent on presidential support for reelection.
14. Presidents are most influential in winning the support of Congress on _____ policy issues.

Knowledge Objective: To analyze symbolic leadership

15. The president has greatest inherent power in matters involving _____ affairs and national security.
16. The president's power has been greatly increased by the mass media, especially _____ .
17. The swelling of the presidency in part results from the _____ expectations.
18. Presidents face a conflict between their role as chief of state and their role as _____ leader.
19. In acting for all the people, the president is a symbolic leader and _____ of state.

Knowledge Objective: To examine the presidential establishment and constraints on the President

20. The Supreme Court in the Curtiss-Wright case decided that the president (did, did not) _____ have exclusive powers in the field of international relations.
21. Since presidents appoint over 4,000 top officials, one of the chief presidential duties is _____ .
22. The War Powers Resolution of 1973 reflects the determination by Congress to control the president's formerly unlimited discretion to use _____ abroad.
23. For economic policy the president depends on the Secretary of the Treasury, the Council of Economic Advisers, and the Director of the _____ .
24. A president who is a successful leader knows where the _____ are.
25. Recent presidents have asked for a constitutional amendment that would give them _____ veto power.
26. To influence media coverage, the president holds _____ _____ .
27. To gauge public opinion, presidents commission private _____ _____ .
28. Presidential candidates depend less on the organized _____ than on their personal political organization.
29. In recent years presidents have come to rely heavily on their personal _____ .
30. The office of _____ and _____ continues to be the central presidential staff agency.
31. Presidents seldom turn to the _____ as a collective body for advice.
32. The vice-president serves as president of the _____ .
33. The number of our presidents who were once vice-presidents is approximately one-_____ .
34. The modern media is the Number One _____ of the presidency.
35. The American people regard television as (more, less) _____ trustworthy than most other American institutions.

Knowledge Objective: To review the search for a proper balance between congressional and presidential power

36. The American people quite clearly (do, do not) _____ want strong purposeful leadership in the 1990s.
37. Most people believe that Congress (can, cannot) _____ furnish the necessary leadership.
38. To make the presidency safe for democracy, we should revitalize _____ _____ such as Congress, the courts, the press, and political parties.

PART V — POST-TEST

1. The American public today gives priority to one aspect of the president.
    a. leadership
    b. honesty
    c. wisdom
    d. policy positions

2. Presidents have the most leeway in
    a. foreign and military affairs.
    b. domestic appropriation matters.
    c. budget appropriations.
    d. social policy.

3. Often a president's "new initiatives" in domestic policy are
    a. highly creative.
    b. previously considered in Congress.
    c. previously thought of by past presidents.
    d. a response to grassroots demands.

4. The functions of the White House staff include *all but*
    a. domestic policy.
    b. economic policy.
    c. congressional relations.
    d. intelligence operations.

5. If the president is to be a successful politician, he must be able to
    a. give commands.
    b. manage conflict.
    c. stand on principles.
    d. rise above politics.

6. Modern presidential cabinets as a collective body have been used by presidents
    a. as high-level advisers.
    b. to create a quasi-parliamentary system.
    c. very infrequently.
    d. to assess new policy proposals.

7. Divided government is encouraged by all but
    a. strong political parties.
    b. varying terms of office.
    c. different constituencies
    d. constitutional ambiguities.

8. Critics who question the twentieth-century evolution of the presidency have named the modern office the _____ presidency.
    a. imperial
    b. dictatorial
    c. fragile
    d. flub dub

9. The president's veto power over bills *does not include* one of the following actions
    a. returning it unsigned with objections.
    b. taking no action for five work days.
    c. taking no action if Congress adjourns in 10 days.
    d. threatening to veto a bill before passage.

10. The arrangement whereby Congress and the President share powers is called
    a. intermingling
    b. bipartisan
    c. check and balance
    d. limited

PART VI — POLITICAL DIALOGUE: THE CLASH OF ISSUES AND IDEAS

1. Woodrow Wilson is reported to have said, "Only prudent athletes should run for the Presidency." Would you agree? How would you lighten the burden of the Presidency without diminishing the powers of the President?

2. Richard Neustadt writes, "the power to persuade is the power to bargain." Cite examples of a President bargaining in order to secure the enactment of his program.

3. President Truman is identified with the quotation, "the buck stops here." Is this a realistic description of the role of the Presidents?

4. Theodore Roosevelt referred to the White House as "a bully-pulpit." Discuss the meaning of this phrase in terms of contemporary politics and current issues.

5. Woodrow Wilson is associated with the quotation, "the President is at liberty, both in law and conscience to be as big a man as he can be." Do you think that this is a good guideline for the modern Presidency?

6. Warren Harding is associated with the quotation, "the White House is a prison." Comment.

7. "The media destroy every hero ... they strip them naked."

8. "... If it were left to me to decide whether we should have a government without newspapers or newspapers without a government, I prefer the latter."

9. David Halberstam in *The Best and the Brightest* advances the theory that we become deeply involved in the Vietnam War because presidential advisers ("the best and the brightest") were almost unanimous in recommending escalation of that war. What legislation has now been enacted to prevent a recurrence of such involvement? Will these restrictions work? Do they limit the president too much?

10. Frequently it is said that Congress has reasserted itself. In fact, some scholars believe that it has shifted the balance of power too much in its own favor. Do you believe that the average American views Congress as an "equal among equals" in its relationship with the president?

11. Our historical experience as a nation abounds with examples of military and diplomatic initiatives taken by presidents without Congressional support or approval. President Reagan's Central American politics are a recent case in point. Can you suggest any restrictions on presidential power that would not endanger our national security?

PART VII — POLITICAL SCIENCE TODAY

1. Because the President is the central actor in the American political system, his policy proposals can sometimes stir the public as well as Congress into political action. However. his proposals are frequently controversial and may create heated opposition as well.

   This was the case in July of 1989 when President George Bush proposed that the United States establish a base on the Moon, launch an expedition to Mars, complete an orbiting space station above the Earth, and in general restore the nation's once preeminent position in space exploration. The President's speech was made at the commemoration of the July, 1969 Apollo 11 moon landing. However, unlike President Kennedy's famous speech of 1961 challenging the nation to land a man on the moon before the end of the decade, President Bush set no timetable for any of the particular missions. His general proposals along with the lack of precise cost estimates seemed to unleash a torrent or criticisms as described in the July 21, 1989 *The New York Times* article written by Bernard Weinraub (p. l).

   The estimate of some 400 billion to reach both the Moon and Mars led to anger on the part of some congressmen in an era of budgetary scarcity:

   Senator Al Gore, chairman of the Committee on Space, Science and Technology stated that 'by proposing a return to the Moon and manned base on Mars, with no money, no timetable, and no plan President Bush offers the country not a challenge to inspire us, but a day-dream.' Senator Jim Sasser, chairman of the Budget Committee, said, 'The President took one giant leap for starry-eyed political rhetoric, and not even a small step for fiscal responsibility.' Rep. Robert G. Torricelli, a member of the House Science and space committee said. 'There is a bitterness over repeated efforts by this Administration to set ambitious goals and then not to providing funding.' Finally, Rep. Bill Green, the ranking minority member of the Appropriations committee that directs funding for NASA, stated that 'Given the Federal budget deficit and earthly demands, I don't see how we can afford expensive manned programs in space in the near future.'

   Research what happened to President Bush's proposals in the subsequent months after his "Moon-Mars" speech. Did Congress or the general public respond to the proposals more favorably after the initial fiscal shock wore off - why or why not? Also, do you believe President Bush could have "packaged" his space proposals more effectively, perhaps by reemphasizing joint missions with the Soviet Union or the technological spinoffs which could benefit American society directly or indirectly? Or was President Bush's political timing off, i.e., should he have waited to push these proposals when the economy was clearly improving? Conversely, do you think the President was correct in trying to challenge all Americans to consider the future exploration of space, regardless of the political outcry?

2. What factors do you believe are responsible for presidential "greatness" or failure? Despite the surveys of great presidents available in the chapter, which president do you believe was truly effective and why? Do most Americans want presidents who offer a vision of the future, who inspire them, who display political courage and daring? Or, depending upon the era, can the American people be satisfied with a president who preserves the status quo with few examples of dramatic policy pro-posals or changes? Research these questions carefully and come up with your own conclusions.

3. Because presidents frequently collide with congressional wishes, some political observers would like to see presidents behave more like British prime ministers vis-á-vis the loyal opposition. For example, would it be helpful if a future president adopted the British practice of actually going to Congress periodically and facing direct questions from leaders of the opposing party, in both the House and Senate? A skillful president might be able to galvanize support for his programs, help his own party, and even win adherents from opposing party congressmen. Conversely, the whole process could result in political disaster. What do you think would happen?

A second idea to win support from opposing congressmen and senators would be for a president to select cabinet officers from both political parties in order to truly create bipartisanship in the executive branch. However, such an approach could weaken party loyalties for a new president. Again, what are some other pros and cons of the bipartisan cabinet concept?

4. If you were president, how would you make sure that you were receiving accurate information and advice from your staff? In other words, would you prefer a loose advisory arrangement where a large number of close advisers and staffers could have access to you on a frequent basis? Or, in order to manage your time effectively, would you prefer trusting only two or three close advisers who in turn would screen out distractions and act as contacts for those wishing to see you directly. These few advisors would also pass on information to you, summarizing data and options from other executive officials. What are the merits or demerits of each approach from the perspective of running an efficient but knowledgeable presidency?

5. President Bill Clinton's popularity with the American people ebbed by late 1994 (one poll showed only a 39% approval rating). The vast midterm GOP gains in Congress certainly did not help him. As another symbol of Clinton's declining popularity, many Democratic candidates for Congress in 1994 had tried to disassociate themselves from their own incumbent president during their own campaigns. Why and how had Clinton reached this low point in his political fortunes?

According to Washington columnist Elizabeth Drew (see USA Today, November 2, 1994, p. 11A), Clinton's problems stemmed from inexperience, poor selection of staffers, and his own personality. Clinton had assembled a White House staff who were largely inexperienced in Washington politics. In addition, scandals among staffers and from Clinton's own past (marital infidelity, Whitewater) sapped the president's time and eroded his reputation. Drew also mentions the issue of gays in the military that hurt Clinton's reputation in the first week or two of his presidency. Finally, Clinton had "squandered the moral authority" of the presidency by being overexposed in the media to the point that the public began ignoring him. Yet, Drew also asserted that Clinton was a "learner" and "resilient"—the "drama of his presidency" was not yet over.

Trace the path of Clinton's presidency from 1994 to 1996 (or to whatever date past 1994 is appropriate). Did Clinton "bounce-back" from his 1994 doldrums—why or why not? Be sure to include both his policy failures and successes during this time frame.

6. In his book, *The Imperial Presidency*, Arthur Schlesinger, Jr., argued that presidential powers had grown so quickly and so extensively that the traditional conception of checks and balances had been jeopardized. Schlesinger states that this destabilizing process had its origins with Franklin D. Roosevelt. The process was reinforced by economic depression, the second World War, Korea, Vietnam, the Cold War, and the threat of nuclear devastation. However, after the Vietnam War and the Watergate scandal, Congress began to reassert itself. Schlesinger asserted that it was very important to strengthen Congress even further. He listed the following proposals directed at transforming the traditional constitutional role and structure of the presidency:

(a) Change the current four-year term of the president to one six-year term. Under this plan, a president could not run again for reelection. In other words, a maximum presidential term would be six years rather than eight (two full terms).

(b) Replace the one-man president form with a six-man directorate, a directorate that would have a rotating chairman. Each directorate member would serve for a year.

(c) Give to the president a Council of State, a body that he would be bound by law to consult. Half of the Council's members would come from Congress and some from the opposition party.

(d) Adopt a version of the British parliamentary system. In other words, a president would be compelled at regular intervals to explain and defend his policies to key members of the political opposition. If the Congress, by a two-thirds or three-fourths vote, issued a vote of "no confidence," a new national election would have to be called within six weeks.

Consider these proposals carefully. Try to jot down what the implications for congressional-presidential relations would be if any or all were adopted. The proposals would fit in nicely with a research paper and/or class discussion.

PART VIII — DATA ANALYSIS

1. Presidents deliver annual State of the Union Addresses where, before a joint session of Congress. they attempt to tell legislators and the public what are the problems facing the nation, how those problems might be resolved, and what the international position of the nation is at the time of the Address.

State of the Union Addresses do differ from president to president, from era to era as new controversies and issues enter and leave the national agenda. In order to understand some of these changes, compare the following four State of the Union Addresses: President Jimmy Carter's Address in January of 1978, President Ronald Reagan's Address in January of 1982, President George Bush's Address in January of 1992, and President Bill Clinton's Address in January of 1995. What differences existed in terms of policy emphasis, solutions, drama and idealism? Were the two Republican Addresses (Bush and Reagan) more alike than dissimilar? Similarly, could you detect any similarities between the Carter and Clinton Addresses (both Democratic Presidents)? Finally, note any major differences among the four speeches. Such sources as *Facts on File* or *The New York Times* (on microfilm) will have complete transcripts of each Address.

2. As measured by public opinion polls, a president's popularity can change substantially from month to month or drastically from year to year. Note George Bush's 80 percent plus approval ratings after the successful Persian Gulf War in 1991. A little more than one year later, the rating had dropped to the 40 percent approval level. However, most presidents have high approval scores upon entering office with popularity declining over time. Look below at the poll data trends of Presidents Truman through Reagan. First, which presidents seemed to retain a great deal of their popularity during their stays in office? Conversely, which two presidents suffered the greatest overall drops in popularity? Finally, construct a graph for George Bush's 1988-1992 and Bill Clinton's 1993-1996 terms in office. Are the patterns for Bush and Clinton similar to or markedly different from the other presidents?

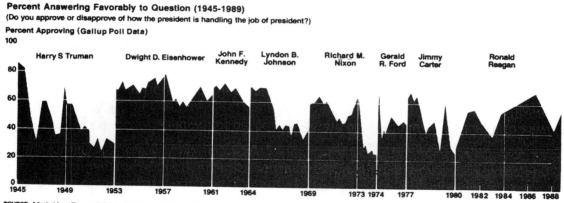

Percent Answering Favorably to Question (1945-1989)
(Do you approve or disapprove of how the president is handling the job of president?)
Percent Approving (Gallup Poll Data)

SOURCE: Adapted from Thomas E. Cronin, The State of The Presidency
(Boston: Little, Brown and Company, 1980), pp. 328-329. Updated with Gallup Poll Data.

PART IX — TEST ANSWERS

Pretest

1. b
2. c
3. a
4. a
5. a

6. c
7. b
8. c
9. b
10. c

Programmed Review

1. abuses
2. leadership
3. character; integrity
4. Vietnam
5. intermingling
6. checks & balances
7. character; energy
8. executives
9. does
10. foreign
11. do
12. different
13. are not
14. foreign
15. foreign
16. television
17. public's
18. party
19. chief

20. did
21. recruitment
22. troops
23. OMB
24. followers
25. item
26. press conferences
27. opinion polls
28. party
29. staff
30. Management; Budget
31. Cabinet
32. Senate
33. third
34. adversary
35. more
36. do
37. cannot
38. auxiliary institutions

Post-test

1. a
2. a
3. b
4. d
5. b

6. c
7. a
8. a
9. b
10. a

Data Analysis

1. Each student may emphasize different aspects of the two Addresses, so there is not one perfect answer.

2. Eisenhower and Reagan; Truman and Nixon suffered the greatest popularity drops. But George Bush's precipitous drop in the year after the Persian Gulf War is comparable. Clinton's drop in popularity (a 39% approval rating) by late Fall 1994 was also significant.

CHAPTER 16
THE JUDICIARY: THE BALANCING BRANCH

The Supreme Court leads an independent existence, in many ways removed from the partisan politics of Congress and the presidency. Yet this isolation from politics is far from total and the Court is sooner or later drawn into those political debates that sweep across the nation. Eventually the Court responds to shifts in the public mood, although the changes are seldom instantaneous or dramatic.

The Warren Court of the 1950s and 60s was replaced by the Burger Court of the 1970s. These leaders were replaced in the late 1980s and 90s by a conservative (libertarian) Court headed by William Rehnquist. Perhaps the most distinctive fact about the Court is the longevity of its members. Those beyond normal retirement age (65) are commonplace. Many are in their 70s. Those over eighty are not uncommon. For the most part their decisions do not make headlines, but the impact is tremendous. Their decision of 1989 legalizing flag burning produced a national storm of protest. Their 1973 decision legalizing abortion divided the nation into two warring camps. School prayer was banned by the Court. The right of Congress to use a legislative veto was declared unconstitutional, thereby invalidating over 200 pieces of legislation. The trend toward a conservative Court was given a great thrust by President Reagan, who named four members. The election of George Bush made it possible for him to name David H. Souter, a relatively obscure man who had written or spoken little. He was overwhelmingly confirmed. Bush's nomination of Clarence Thomas, a black jurist, prompted a storm of protest after a former employee, Anita Hill, charged him with sexual harassment. Thomas was narrowly confirmed, 52-48, after Hill's charges became a rallying point for many women's groups. Shortly after taking office President Clinton named to the Supreme Court Ruth Bader Ginsberg, a woman with a reputation for fairness and moderation and Stephen G. Breyer, a noncontroversial judicial moderate.

PART I — GUIDEPOSTS

1. Judges: The Balancing Branch
    a. How did the first judges of the Supreme Court shape its authority and scope?
    b. Why is our system called adversarial?
    c. What kinds of disputes do they hear?
    d. Why have class action suits become so important?
    e. Do judges make law?
    f. What is *stare decisis*? How does it affect what the judges decide?

2. Federal Justice
    a. By what body was the federal court system established?
    b. What courts form the base of the federal judicial system? What do they do?
    c. What cases reach the Courts of Appeal? How do they relate to the state court systems?

3. Prosecution and Defense: Federal Lawyers
    a. What key role in the system do federal prosecutors play?
    b. What is the function of the Solicitor General?
    c. How are the rights of poor defendants protected?

4. How Federal Judges Are Selected
   a. What groups have an input in the selection process?
   b. Why is the Senate Judiciary Committee so important?
   c. How much attention is paid to party, race, and sex in nominating judges?
   d. How important is ideology?
   e. Why is age such a vital factor?
   f. What role does ideology play? When applied to the Court, what is the meaning of activism and restraint?
   g. How did the nomination hearings of Bork, Souter, and Thomas differ? What was the public's reaction?
   h. Is change likely for the selection process of judges?
   i. How much authority does Congress have over the Court's jurisdiction and membership?

5. How the Supreme Court Operates
   a. What devices give the Court an air of authority and respect?
   b. How does the Supreme Court decide what cases it will hear?
   c. What is the "rule of four"?
   d. What procedure is used by the Court in hearing cases?
   e. Why are Court conferences so important?
   f. Who writes the Court opinion? What if the vote is split?
   g. Why is such an effort put into consensus voting?
   h. How has the style of recent chief justices varied?
   i. Why is the implementation of many Court decisions long delayed?

6. Judicial Power in a Democracy
   a. Does our system of justice put power in the hands of unelected officials?
   b. Does public opinion have any impact?
   c. Who favors judicial activism? Judicial restraint? Are conservatives and liberals apt to change roles in this argument? Why?
   d. What can Congress do if it disagrees with a Court decision?

PART II — GLOSSARY

JUDICIAL REVIEW - The Supreme Court authority, established in <u>Marbury v. Madison</u>, to declare acts of Congress unconstitutional.

JUDICIAL ACTIVIST - A judge who believes that judges should play a part in shaping public policy.

JUDICIAL SELF-RESTRAINT - A theory that judges should not be involved in policy-making.

EQUITY - Judge-made law that goes beyond normal procedure to ensure justice.

STATUTORY LAW - Law based on acts of legislatures or Congress.

COMMON LAW - Judge-made law developed from medieval English precedents.

CIVIL LAW - In contrast with common law, the legal code based on legislative acts.

CONSTITUTIONAL LAW - The law developed from Supreme Court, decisions interpreting the Constitution.

ADMINISTRATIVE LAW - Law developed from rules and decisions of administrators.

CRIMINAL LAW - Law enacted by state legislatures and Congress that defines crime and punishment.

ADVERSARY SYSTEM - Theory that suggests truth will be found by the two contending parties fighting out their differences before a court as an impartial arbiter.

JUSTICIABLE DISPUTES - Disputes that grow out of actual cases and are capable of settlement by legal methods.

STARE DECISIS - The rule of precedent whereby a judicial decision is based on an earlier court

DISTRICT COURTS - The basic federal courts of original jurisdiction.
ORIGINAL JURISDICTION - The authority of a court to consider a case in the first instance.
COURT OF APPEALS - One of twelve federal courts having only appellate jurisdiction.
APPELLATE JURISDICTION - The authority of a court to review the decisions of courts of
    original jurisdiction.
U.S. MARSHAL - A federal police officer attached to each district court.
WRIT OF CERTIORARI - An order issued by the Supreme Court agreeing to review a case from a
    lower court.
MAJORITY OPINION - The judicial statement supporting a verdict filed by the majority justices.
DISSENTING OPINION - The judicial statement questioning the majority verdict filed by minority
    justices.

PART III — PRETEST

1. Procedure in the Supreme Court is surrounded by considerable ceremony. *All but one* of the
   following procedures is customary.
       a. The justices are always attired in their robes of office.
       b. Government attorneys wear morning clothes.
       c. All judges are seated in alphabetical order.
       d. Judges are introduced by the Clerk of the Court.

2. The chief basis for judicial decisions is probably
       a. precedent.   c. the party in power.
       b. public opinion.   d. checks and balances.

3. The judicial doctrine of *stare decisis* provides that the courts decide cases largely on the basis of
       a. present economic and social conditions.
       b. earlier court decisions.
       c. interpreting the will of Congress.
       d. equity.

4. Federal courts of appeal normally have
       a. original jurisdiction.
       b. grand juries.
       c. three-judge jury.
       d. judges with ten-year terms.

5. No decision can be rendered by the Supreme Court unless
       a. all nine judges participate.
       b. a quorum of five is present.
       c. six judges participate.
       d. at least two judges represent majority opinion.

6. At the Friday conference of Supreme Court justices, *all but one* of the following is true
       a. The chief justice presides.
       b. The chief justice votes first.
       c. Each justice carries a leather book.
       d. A majority decides the case.

7. The powers of the chief justice include *all but one* of the following.
    a. presiding over the Court
    b. choosing the opinion writer if Justice has voted with the majority
    c. barring dissenting justices from the Friday conference
    d. leading conference discussion

8. The "rule of four" in Supreme Court procedure provides that four judges
    a. may adjourn the Court.
    b. grant a writ of *certiorari.*
    c. give priority to the order of hearing a case.
    d. are a quorum.

9. Critics of judicial activism believe that the courts should not try to make policy because
    a. judges are not elected.
    b. they do not represent all regions of the country.
    c. their terms do not coincide with that of the president.
    d. they do not have the necessary expertise.

10. After a grueling hearing that outraged women and liberal groups, the Senate Judiciary Committee narrowly confirmed
    a. Antonin Scalia.   c. Clarence Thomas.
    b. David Souter.   d. Sandra O'Connor.

PART IV — PROGRAMMED PREVIEW

Knowledge Objective: To describe the differing forms of law on which the American legal system is based

1. Law based on judicial decisions of medieval English judges is _____ law.
2. Law based on judicial interpretation of the Constitution is _____ law.
3. A specific act of legislative body is _____ law.
4. Law based on exceptions from the common law in the interests of justice is _____ law.
5. The code of law emerging from bureaucratic decisions is _____ law.
6. The rule of precedent under which federal courts operate is called _____ _____ .
7. The concept that the courts should serve as a neutral referee between two contending parties is called the _____ system.

Knowledge Objective: To gain an overview of the organization of the federal court system

8. The lowest federal courts, in which nearly 700 judges preside, are _____ courts.
9. The federal courts that review district court decisions are courts of _____ .
10. The highest federal court, with both original and appellate jurisdiction, is the _____ .
11. The right to review cases already considered is _____ _____ .
12. The top U.S. prosecutor is the _____ _____ .
13. State and federal courts (do, do not) _____ exist in a superior-inferior relationship.
14. Much of the lower judicial work of the U.S. district is now carried out by _____ .
15. Decisions of regulatory agencies can be reviewed by courts of _____ .
16. Persons charged with a crime may get a reduced sentence by agreeing to a(n) _____ _____ .
17. The court officer who determines most appeals heard by the Supreme Court is the _____ _____ .

Knowledge Objective: To study the major participants involved in selection of federal judges

18. The custom that requires the president to consult with a state's senators before nominating a federal judge is called _____ _____ .

19. All potential nominees for federal judgeships are_____ by the American Bar Association.

20. In naming federal judges, the political affiliation of the nominee may be less important than the person's _____ .

21. Presidential nominations to the Supreme Court are reviewed by the Senate _____ _____ .

22. In an attempt to avoid another Bork nomination battle, Bush nominated Souter, who had no _____ past record.

23. Bush's most controversial nomination to the Supreme Court was _____ .

24. Congress controls the _____ and _____ of federal courts.

Knowledge Objective: To discover how the Supreme Court operates

25. The only cases heard by the Supreme Court are those selected by the _____ _____ .

26. Cases previously decided by lower courts are called up to the Supreme Court by writs of _____ .

27. The normal upper time limit granted to counsel for each side in arguing a Supreme Court case is _____ _____ .

28. Supreme Court decisions are made in secret each week at the _____ _____ .

29. One use of published Supreme Court _____ is to communicate with the general public.

Knowledge Objective: To evaluate the role of judicial review in a democratic society

30. Over the past forty years more than 400 acts of _____ and _____ _____ have been invalidated by the Supreme Court.

31. When the Supreme Court becomes greatly involved in political life, it is known as an _____ court.

32. Critics who believe that the Supreme Court has become too activist charge it with engaging in _____ _____ .

33. The opponents of judicial activism believe that the Court should not become involved in _____ making.

PART V — POST-TEST

1. An activist court, the critics say, is overly zealous in protecting the
   - a. poor.
   - b. property owners.
   - c. state officials.
   - d. military officers.

2. The federal court that has only original jurisdiction is
   - a. the Supreme Court.
   - b. district courts.
   - c. courts of appeal.
   - d. lower courts.

3. An adversary system of justice is one in which
   - a. the police bring charges.
   - b. the court is a neutral referee.
   - c. judges are political appointees.
   - d. justice is based on majority vote.

4. The top national official who has openly favored minority considerations in the judicial selection process has been
   a. Carter.
   b. Burger.
   c. Ford.
   d. Reagan.

5. The law that evolved from decisions interpreting our basic national governing document is
   a. constitutional law.
   b. administrative law.
   c. equity law.
   d. statutory law.

6. Several justices have timed their retirement to
   a. ensure a replacement by a president sharing their views.
   b. increase their retirement benefits.
   c. bring fresh ideas to the Court.
   d. avoid ruling on an issue where they have no competence.

7. Elections eventually influence Supreme Court decisions because
   a. the judges try to do what the people want.
   b. judges who are out of step are impeached.
   c. new judges are appointed.
   d. interest groups influence decisions.

8. In federal courts, justifiable disputes are
   a. all constitutional questions.
   b. those involving actual cases.
   c. all administrative decisions.
   d. those involving political questions.

9. The relationship between the state and federal court systems is
   a. federal courts are always superior.
   b. state courts have original jurisdiction.
   c. they have interrelated responsibility.
   d. they are completely separate.

10. If a Supreme Court justice agrees with the majority decision but differs on the reasoning, he files
    a. a concurring opinion.
    b. a dissenting opinion.
    c. articles of agreement.
    d. a minority opinion.

PART VI — POLITICAL DIALOGUE: THE CLASH OF ISSUES AND IDEAS

1. "Supreme Court judges should be chosen in national conventions, run for office, be elected for stated terms (say 10 years), and have the right to reelection if they can win a majority vote." What impact would such a program have on the voting record of judges? What kind of campaign would a judge be apt to wage?

2. In recent years our great ocean-going ships have carried gyroscopes to provide stability and lessen passenger discomfort in stormy weather. So, too, does the Supreme Court provide stability within our political system for the Ship of State, like the gyroscope, the Court does not determine the direction of the voyage or the speed of passage. But it does prevent erratic, ill-considered moves. Do you agree? Disagree? Cite illustrations or evidence to support your position.

3. You are the President of the United States. A vacancy has just occurred on the Supreme Court, and you must fill it. What criteria will you use in searching for an appointee? Whom will you consult?

4. Evaluate Critically: "A Supreme Court Justice is supposed to have said to a group of students, 'I want to say to you, young gentlemen, that if we don't like an act of Congress, we don't have much trouble to find grounds for declaring it unconstitutional.' Do you consider the Justice's statement true? (Answer "yes" or "no.") What evidence can you cite to support your stand? If your answer is "yes," does this mean the judges are governed only by personal bias?"

5. "Forget about tradition and habit. Take a fresh look at the Supreme Court. In no sense is it a democratic institution. Its members are appointed, rather than elected. They hold office for life. They meet privately, with no chance for public scrutiny. At best they are an aristocratic body, dressed in black robes and spouting legal jargon such as *stare decisis.* Actually such groups, cut off from the public should have no place in democratic theory or practice." Do you agree? Disagree? Why?

6. "Most private and public employers have ground rules on retirement that are wise and humane. They recognize that aged people are not as mentally astute as the young. So they have upper limits on age, give retirees a dinner and a gold watch, and wish them well in their retirement years. The Supreme Court should be no exception to this practice. We don't need "Nine Old Men" (or women) to govern the United States." Defend or criticize this view.

7. Justice Clarence Thomas destroyed his impartiality on women's issues for all time after the Hill testimony. A sensitive man would have withdrawn his name for consideration at that point. Instead, he became an issue in the 1992 Pennsylvania senate election when Lynn Yeakel made the foundation of her campaign against Arlen Spector his ruthless questioning of Anita Hill. Do you agree? Would withdrawal of his name have been a tacit confession of guilt?

PART VII — POLITICAL SCIENCE TODAY

1. After the 1988-1989, 1989-1990, and 1990-1991 terms of the Rehnquist Supreme Court, judicial experts agreed that the Court was slowly being dominated by an emerging "conservative" majority. President Bush's selection of conservative Clarence Thomas in 1992 seemed to strengthen the validity of this observation. This conservative orientation suggested that Roe v. Wade might be overturned by the Rehnquist Court.

But in June of 1992, the Court's "conservative majority" fragmented in Planned Parenthood v. Casey. Three Reagan-appointed Justices—Sandra Day O'Connor, Anthony Kennedy, and David Souter—joined with the Court's most liberal survivors—Harry Blackmun and John Stevens—to uphold Roe v. Wade. Rehnquist, White, Scalia, and Thomas voted basically to overturn Roe. New curbs on abortion were upheld such as girls under 18 needing parental consent before an abortion could be upheld. In the final analysis, it appeared that 83-year-old Blackmun would likely be the next Justice to retire. The "fifth vote" to overturn Roe thus became a political possibility.

Not one, but two new Supreme Court vacancies occurred under the Clinton Administration in 1993 and 1994 (see chapter text). President Clinton first appointed Ruth Bader Ginsburg to replace Justice White and then Stephen G. Breyer to replace Harry Blackmun. The "expectation" was that the Clinton appointments would preserve the Court's support for Roe v. Wade. Try to find the most recent material possible on Ginsburg's and Breyer's attitudes toward abortion before their confirmation as Justices and after they were placed on the Court. From your research, does it appear that the "expectation" was accurate or not?

2. Review some of the specific reasons why Judge Bork and Judge Ginsburg were rejected by the U.S. Senate. Cite a few articles from key newspapers and journals of opinion during the time period. What conclusions do you arrive at regarding the nature of "confirmation politics"?

3. Notice the importance of appeals in the American judicial system. The opportunity to appeal one's case to a higher court is a key component of due process. However, appeals take time and can be financially exhausting. Similarly, critics of the appeal process contend that the process basically prevents swift justice. It is not at all uncommon that convicted criminals, such as those on death row, are able to avoid execution for years through the clever use of the appeal.

   Where would you stand on this debate? Would you favor a time limit for all appeals to be exhausted? Why or why not?

4. Would you favor a professional jury system? In other words, instead of picking jurors from a community, individuals would be educated in the law and court procedures to decide dispassionately on the guilt or innocence of the defendant. These highly-trained people would have the ability to sift evidence and listen critically. They would serve on a number of trials each year. What would be the pros and cons of such a system? Would professional jurors really represent one's "peer"? Conversely, would professional jurors be more capable, intellectually, of deciding a case on its objective merits rather than emotion?

5. Plea bargaining is another controversial practice in the American judicial system. Because our courts are so overcrowded with unheard cases, advocates of the practice argue that plea bargaining is an efficient, common-sense approach. By having the defendant plead guilty to a lesser offense, a prolonged trial is avoided and taxpayer dollars are spared. However, is it desirable for an individual to be punished to a lesser extent simply because of expediency?

   Try to talk with a lawyer about the practice of plea bargaining. What appears to be the legal community's views on the subject?

PART VIII — DATA ANALYSIS

1. Review the organization of the federal courts. Chief Justice Burger once argued that too many cases were flowing upward to the Supreme Court. There should be some structural mechanism by which relief could be granted to the Court. He proposed a new court of appeals composed of nine federal appellate judges who should review conflicting rulings of the various courts of appeals. Where would you place this new court on the chart and why?

2. Look at the data from Table 16-1 on "the party affiliation of judges appointed by presidents from FDR to Clinton." What generalizations can you derive from the data shown and why do you think the data follows such a consistent pattern?

PART IX — TEST ANSWERS

Pretest

1. c
2. a
3. b
4. c
5. c

6. b
7. c
8. b
9. a
10. c

Programmed Review

1. common
2. constitutional
3. statutory
4. equity
5. administrative
6. stare decisis
7. adversary
8. district
9. appeal
10. Supreme Court
11. Appellate jurisdiction
12. Attorney General
13. do not
14. magistrates
15. appeal
16. plea bargain
17. solicitor general

18. senatorial courtesy
19. evaluated
20. ideology
21. Judiciary Committee
22. visible
23. Thomas
24. structure; jurisdiction
25. Supreme Court
26. certiorari
27. thirty minutes
28. Friday conference
29. opinions
30. legislatures; city councils
31. activist
32. judicial legislation
33. policy

Post-test

1. a
2. b
3. b
4. a
5. a

6. a
7. c
8. b
9. c
10. a

Data Analysis

1. The new appeals court would have to be inserted between the Supreme Court top level and the level of the U.S. Courts of Appeals. Burger's concept would ultimately restrict the number of cases flowing to the Supreme Court. However, critics assert that the Court can already pick and choose the cases they will hear, so why is this new court needed?

2. Clearly, presidents overwhelmingly selected judges from their own party affiliation. Presidents usually assume that judges from their party will have similar (if not identical) ideologies. Also, their parties will be strengthened by penetrating the judicial branch as much as possible. To run counter to this pattern would mean possible political retaliation against a president from supporters within his own party.

CHAPTER 17
BUREAUCRATS: THE REAL POWER?

Most activities of the federal government are carried out by bureaucrats. Hence the selection, organization, and control of these people is a central issue of government. Today most elected officials join the public in being critical of the bureaucrats and bureaucracy. Ronald Reagan promised to curb the bureaucracy by eliminating the Departments of Education and Energy, cutting pay-raises and fringe benefits of workers, and placing a ceiling on the number of federal employees. A commission appointed by him (Grace Commission) claimed that $424 billion could be saved in three years if its recommendations were followed. Critics scoffed! Supporters cheered!

And not much happened. In fact, another Cabinet post, Veterans Affairs, was added and none were cut. President Bush, in contrast, did not denounce the bureaucracy, recognizing that if he were to be successful, he needed a loyal, efficient corps of government workers.

The Clinton administration attempted to downsize the bureaucracy. Vice-President Gore was assigned the task of reinventing government which proved to be difficult. Still the negative image of government workers persists. In basic terms it boils down to this:

Are bureaucrats productive people, or are they a kind of parasitical growth attached to the nation's long-suffering taxpayers?

One Answer: Yes! Bureaucrats are productive people - very important people: they make the American political system work.
Another Answer: No! Government work attracts people interested chiefly in security, routine, and carefully defined rules. It repels those with drive and initiative.

Another question concerns the organization of governmental machinery. Are bureaucrats over-organized, so that any constructive suggestions are finally lost somewhere along the chain of command? Or is the system under organized and badly controlled, so that bureaucrats become free agents, responsible to no one?

A final question concerns the recruitment and retention of government personnel: How can government assignments be made attractive to young people of ability?

Option 1: Government should compete with private industry for personnel in terms of salary and advancement.
Option 2: Government recruitment officers should emphasize steady employment, long vacations, and a multitude of fringe benefits as counterweights to relatively low salaries.

PART I — GUIDEPOSTS

1. Overview of the Federal Bureaucracy
   a. What is a bureaucratic organization?
   b. What do bureaucrats do?
   c. Why is the bureaucracy an inviting target for critics?
   d. What are the basic facts about the present size, location, background, and types of jobs in the federal bureaucracy?

e. Describe the formal way in which the federal bureaucracy is organized.

f. How does the organization differ?

2. The United States Civil Service

a. Why was the original spoils system replaced by a merit system?

b. How was the Civil Service changed by legislation of 1978?

c. What was the objective of the Hatch Act? What criticisms and defenses has it provoked?

3. Bureaucracy In Action

a. On what assumptions is the classical model of organization based?

b. In reality how is this classical model affected by politics?

c. What essential points about the bureaucracy are illustrated by the careers of:

J. Edgar Hoover

Admiral Rickover

George Brown

4. Public View of the Bureaucracy

a. Why is there widespread public hostility toward bureaucrats?

b. Do the common complaints about bureaucracy have a factual base?

c. Why do we have red tape in our system?

d. Do government agencies ever fade away?

e. How does the existing U.S. bureaucracy compare with that of other major nations?

5. Bureaucratic Responsiveness and Accountability

a. On the broad scene, is our bureaucracy responsive to citizen needs?

b. What is privatization, who are the supporters, who are the critics?

c. What leverage do Presidents have in controlling bureaucrats?

d. Why is the OMB such a major force?

e. What form does bureaucratic resistance to change take?

f. How does Congress exert control over bureaucrats?

g. What is the major reason that Congressional oversight is often weak?

h. Why do we lack a simple answer to the questions of bureaucratic reform and control?

PART II — GLOSSARY

BUREAUCRATS - Government officials, normally those who receive office through appointment rather than election.

RED TAPE - The procedure and forms used in carrying out policies, often, by implication, unnecessary steps.

BUREAU - Generally the largest subunit of a department or agency.

GOVERNMENT CORPORATIONS - A cross between business corporations and government agencies, created to secure greater freedom of action.

INDEPENDENT AGENCY - A government agency not subordinate to a regular executive department.

REGULATORY AGENCY - A board or commission responsible for controlling some aspect of national life which generally has judicial, legislative, and executive powers.

QUASI-JUDICIAL - The power held by some agencies to both execute and interpret regulations.

QUASI-LEGISLATIVE - The power held by some agencies to both make and execute regulations.

CHAIN OF COMMAND - A clear line of authority and responsibility.

LINE AND STAFF - A dual type of organization in which line officers execute orders, while staff officers are executive advisers.

HATCH ACTS - Laws of 1939-1940 that barred federal employees from active participation in politics.

SPAN OF CONTROL - Formula for determining the maximum number of people that any administrator can effectively deal with.

CLASSIC MODEL - A theory of organization developed early in this century, often referred to as the rational approach.

PRIVATIZATION - Shifting government functions to the private sector.

PART III — PRETEST

1. Depending on the observer, red tape can be described in *all but one* of the following ways.
   a. senseless regulations that prevent prompt action
   b. civil service employees who serve under the merit system
   c. an established procedure for a particular operation
   d. a bureaucracy that is more interested in means than ends

2. Almost one third of all civilian employees of the federal government work for
   a. defense agencies.
   b. the Social Security Administration.
   c. welfare agencies.
   d. the Interstate Commerce Commission.

3. Which group is not a member of the iron triangle?
   a. bureaucrats   c. interest groups
   b. federal judges   d. congressional subcommittees

4. An example of a government corporation is the
   a. Securities and Exchange Commission.
   b. U.S. Mint.
   c. Government Printing Office.
   d. Federal Deposit Insurance Corporation.

5. Independent regulatory boards have *all but one* of these special characteristics.
   a. They do not report directly to the president.
   b. They perform legislative functions.
   c. Their members are political appointees whose terms coincide with the president's.
   d. They have judicial functions.

6. A landmark law creating a merit system of civil service was the _____ Act, named for its sponsor.
   a. Garfield   c. Pendleton
   b. Sedman   d. Hatch

7. The OMB plays *all but one* of the following roles in recruiting new civil service employees.
   a. administers and scores tests
   b. designates the individual an agency must hire
   c. creates a ranked register of successful applicants
   d. certifies three names for each agency vacancy

8. The Hatch Act provides that government employees can
   a. make campaign contributions.
   b. remain neutral in campaigns.
   c. solicit votes of their friends.
   d. not vote.

9. The classical model of public administration theory emphasized *all but one* of the following
    a. friendship patterns   c. chain of command
    b. line and staff   d. span of control

10. The weakest relationship of most federal administrators is with
    a. fellow colleagues.   c. congressional committees.
    b. lobbyists.   d. the president.

PART IV — PROGRAMMED REVIEW

Knowledge Objective: To examine the shape of federal bureaucracy

1. Bureaucrats are accused of being inefficient and too _____ at the same time.
2. Nearly _____ of all federal civilian employees work for the defense agencies.
3. Over 85 percent of the bureaucrats work _____ the Washington area.
4. Most federal employees are _____ collar workers.
5. The federal level of bureaucracy has (grown, decreased) _____ in the past few years.
6. Federal employees are _____ representative of the nation as a whole than legislators.
7. The common basis for organization of a department is _____ .
8. An example of a government _____ is the F.D.I.C.
9. _____ organization emphasizes structure; _____ organization emphasizes personal relationships.

Knowledge Objective: To trace the evolution of the U.S. Civil Service

10. The _____ system permitted newly elected presidents to appoint their supporters.
11. Restrictions on the political activities of federal employees were imposed by the _____ Act.
12. Federal employees (may, may not) _____ take an active part in partisan politics.
13. _____ _____ was a noted German sociologist who advocated an efficient, nonpolitical bureaucracy.
14. Under the "real bureaucracy" model, civil servants are involved in the _____ of policy.

Knowledge Objective: To analyze the criticisms of bureaucracy

15. Most Americans support bureaucracy that operates in their interest while being critical of big bureaucracy in the _____ .
16. A highly criticized aspect of the federal bureaucracy is the public employee's job _____ .
17. The object of Gore's 800 recommendations to reinvent government was to eliminate bureaucratic _____ and _____ .
18. The _____ of a federal agency is the _____ rather than the rule.
19. One major problem of big government has been that _____ exceed performance.
20. The complex rules and regulations under which bureaucracy functions is called _____ _____ .
21. The performance of the U.S. bureaucracy compares (favorably, unfavorably) with the rest of the world.
22. The process of contracting out public services to private organizations is called _____ .

Knowledge Objective: To discover the controls under which bureaucrats operate

23. Major control of bureaucracy is shared by _____ and the _____ .
24. The Civil Service Reform Act (1978) created a top grade of career bureaucrats, the _____ _____ _____ .

25. Supporters of the patronage system believe that the existing _____ system of federal employment encourages deadwood.
26. _____ is the executive office responsible for managing the federal bureaucracy.
27. The responsiveness of bureaucrats is limited by the procedures that make them _____ .

V — POST-TEST

1. The largest subunit of a government department is usually called a
   - a. bureau.
   - b. division.
   - c. commission.
   - d. cabinet.

2. In the give and take of Washington politics, the welfare of _____ is the least protected.
   - a. doctors
   - b. the poor
   - c. the middle class
   - d. the wealthy

3. Congress normally controls the bureaucracy in all of the following ways *except*
   - a. budgetary appropriations.
   - b. holding hearings.
   - c. confirmation of personnel.
   - d. firing civil servants.

4. Which term *does not* describe the same model of public administration?
   - a. textbook
   - b. incremental
   - c. classical
   - d. rational man

5. An example of informal organization would be when a superior and his subordinates
   - a. hunt and fish together.
   - b. confer over bureau policy.
   - c. jointly evaluate employees for promotion.
   - d. establish long-range budget plans.

6. Who controls the bureaucracy?
   - a. the president
   - b. Congress
   - c. no single power source
   - d. the voters

7. In practice the Senior Executive Service has
   - a. been successful.
   - b. been a failure.
   - c. had little impact.
   - d. transformed the Civil Service.

8. An effective device for implementing the president's wishes is the
   - a. Senior Executive Service.
   - b. Office of Management and Budget.
   - c. Civil Service Reform Act.
   - d. Assistant Secretaries.

9. The responsiveness of a bureaucracy is closely linked to its
   - a. accountability.
   - b. security.
   - c. clientele.
   - d. computer capability.

10. Privatization is
    a. the commissioning of merchant ships as a part of the navy.
    b. secrecy of interoffice memos.
    c. the president's right to withhold his IRS return.
    d. placing certain government functions in the private sector.

PART VI — POLITICAL DIALOGUE:
THE CLASH OF ISSUES AND IDEAS

1. Gore's Report of 800 Recommendations to Reinvent Government was a step in the right direction. Agree or disagree?

2. The Case of J. Edgar Hoover. Why did Hoover have a unique position that made him "untouchable" by his superiors? What illegal action did he take against Martin Luther King, Jr. and other prominent Americans whom he disliked? How did he thwart President Nixon and his aides? Why could he be described as a "loose cannon"?

3. The Case of Admiral Rickover. What were his achievements? What unorthodox methods did he employ? Why was he able to "get away with" his defiance of those who were his nominal superiors?

4. The Case of George Brown. How did he get his job? What was his first reaction when he was told to cut his budget? Why did he reconsider his initial reaction? What action did he finally take? Justify or criticize his decision.

5. "Americans invoke Jeffersonian values - decentralization, local control, small and amateur government - in shrill terms - as these goals become increasingly unworkable." Discuss.

6. "Government is not the solution to our problems. Government *is* the problem." Is this statement true?

7. "We need to get the bureaucracy off our backs and the IRS out of our pocketbooks." Discuss.

8. The Grace Commission was composed of unbiased patriots - experienced business leaders who had met payrolls and paid taxes. Unfortunately their major recommendations have been largely ignored or implemented only half-heartedly. This proves only one thing - that the bureaucracy is running amuck, with no elected leader to curb it.

9. "Compared to any other highly industrialized country with a world-wide military presence, the United States runs a tight ship, if we measure the size and cost of our bureaucracy against our population and GNP." Defend or criticize this statement.

PART VII — POLITICAL SCIENCE TODAY

1. Before reading this chapter, what stereotypes or images did you have of federal bureaucrats and bureaucratic agencies? Have any of those original impressions been modified after finishing the chapter? If so, which ones and why the change in viewpoint? Conversely, if you feel that your original images of bureaucracy have remained essentially the same, then explain why you feel the way you do. You may wish to incorporate the contrasting views held by liberals (federal bureaucracy is too status-quo oriented, lazy, and unimaginative) and conservatives (federal bureaucracy

is too liberal, too large, powerful, and unaccountable) regarding the merits or demerits of the bureaucracy.

2. One crucial problem facing the federal work-force is whether pay scales are going to stay high enough in order to retain trained, skilled personnel. This basic problem was highlighted in the July 23, 1989 Sunday edition of the *The New York Times*. Two staff writers, Andrew Rosenthal and Robert D. Hershey Jr. on page 4E amplified on these fundamental problems. Rosenthal's article, entitled "It's Loneliest at the Top of the Bureaucracy," stressed the "shortage of officials" theme by asserting the following points:

(a) NASA, the National Aeronautics and Space Administration, had lost nearly 200 managers and scientists in the three months prior to President Bush's announcement of a manned mission to Mars space goal.

(b) The NASA exodus had parallels in nearly every Cabinet Department and Government agency. As Rosenthal put it, "After six months, President Bush has not been able to place his appointees in 45 percent of the Government's top jobs - because of political haggling, the salary gap, the new revolving-door rules, increased scrutiny of public officials' private lives and the time it takes the FBI to do background checks."

(c) Furthermore, "Administration officials believe the biggest obstacles have been the failure of an executive pay raise earlier this year and the tightened limits on future employment for officials involved in procurement." While President Bush had proposed raises of close to 25 percent for some 7900 executive branch officials, the current situation for the Government was that it was being cut out of the market for the most desirable specialists, especially those between the ages of 45 and 55.

Hershey's article, "The Civil Service: Doubts From Within and Without," amplified on some of the themes in the Rosenthal analysis.

(a) Some government researchers insisted that the Civil Service system was facing a "quiet crisis" which could lead to a total breakdown of governmental performance. However, other experts maintained that there was no cause for alarm, since the Government was continuing to get qualified people for the vast majority of jobs available.

(b) A skeptic, Terry W. Culler, who was a former associate director of the Office of Personnel Management from 1981 to 1986, argues that it is impossible to prove conclusively that there has been an erosion in the quality of the Federal work force. Mr. Culler noted that "there are many applicants for most jobs and that just over 5 percent of federal employees each year quit their jobs, as against 10.9 percent in the private sector. What's more, Federal workers suffering the biggest pay disparity with their private counterparts had low attrition while clerical workers, with the smallest pay gap, quit most often."

(c) As another point of view, Hershey quotes Alexander B. Trowbridge Jr., a former Commerce Secretary, who "believes that the Civil Service has deteriorated but that higher pay is not necessarily the best remedy. He notes that in addition to job security, the Government offers to many a valuable training ground and 'a lot of psychic income.'

You may wish to consult the *The New York Times* and read both articles in their entirety to gauge the possible problems and potential solutions for those problems vis-à-vis the federal workforce. In addition, peruse the New York Times Index or other reference sources for related articles that have been published from 1990 to the present. After finding this more recent material, would you change any of Hershey and Rosenthal's findings from their 1989 articles? If so, why? If not, why not?

3. Research the procedures you would have to follow to apply for a civil service job with the federal government. What pay scales and/or grade classification might you reasonably expect as a first year federal employee, assuming a college degree in your chosen field? How would pay and benefits compare with comparable salary and benefits in a private sector-equivalent position?

4. There have been government "success stories" regarding beneficial regulations. For example, the Environmental Protection Agency's rule to lower the lead content in regular gasoline has reduced birth defects. The FDA's testing of drugs before they go on to the market is an obvious benefit to society. The NHTSA (National Highway Traffic Safety Administration) has saved countless lives by forcing auto manufacturers to recall unsafe cars. Similarly, OSHA's regulations mandating removal of asbestos standards from the workplace has reduced the risk of cancer.

What other federal regulations can you list of comparable benefit? Try to think of some. A possible research paper could result from your research. To help you, read #5 below.

5. In 1992, OSHA issued new rules designed to protect healthcare workers from contracting or spreading AIDS. In particular, dentists and doctors nationally would have to spend millions of dollars in order to comply with the rules. Critics of the rules charged that these costs would be passed on to patients and the costs of medical care would skyrocket. As a possible outside project, interview your own doctor/dentist to gain their perspective of these rules. Try to obtain a copy of the regulations by contacting OSHA.

Part VIII — Data Analysis

1. Look at the charts involving pay for federal civil servants as taken from the *The New York Times* of July 23, 1989, p. 4E (see "Political Science Today" section, part #2). What conclusions can you reach regarding the attractiveness of salaries in the Civil Service? What factors should be considered in seeking a federal job other than formal pay scales?

Contact Civil Service and obtain the most current pay scales for federal civil servants and Assistant Secretaries in major Cabinet agencies. Then compare these pay scales to the charts from the 1989 *The New York Times*. Have federal salaries increased substantially? Have those salaries kept pace with the rate of inflation?

2. Regarding the "Thinking it Through" insert material on "Unannounced Drug Testing." how would you rule on the practice if you were a member of the Supreme Court in 1995? If the Court has ruled on the issued recently, then research what the decision's content was and the judicial reasoning behind the ruling.

Pay: public vs. private

Average annual salaries in 1988 for selected Federal civil servants and private-sector employees in jobs involving comparable training and responsibility. Federal figures describe a range, from starting to highest available salary, in job categories from GS-1 to GS-15. Private-sector figures are national averages based on a Federal survey. Pensions and other benefits are not included.

Occupation	Federal	Private sector
File clerk GS-1 (entry level)	$9,811-$12,275	$11,461
Chemist GS-5 (entry level)	15,118-19,654	25,314
Secretary GS-5 (mid-level)	15,118-19,654	19,504
Computer operator GS-8 (mid-level)	16,851-21,480	22,682
Systems analyst GS-9 (entry level)	22,907-29,783	31,130
Chief accountant GS-14 (senior level)	46,679-60,683	88,223
Engineer GS-5 (entry level)	15,118-19,654	29,222
Engineer GS-15 (top level)	54,907-71,377	85,725
Attorney GS-15 (top level)	54,907-71,377	110,489

Source: Bureau of Labor Statistics

PART IX — TEST ANSWERS

Pretest

1. b	6. c
2. a	7. b
3. b	8. b
4. d	9. a
5. c	10. d

Programmed Review

1. powerful	15. abstract
2. one-third	16. security
3. outside	17. waste; inefficiency
4. white	18. death; exception
5. decreased	19. promises
6. more	20. red tape
7. function	21. favorable
8. corporation	22. privatization
9. Formal; informal	23. Congress; President
10. spoils	24. Senior Executive Service
11. Hatch	25. tenure
12. may not	26. OMB
13. Max Weber	27. accountable
14. politics	

Post-test

1. a	6. c
2. b	7. c
3. d	8. b
4. b	9. a
5. a	10. d

Data Analysis

1. An obvious conclusion from the pay charts is that salaries in the private sector appear far higher in job categories ranging from GS-l to GS-15. Assistant Secretaries in Cabinet agencies also appear to be losing ground in terms of salaries adjusted for inflation. However, on the plus side, pensions, sideline benefits, and job security may be better than in the private sector.

2. The "ruling" over mandatory drug testing will depend upon your individual reasoning and values vis-à-vis civil liberties.

CHAPTER 18
MAKING ECONOMIC POLICY

In recent years political scientists have turned their attention to the complex study of public policy - its initiation, formulation, implementation, and evaluation. They have asked such questions as: How do new issues first emerge on the national scene? Who has a voice in drafting policy to deal with the issue? How are new policies best implemented? What criteria should be applied to measure a policy's effectiveness?

There are sometimes built-in tensions between political leaders concerned with balancing off conflicting voter demands and the professional experts who deal in statistical data, cost effectiveness, and experimental models.

But this debate ignores an important ingredient of all policy decisions — money. Although government has a greater ability to borrow money than private individuals do, in the long run its ability to do things is limited by its revenues. And, to a great extent government is not a free agent, starting with a blank slate. It must pay interest on the money previously borrowed. Certain obligations are in a "must" category, such as Social Security payments. And national defense has a very high priority. Hence, government finds itself with limited choices, after these obligations are met.

Government taxation and spending were a major theme during the Reagan-Bush years. Congress attempted to control run away deficits by passing the Gramm-Rudman-Hollings bill and then evading it by placing part of the deficit outside the agreement. The result was a strange mixture. Prices stabilized, but yearly deficits ran so high that the total exceeded that incurred by all previous presidents.

After taking office, Clinton quickly sought a tax package which increased the taxes of the wealthy. After passage of his tax program, Clinton turned his attention to the passage of NAFTA.

PART I — GUIDEPOSTS

1. Making Public Policy
      a. What is public policy?
      b. What are the major stages of public policy?
      c. Who participates in public policy?
      d. What is a nondecision?
      e. What are four different policy models?

2. The Budget: Policy Blueprint
      a. How great is the federal budget?
      b. How large is our debt?
      c. What percentage of the national income is spent by government?
      d. Where does the national government raise its tax revenues?
      e. How does the government divide the budget dollar?
      f. What parts of the budget are untouchable? Controllable?
      g. Who are the chief actors in the budget process?
      h. What limits were established by the Budget Reform Act of 1974?
      i. Why was the General Accounting Office created?

3. The Politics of Taxing and Spending
    a. Which taxes are the fairest?
    b. How widespread is the antitax movement?
    c. How was the tax system reformed in 1986?
    d. How was the tax burden shifted by this change?
    e. How was tax policy changed in the Clinton administration?

4. Managing the Economy
    a. What is monetary policy?
    b. How was the role of government permanently changed by the Great Depression?
    c. What devices does government use to manage the economy?
    d. What theory of management was advanced by John Maynard Keynes?
    e. How does supply side theory differ from Keynes?
    f. What assumptions underlie that theory of monetarism?
    g. Who supports and who questions a proposed balanced budget amendment? Who would benefit? Who would be hurt?

5. Promoting Commerce
    a. How does government aid business?
    b. How are farmers benefited by subsidies?
    c. What is the purpose of GATT?
    d. What are the pros and cons of NAFTA?

PART II — GLOSSARY

PUBLIC POLICY - The actions taken by government to prevent or encourage specific goals.

INCREMENTALISM - The theory that public policy is a process of slow, piecemeal decisions.

OFFICE OF MANAGEMENT AND BUDGET - A presidential staff agency that serves as a clearinghouse for budgetary requests.

GENERAL ACCOUNTING OFFICE - The independent agency that audits government expenditures.

TARIFF - A tax on imported goods.

FISCAL POLICY - Government taxing and spending policy to manage the economy.

SUPPLY SIDE ECONOMICS - The theory that tax cuts will expand private economic activity.

JOHN MAYNARD KEYNES - English economist who advocated a positive role for government in promoting national prosperity.

FEDERAL RESERVE BANK - One of the twelve regional "banker's banks" that in combination make up the Federal Reserve System.

EXCISE TAX - A consumer tax on a specific kind of merchandise, such as tobacco.

SALES TAX - A general consumer tax.

REGRESSIVE TAX - A tax that weighs most heavily on those least able to pay.

MONETARISM - The theory that money supply is the key factor in the economy's performance.

BALANCED BUDGET AMENDMENT - An amendment that would restrict government spending to total revenues.

SUBSIDY - A government payment to a specific group.

PROTECTIONISM - A policy that favors domestic producers or workers.

PART III — PRETEST

1. The national debt by 1994 was approximately
   a. $4.5 trillion.
   b. $200 million.
   c. $1600 billion.
   d. $1 billion.

2. The total budget of the United States government for 1990 was over
   a. $100 billion.
   b. $450 billion.
   c. $650 billion.
   d. $1.5 trillion.

3. The Federal Reserve banks serve *all but one* of the following functions.
   a. insures bank deposits
   b. determines money supply in economy
   c. regulates banks
   d. influences interest rates

4. The economist who first urged that government should fill any gaps left by a deficit of private spending and investment was
   a. Adam Smith.
   b. John M. Keynes.
   c. John K. Galbraith.
   d. Paul Samuelson.

5. An estimate of the total output of all U.S. economic activity is the
   a. GNP.
   b. OMB.
   c. GAO.
   d. VAT.

6. Critics of NAFTA worry about all but one of the following.
   a. Mexican antipollution laws are lax.
   b. Mexican products are inferior.
   c. Mexican workers accept low wages.
   d. U.S. companies will move to Mexico.

7. The substance of what government does is called
   a. lobbying.
   b. lawmaking.
   c. bargaining.
   d. public policy.

8. Policy subsystems develop in Washington between political activists and
   a. research institutes.
   b. lobbyists.
   c. the media.
   d. all of the above

9. The passage by Congress of a clean air act is an example of
   a. evaluation.
   b. implementation.
   c. adoption.
   d. formulation.

10. Policy-making leadership is best described as
   a. shared.
   b. unilateral.
   c. concentrated.
   d. nonexistent.

PART IV — PROGRAMMED REVIEW

Knowledge Objective: To examine the nature of policy making
1. The first step in policy-making is problem _____.
2. The process during which alternative solutions to a policy problem are explored is called policy _____.
3. Much scholarly work on policy issues is performed at _____ such as Brookings Institute.
4. The process during which policy is translated into practice is called policy _____ .

Match the items in the left hand column with those on the right
5. There is an American ruling class
6. Emphasis on inputs and outputs
7. Piecemeal policy change

   a. incrementalism
   b. policy system
   c. bureaucratic-politics
   d. rational man
   e. power elite

8. The _____ government is the biggest spender of all.
9. All levels of government today spend approximately (one-quarter, one-third) _____ of the national income.
10. Benjamin Franklin once said that nothing was certain but death and _____ .
11. The greatest single source of income for the federal government is the _____ tax.
12. An income tax that has higher rates for higher incomes is called _____ .
13. Social Security taxes are _____ because they fall most heavily on low income people.
14. The _____ usually originates tax legislation.

Knowledge Objective: To analyze the budget: income and expenditures
15. Approximately _____ percent of the national budget goes to pay interest on the national debt.
16. The two largest categories of spending in rank order are _____ and _____ .
17. Each year the national government spends over _____ per capita.
18. Total expenditures of the national government are _____ billion annually.
19. Departmental budgets are coordinated by the Office of _____ .
20. The congressional agency that runs a check on government expenditures (including performance auditing) is the _____ .

Knowledge Objective: To examine politics of taxing and spending
21. The _____ tax hits those most able to pay and hardly touches those at the bottom of the economic ladder.
22. The _____ tax is the most controversial.
23. Reagan's answer to the antitax movement was _____ economics.
24. Supply-side economics held _____ can be stimulated by tax cuts.
25. Under the Clinton administration taxes were (cut/raised).
26. Technically, a tax deduction is called a tax _____ .
27. As a result of the 1986 tax reform, most taxpayers now pay _____ income taxes and most corporations pay _____
28. Our debt is a result of spending more for _____ and _____ programs than current tax _____ can afford.

Knowledge Objective: To analyze policies used by the national government to manage the economy

    29. The British economist _____ urged government intervention if private investment was inadequate.

    30. The economic theory that advocates control by regulating the supply of money is called _____ .

    31. Those who believe that neither Congress nor the president have the political courage to curb spending or taxes advocate a _____ _____ amendment.

    32. The Department of Commerce promotes economic growth and encourages business _____ and _____ .

    33. American farm productivity is a direct result of _____ programs.

    34. Most farm subsidies go to _____ farmers.

Knowledge Objective: To examine the arguments between protectionists and free traders

    35. Most economists and diplomats favor _____ trade.

    36. American automobile manufacturers have supported _____ on imports of Japanese automobiles and European steel.

    37. Advocates of free trade argue that protectionist devices (raise, lower) _____ prices for U.S. consumers.

    38. The principal device used by governments to protect their industry against foreign imports has been the _____ .

    39. GATT has had (some, no) success in lowering tariffs and quotas to increase fair trade.

    40. The largest free trade zone was formed by the _____ _____ _____ _____ Agreement.

PART V — POST-TEST

1. The U.S. government levies excise taxes on *all but one* of the following.
    a. gasoline
    c. liquor
    b. real estate
    d. plane tickets

2. Spending by all levels of government today represents _____ of American income.
    a. one-half
    c. one-fifth
    b. one-third
    d. one-tenth

3. In rank order, the largest tax sources of government income are
    a. personal income, social insurance, and corporations.
    b. corporations, excises, and personal income.
    c. social insurance, corporations, and personal income.
    d. personal income, corporations, and excises.

4. Opponents of the balanced budget amendment believe that the responsibility for budget making should remain with the
    a. president.
    c. GAO.
    b. Congress.
    d. Treasury.

5. The losers (who will pay more taxes) in the tax reform law of 1986 are
    a. low income people.
    c. high income people.
    b. upper-middle income people.
    d. the poor.

6. The Clinton program raised taxes in *all but one* of the following ways.
   a. VAT
   b. raised top taxes to 36 percent
   c. 4.3 cents gas tax increase
   d. increased taxes for wealthy Social Security recipients

7. Supply-side economics places its chief emphasis on
   a. production.
   b. consumption.
   c. conservation.
   d. regulation.

8. The result of government farm programs has been
   a. massive bankruptcies.
   b. higher production.
   c. cheap food.
   d. elimination of surpluses.

9. The U.S. government does *not* provide one of the following services to aid the business community.
   a. forecasting the weather
   b. issuing patents
   c. operating an exchange for the sale of stock
   d. providing technical assistance to corporations

10. While most economists favor free trade, many taxpayers favor
    a. a lowering of tariff barriers.
    b. increased protectionism.
    c. more cooperation with the Common Market.
    d. a closer working relationship with Japan.

Part VI — Political Dialogue: The Clash of Issues and Ideas

1. In the early 1960s Richard Rovere authored a book *The American Establishment* in which (half in jest) he suggested that men drawn from the same select colleges, family backgrounds, and financial circles run the country, no matter which party wins the elections. Later an attack on "The Establishment" became one of the battle cries of the New Left. Earlier C. Wright Mills had written about a "Power Elite." Still earlier, American protesters had denounced "International bankers," or "Wall Street."
   a. How valid is the elitist model of American society? Is power highly centralized? Who has it?
   b. Are we today merely exchanging one elite for another? If spokesmen for women, young people, the poor, and blacks gain power, what devices can be created to make them responsible to the rank and file?
   c. Do we have any assurance that such leadership will be concerned with the public good?
   d. Is there any chance that we will get true philosopher-kings if great authority is shifted to today's student leaders?
   e. Does someone other than elected officials run the country?
   f. Do the "Lords of the Press, TV and Radio" control what people read and see? Can they determine elections?

2. *Policy models*: Select an issue that has sharply divided the American people over a considerable period of time. Try to apply all the policy-making models to the issue that is selected, to demonstrate how it is possible to believe in each theory. Possible issues that lend themselves to this treatment include:

a. Affirmative action programs
b. National health insurance
c. Federal aid to education
d. Abortion
e. Crime and violence

3. Farmers appear to be favored in the part of the national government's budget that is given over to nondefense expenditures.
   a. Is this because their problems and needs are greatest?
   b. Do they have greater voting strength than slum residents, school children, and migratory workers?
   c. Review what you know about the voting habits of low income groups. Does this throw any light on Congressional appropriations?
   d. Does the American system guarantee that the greatest need will get the greatest attention? Why? Why not?

4. You are a US Representative from a large industrial state. Among your committee assignments is one involving tariff revisions. Testimony before your committee has demonstrated that foreign automobile imports have now captured a high percent of the U.S. market and that the percentage is steadily rising. The American companies want quotas placed on foreign imports. They are particularly concerned about Japan, which has an efficient, expanding automobile industry that now has the bulk of the U.S. import market. However, a spokesman for Japan has pointed out that she is the second-biggest customer for U.S. made products and that to buy she must sell.

How will you make your decision? Are American consumers benefitting from cheap Japanese autos? Should countries with low labor scales be barred from the U.S. market? Should the government protect a high price industry? What do you think would happen to energy consumption if all foreign autos were barred from the U.S.? What should we do as Korea and Yugoslavia enter the American market?

PART VII — POLITICAL SCIENCE TODAY

1. Whenever the "Fed" raises or lowers interest rates, the impact upon the economy in general and more specifically the securities markets, mortgage rates, car loans, etc. is considerable. In November of 1994, the "Fed" raised rates significantly, claiming that this action was necessary to curb inflation. Other economists disagreed, claiming that the rate increase would choke-off economic recovery. Research this action and other Fed moves. It could serve as the focus of an interesting term paper.

2. In recent years, there have been growing trading strains between the United States and its allies, most notably Japan and Europe. The massive trade deficit has prompted some members of Congress and the business community to demand "protection" from the influx of goods from foreign producers.

Hypothesize for a moment on what might happen if the United States became strongly protectionist against Japan. Would this help American producers? Would protectionism help or hurt American consumers in terms of the prices they would have to pay for autos, electronic equipment, and so forth? How would the Japanese retaliate? In short, assess the pros and cons of extensive protectionism and arrive at your own conclusion regarding the relative wisdom of such a move. The chapter section should help you to think through the problem.

PART VIII — DATA ANALYSIS

1. Review the data on "Presidents and Total Deficits, 1934-1993."
Complete the data on the deficit by finding what the current deficit is *this fiscal year*. Does the amount of the current deficit represent a reduction or increase over previous years? Can you find any information in terms of the Clinton Administration predicting what the deficit will be a year or two from now? Do those projections seem realistic to you — why or why not? Finally, will taxes have to be raised and/or federal spending reduced in order to shrink the deficit in the near future — why or why not?

2. In relation to Exercise #1 above, the idea of a Balanced Budget Amendment (BBA) surfaced again in 1994 after the Republicans gained control of both houses of Congress. In particular, the new House Speaker, Newt Gingrich of Ga., asserted repeatedly in November and December of 1994 that he intended to ask the House and his GOP colleagues in the Senate to vote again on the Amendment early in 1995. Review the action that Congress took on the Amendment in 1995.

3. Look at the text material on problem identification, formulation, adoption, implementation, and evaluation. Then proceed to look through several weeks of *Time, Newsweek,* and *U.S. News and World Report.* Try to isolate policies which can be synchronized with each of the five stages of the policy-making process. After doing this, can you determine what factors move a policy proposal through each of the stages, i.e., from one stage to the next? Jot down a few of your findings in the space below or in your notebook.

PART IX — TEST ANSWERS

Pretest

1. a
2. d
3. a
4. b
5. a

6. b
7. d
8. d
9. c
10. a

Programmed Review

1. identification
2. formulation
3. think tanks
4. implementation
5. e
6. b
7. a
8. national
9. one-third
10. taxes
11. personal income
12. progressive
13. regressive
14. President
15. 14
16. social programs; defense
17. $5800
18. $1518
19. Management and Budget
20. General Accounting Office

21. progressive
22. sales
23. supply-side
24. production
25. raised
26. expenditure
27. lower; more
28. defense; domestic; revenues
29. John Maynard Keynes
30. monetarism
31. balanced budget
32. research; development
33. government
34. wealthy
35. free
36. limits
37. raise
38. tariff
39. some
40. North American Free Trade

Post-test

1. b
2. b
3. a
4. b
5. b

6. a
7. a
8. b
9. c
10. b

Data Analysis

Answers to all three data analysis problems will depend upon each student's research effort.

CHAPTER 19
MAKING REGULATORY POLICY

The direction of government regulation has changed once again. After the Reagan-Bush years of declining regulation, Clinton created a more complicated pattern. Clinton tends to view each area separately. In the telecommunications area he pushed for deregulation while he pushed for more regulation of guns, smoking and seafood.

But although emphasis has shifted, a demand remains for much of the regulatory machinery. Americans do need to be protected against a polluted environment, unsafe equipment, on-the-job dangers, and monopoly price fixing. Our dilemma, then is to maximize cost-effective beneficial regulation while minimizing overly zealous nitpicking. In a world where technology is increasingly widespread and corporations are international, protection for average citizens can come only from government.

PART I — GUIDEPOSTS

1. What is Regulation?
   a. Why do we have regulation?
   b. Do we have too much or too little regulation?
   c. What has been Bush's stand on regulation?
   d. How does regulation modify the free market concept? How does it differ from socialism?
   e. What case can be made for regulation?
   f. What are the basic criticisms of regulation?
   g. How do we try to curb monopoly? Why do we accept it in some areas?
   h. Why do market imperfections arise? Can we justify efforts to correct them?
   i. Why does government become involved in protecting the weak?
   j. Why does cost effectiveness become a central issue in regulation?

2. Regulating Business
   a. Why did business practices of the late 19th century bring about antitrust legislation?
   b. How effective has it been?
   c. How has US competition in world markets modified our views on antitrust curbs?
   d. What has been the attitude of the Reagan-Bush administrations toward antitrust enforcement? The Clinton administration?
   e. What consolidation trend has prevailed in recent years?
   f. Does the growth of mergers diminish the free market place and competition?
   g. What conflicting proposals are offered to curb or regulate bigness?
   h. What has been the impact of the breakup of AT&T?

3. Regulating Labor-Management Relations
   a. Why does labor generally favor government intervention?
   b. How does government protect workers by establishing wage-hour laws? Minimum wages? Restricting child labor? Safety legislation?
   c. How has the right to organize been protected?
   d. How did the Taft-Hartley Act curb union power?
   e. What developments seem to be promoting labor-management harmony?

4. Regulating the Environment
    a. Why does cost become a central issue in pollution control?
    b. In what ways is our environment polluted?
    c. How have we tried to clean up the air?
    d. What is the major source of acid rain? What damage does it do? What costs does its control entail?
    e. What are the major provisions of the 1990 Clean Air Act?

5. Regulating Occupational Safety and Health
    a. Why has OSHA been subject to so much criticism?
    b. Where are the most dangerous jobs?
    c. How valid have criticisms of OSHA been?
    d. Do workers need the protection of OSHA?

6. Regulatory Outcomes and Issues
    a. What positive impact do supporters of regulation offer?
    b. What criticisms of regulation are offered?

7. The Deregulation Debate
    a. What benefits do advocates of deregulation claim?
    b. What do the critics say?
    c. Has airline deregulation been more beneficial to the airlines? The consumers?
    d. What has been the upshot of railway deregulation? Trucking deregulation?
    e. How does deregulating banking offer special problems?
    f. In a general debate over deregulation, who has the better case?

PART II — GLOSSARY

MERGER - The consolidation of two or more companies.

ACID RAIN - The fallout of sulfur dioxide from utilities and other sources down wind from the source, damaging forests, wild life, and fish.

ENVIRONMENTAL IMPACT STATEMENT - The statement required in all proposals, using federal funds, analyzing their result on the environment.

TAFT-HARTLEY ACT - The national law (1974) that restricted union rights.

COLLECTIVE BARGAINING - Direct negotiations between an employer and a union over employment conditions.

OSHA - The federal agency concerned with employee safety and health.

TOXIC WASTE - A byproduct of manufacturing involving nuclear and chemical residues.

MONOPOLY - Technically, a market in which only one supplier exists. Commonly, a market with few suppliers (oligopoly).

SHERMAN ANTI-TRUST ACT (1890) - The first major national law designed to prevent business monopoly and preserve competition.

CLAYTON ACT (1914) - The law that specifically exempted labor from its provisions while closing loopholes in the Sherman Anti-Trust Act.

FEDERAL TRADE COMMISSION - Established in 1914 to prevent unfair, unethical business practices.

*CONGLOMERATE - A corporation that controls many noncompetitive units.

NATIONAL LABOR RELATIONS ACT (Wagner Act) - The 1935 law recognizing the right of workers to organize and bargain collectively.

CLOSED SHOP - A union-employer arrangement outlawed by the Taft-Hartley Act, which restricted employment to union members.

UNION SHOP - A union-employer arrangement providing that all employees must join a union within a specified time after employment.

JURISDICTIONAL STRIKE - A strike arising from a dispute between unions over which has the right to do a job.

RIGHT-TO-WORK LAW - State law forbidding union shops.

CLEAN AIR ACT - The law of 1990 that sets air standards, provides research funds, and establishes target dates for automobile emission controls.

NATIONAL ENVIRONMENTAL POLICY ACT - The basic law (1969) that established the primacy of the national government in environmental issues.

INDEPENDENT REGULATORY COMMISSIONS - The twenty agencies created by Congress over the past century to control segments of the economy. They are independent in the sense that they are immune to immediate political pressure from the President or Congress.

PART III — PRETEST

1. _____ is not a new regulatory activity.
   a. Antitrust
   b. Pollution
   c. Toxic waste
   d. Industrial health

2. The alternative to regulation is
   a. socialism.
   b. mercantilism.
   c. *laissez faire.*
   d. incrementalism.

3. Regulation generally involves government's use of its
   a. taxation power.
   b. general welfare power.
   c. police power.
   d. economic power.

4. The basic law designed to control monopolies is the
   a. Clayton Act.
   b. Taft-Hartley Act.
   c. Sherman Act.
   d. Wagner Act.

5. The most common forms of business concentration today are
   a. monopolies and conglomerates.
   b. conglomerates and natural monopolies.
   c. natural monopolies and oligopolies.
   d. oligopolies and conglomerates.

6. Responsibility for protecting the free enterprise system against monopoly is assigned to which Cabinet department?
   a. Commerce
   b. Justice
   c. Treasury
   d. Labor

7. Labor's basic struggle was over
   a. the right to organize.
   b. minimum wages.
   c. health care benefits.
   d. pension payments.

8. Most regulation of union activity is assigned to the
   a. Federal Trade Commission.
   b. Antitrust Division of the Justice Department.
   c. National Labor Relations Board.
   d. Department of Labor.

9. After a rather bad start, OSHA appears to be concentrating on
   a. industrial accidents.
   b. fire prevention.
   c. sanitary facilities.
   d. hazards.

10. What is the final question in all debates over environmental pollution?
   a. Do we want clean air?
   b. What price will we pay?
   c. Have you filed an environmental impact statement?
   d. Will it create jobs?

PART IV — PROGRAMMED REVIEW

Knowledge Objective: To examine the reasons for and trends in regulation

1. Regulations exist to encourage economic _____ and _____ objectives.
2. Regulation is a _____ ground between laissez faire and socialism.
3. Most wages, prices and allocation of goods and services in the United States are determined by the laws of _____ and _____ .
4. Supporters of regulation argue that it (improves, limits) _____ the quality of American life.
5. Critics of regulation say that it is _____ and _____ .
6. _____ is an economic market where power is concentrated in a few units.
7. The aim of antitrust laws is to encourage _____ .
8. Electric utilities are an example of a _____ monopoly.
9. Cable TV is an example of a _____ monopoly.
10. _____ regulation attempts to provide clean air and consumer safety.
11. Rather than aiming for absolute standards, most policy-makers aim for regulation that is balanced against "reasonable" _____ .
12. Performance standards would shift the means of achieving required social goals from government to _____ .
13. The social costs of regulation are relatively (difficult, easy) _____ to establish.

Knowledge Objective: To trace government attempts to maintain business competition

14. Congress in 1890 attempted to curb monopolies by passing the _____ _____ Act.
15. Many antitrust suits are settled by _____ decrees.
16. Today business concentration has been largely (eliminated, unchanged) _____ .
17. Americans believe in business competition, but they also believe in _____ .
18. Regulation of US business has become more difficult in recent years because the marketplace has become _____ .
19. The national government brought suit against AT&T, charging it with being a _____.
20. The Reagan-Bush administrations generally adopted a _____ policy toward mergers.

Knowledge Objective: To consider the major legislation affecting labor management relations

21. Labor leaders generally _____ federal regulation.
22. Most labor laws regulate the relationship of workers with _____ .
23. The Taft-Hartley Act placed limitations on _____ .
24. In recent years unions have lost members and _____ clout.

Knowledge Objective: To review the politics and technology of environmental protection

25. The most active pollution control effort is being made by the _____ level of government.
26. The government has chosen a _____ approach to pollution.
27. The _____ _____ Agency is responsible for enforcement of antipollution laws.
28. Most pollution arguments center around the issue of _____ .

29. The cost of cleaning up the environment will be borne chiefly by _____ sources.
30. An environmental _____ statement must be filed for any new project using federal funds.
31. The 1990 Clean Air Act has been called the most _____ piece of environmental legislation ever passed.
32. The EPA has pressed for new regulatory strategies that encourage _____ solutions for ecological problems.
33. There is now general agreement that US forests and Canadian water supplies are damaged by _____ _____ .
34. Many Reagan appointees were _____ to environmental concerns.
35. Policy over the control of acid rain has (unified, divided) _____ interest groups.

Knowledge Objective: To evaluate the goals, criticisms and successes of OSHA

36. Perhaps the most criticized of all federal regulatory agencies is _____ .
37. OSHA was established to reduce industrial_____ .
38. The "nitpicking" _____ of OSHA are the source of many complaints.
39. A majority of industrial accidents occur in _____ business.
40. The Reagan administration attempted to (lessen, increase) _____ the authority of OSHA.

Knowledge Objective: To examine current trends in regulatory politics

41. Regulatory agencies are sometimes _____ by the industries that they regulate.
42. The result of regulation has normally been to (increase, decrease) _____ prices.
43. Regulation (encourages, discourages) _____ technological innovation.
44. Small cities have experienced _____ service and _____ fares from airline deregulation.
45. Deregulation of railroads and trucks appears to be (successful, unsuccessful) _____.
46. The FSLIC has resulted in the biggest _____ of government regulation.
47. The net result of deregulation thus far appears to be _____ as far as consumers are concerned.

PART V — POST-TEST

1. Deregulation is being implemented in all of the following areas *except*
   a. education.   c. airlines.
   b. railroad.   d. trucks.

2. The attitude of the Reagan administration toward regulation was best summarized in the slogan
   a. we need more.   c. let's be tougher.
   b. let's have less.   d. practice begins neglect.

3. Reasons for regulation do *not* include
   a. curbing monopolies.
   b. compensating for imperfect markets.
   c. eliminating the "economically weak."
   d. controlling natural monopolies.

4. Our first efforts at regulation were intended to
   a. encourage unions.
   b. preserve competition markets.
   c. protect consumers.
   d. curb pollution.

5. The end result of nearly a century of antitrust legislation is that
    a. business concentration exists.
    b. monopolies are commonplace.
    c. business is widely dispersed.
    d. cutthroat competition is the norm.

6. Clinton's environmental policy included proposals for *all but* one of the following
    a. new rules to reduce the greenhouse effect
    b. new pesticide regulation
    c. eased restriction on cutting timber that housed the spotted owl
    d. major increase of grazing fees

7. The right to organize and bargain collectively was guaranteed by the _____ Act.
    a. Wagner   c. Taft-Hartley
    b. Sherman   d. Walsh-Healey

8. The Taft-Hartley Act does not outlaw
    a. the closed shop.   c. jurisdictional strikes.
    b. the union shop.   d. secondary boycotts.

9. The basic criticism of OSHA appears to be that its regulations are too
    a. lax.   c. trivial.
    b. strict.   d. general.

10. The phrase that best describes the projected environmental policy of the 1990s is
    a. tradeoffs.   c. effluent charges.
    b. whitewash.   d. escalating controls.

PART VI — POLITICAL DIALOGUE: THE CLASH OF ISSUES AND IDEAS

1. Analyze the short and long-term impact of airline deregulation. Cover the following points:
    a. The emergence and disappearance of new airlines (Ozark, Peoples Express, Piedmont, Braniff).
    b. The fare wars.
    c. Passenger safety.
    d. Why the mergers left some communities without adequate service.
    e. What will be the final result
    f. Should we have a national airline, like Japan?

2. Some states have adopted "lemon laws" that give buyers protection against badly built cars, by forcing companies to give free repairs or refunds. We should have a national law that covers all cars sold in the United States. Do you agree? Disagree? Why?

3. "The quickest way to clear up the Savings and Loan mess is to cut the total guarantee on deposits to any one person to $10,000, effective immediately. This would get depositors who have been enjoying a "free ride" to become concerned about the lending policies of their banks, and drive the banks back into their original mission — to finance private homes.

4. You are a member of the Federal Trade Commission. A leading soap company has been char before the Commission with violating the "truth in packaging" laws. Specifically, the deter

boxes for the "giant, economy" size are only half filled. The company contends that the box clearly states that it contains 56 ounces; that overcrowding in the box will damage some of the granules; and, finally, that the box is more attractive and gives the company more space to write directions for use. What ruling will you favor? Why?

5. The general rule in all forms of social regulation is that each restriction has a cost that must be weighed against the social benefit. In the case of energy regulation indicate the social cost involved in each of the following actions:

      a. Requiring increased use of coal
      b. Halting construction of nuclear plants
      c. Improving automobile gasoline mileage
      d. Encouraging the production of shale oil
      e. Lifting the 55 mph speed limit
      f. Increasing oil imports
      g. Building more nuclear plants

6. What are some of the alleged negative effects to consumers of deregulation of airlines, natural gas and banking? Who gets hurt? Are we ending up with a few giant companies that can set prices as they wish?

PART VII — POLITICAL SCIENCE TODAY

1. The conflict between regulation's goals of protecting society and the costs attached to that regulation was well represented in a "debate" entitled "Is Cleaner Air Worth the Cost" appearing in <u>The New York Times</u> of April 22, 1989, p. 15. Two congressmen, Max Baucus (D, Montana) and Joseph I. Lieberman (D, Connecticut), argued in "Ask the Asthmatics" the following points (both men were members of the Senate environmental protection subcommittee):

  a. Smog levels in 1988 were the worst of the past ten years.
  b. All cars should meet the same auto emissions standards as present in California. California's strict limits on emissions for vans and trucks should also be pushed nationally.
  c. It is not true that "more stringent emission controls are too expensive…clean air legislation would cost $7.9 to 8.7 billion in 1993. It's still a lot of money but consider…we spend $6 billion a year each on athletic footwear and lotteries, $8 billion on chocolate, $10 billion on boats, $21 billion on soft drinks and $83 billion on jewelry. Is it worth spending what we spend each year on chocolate for cleaner air? Can we afford not to?"
  d. The estimate of environmental damage caused by air pollution is $60 to $100 billion each year. Taxpayers and consumers spend up to $40 billion each year in health care and other causes of illness and death linked to air pollution.
  e. There is a great deal of suffering by those most vulnerable to air pollution such as people with pulmonary heart disease, pregnant women and their unborn children who cannot tolerate carbon monoxide, the elderly, and asthmatics.

S. Fred Singer, a professor of environmental science at the University of Virginia, argued in "Purity Can't Be Achieved" the following counterparts:

  a. Any clean air bill Congress passes will not be worth the cost to the consumer. The "huge economic cost will be hidden in higher food, electricity, and transportation expenses, which hit the poor hardest."
  b. While average air quality has improved since the passage of the original Clean Air Act back in the 1970s, (sulfur dioxide is down 29 percent, carbon monoxide, 39 percent), the

cost-benefit relationship seems skewed when "it becomes increasingly difficult and expensive to remove the last remnants of pollution - typical of any clean-up project. Costs shoot up exponentially as emission standards are tightened, while benefits show only modest increases."

c. There are other health factors which should be addressed - indoor pollutants like tobacco smoke and radon gas, and formaldehyde and carbon tetrachloride. "Rather than spend all of our money trying to eliminate a few risk factors, we should do what we can to reduce overall risks to our health."

d. "Controlling emissions should be left to local government and the polluters themselves. After all, a 'standard' simply means that only a certain amount of a pollutant can be emitted into the atmosphere. The atmosphere doesn't care whose smoke stack is controlled."

Reflect upon these respective pro and con arguments. Which ones make the most sense to you and why? Note that this debate involving "trade-offs" between the benefits and costs of clean air will continue to be relevant now and in the future, regardless of legislation passed by Congress.

2. As a corollary to the above exercise, you may wish to analyze the proposed overhaul of the Clean Air Act suggested by President George Bush in July of 1989. In that plan, the President set the following goals and/or schedules:

a. *Auto Tailpipes* - The bill set lower overall limits for emissions than did current law, but those limits did apply to an average of all vehicles rather than individual vehicles. NOTE: Environmentalists attacked the idea, arguing that *every car* should meet a standard.

b. *Cities* - The promise in the bill was that all cities except those with the most severe pollution would have clear air by the year 2000. Such cities in the severe category as New York, Los Angeles, and Houston would have an additional 10 years before facing sanctions.

c. *Factories* - President Bush did set a schedule for cutting back the release of poisonous chemicals into the air. However, critics argued that the plan did not mandate utilization of the best emission-control devices.

"What happened to these presidential suggestions in the 1990 Clean Air Act? Did they become integral components of the new law? Were any suggestions modified or eliminated altogether?

3. Unlike the conservative, pro-business Reagan-Bush years, federal regulators in the Clinton Administration pursued a vigorous, activist agenda toward corporate America. Despite being understaffed, OSHA levied millions of dollars in fines against companies that exposed workers to health hazards. The Department of Transportation found defective side-mounted gasoline tanks on General Motors trucks. The Food and Drug Administration charged that public school lunches contained too many calories and too much fat, angering food companies who complained that the cost of compliance with these FDA guidelines would far exceed nutritional benefits. Even banking regulators got into the act, investigating why many savings and loans refused to invest more heavily in low-income neighborhoods.

As a possible research topic, investigate any or all of these Clinton initiatives. Were they necessary and appropriate? Was the cost of compliance too high? Finally, do you believe that much of this "regulatory activity" could be left to the corporations themselves, not government? Why or why not? Write down your reasons.

PART VIII — DATA ANALYSIS

1. In late 1994, the FAA—Federal Aviation Administration—began to question the safety of the nation's civilian jetliners. The airline companies, confronted with shrinking profits, were extending the flight-lives of aircraft rather than investing in new, very expensive planes. Many of these older planes were 20 to 30 years of age. Several had crashed due to in-flight structural failures. The airlines insisted that they were maintaining these aircraft according to FAA guidelines. Furthermore, it was far cheaper to fix these old planes, thus allowing them to fly for additional decades.

   Follow-up this issue into subsequent years. Can you find any evidence of the FAA implementing even tougher regulations again toward aircraft? What steps did the airlines take to resolve this problem, if any? Finally, did consumer organizations and/or Congress begin pressuring the FAA or the airlines to take some action? Your data could form the basis of an oral or written presentation.

2. Look at the "You Decide" insert regarding the issue of the minimum wage and sub-minimum wage for youth in the text chapter. How would you respond to the insert's questions (thoughts about the proposal, benefits and disadvantages)? More specifically, do you believe the minimum wage is essential to a sound economy and especially the poor? Why or why not? Finally, what is the current minimum wage and what action has the Clinton Administration taken regarding this issue?

PART IX — TEST ANSWERS

Pretest

1. a
2. c
3. c
4. c
5. d

6. b
7. a
8. c
9. d
10. b

Programmed Review

1. competition; social
2. middle
3. supply; demand
4. improves
5. inefficient; counterproductive
6. Oligopoly
7. competition
8. natural
9. hidden
10. Social
11. costs
12. industry
13. difficult
14. Sherman Antitrust
15. consent
16. unchanged
17. bigness
18. international
19. monopoly
20. permissive
21. favor
22. employers
23. unions
24. political

25. national
26. regulatory
27. Environmental Protection
28. cost
29. private
30. impact
31. expensive
32. market
33. acid rain
34. hostile
35. divided
36. OSHA
37. accidents
38. rules
39. small
40. lessen
41. captured
42. increase
43. discourages
44. less, higher
45. successful
46. failure
47. positive

Post-test

1. a
2. b
3. c
4. b
5. a

6. d
7. a
8. b
9. c
10. a

Data Analysis

The responses to both exercises will vary depending upon individual research.

CHAPTER 20
MAKING SOCIAL POLICY

The responsibility of the government to solve social problems has been debated since the drafting of the U.S. Constitution. Conservatives believe individuals should take responsibility for their own problems rather than rely on the government for assistance. In addition, they think private agencies such as charities, churches and foundations whose funds are raised via voluntary contributions from individuals and businesses should support services and programs which address health, medical, educational and housing problems for the indigent. And, when government takes responsibility for social programs, it should be at the state or local levels.

On the other end of the philosophical spectrum, liberals believe the government has the responsibility to offer and publicly fund services and programs to attain and maintain some 'minimum standard of living' for all citizens. On a practical level, liberals do not think private agencies are able to raise sufficient resources to respond to all of the educational, medical, employment, housing and nutritional needs of society. In addition, they believe that the national government ought to provide funding and set social policy standards because state and local governments are generally not willing or able to address social problems.

This chapter outlines the elements that have sustained the social policy debate over the past two hundred years and describes four efforts to change the federal government's role during the twentieth century. In two instances significant expansions of the government's role in social programming occurred; one as a result of President Franklin D. Roosevelt's New Deal and the other from President Lyndon B. Johnson's Great Society initiatives. A reduction in the federal government's leadership and funding responsibilities for social programs was sought by Ronald Reagan's administration. And, most recently, President Bill Clinton's attempts to establish new national policy in the areas of health care, welfare, education and crime control are reviewed. The effects of revisions to federal policy on state and local governments are also considered.

Through this chapter, we find that social policy over the last sixty years has not been static. Dramatic changes in social policy represent variations regarding how the president, Congress and American citizens have viewed the government's responsibility for providing and funding social programs. Demands to reduce the federal deficit and a change in the public's basic attitude about governmental responsibility for social programs will likely fuel the social policy debate throughout the 1990s.

PART I — GUIDEPOSTS

1. The Role of Government in Social Policy
   a. What is the proper role of government in the provision and funding of education, health care, housing, job security, care for the elderly and public safety?
   b. Why do conservatives prefer private solutions to social problems?
   c. Why do liberals prefer public solutions to social problems?
   d. Are social policy problems better addressed by the national government or by state and local levels of government?
   e. What impact have federally mandated social programs had on state and local governments?
   f. Should social programs differ among states or should all who benefit receive the same treatment?

2. History of Social Policy in the United States
  a. How does the federal constitution support government's involvement in social policy?

  b. The New Deal
    1. How did the New Deal expand the government's social policy responsibilities?

  c. Social Security
    1. What benefits are provided by the Social Security Act of 1935 and subsequent amendments?
    2. Why is Social Security politically popular?
    3. How is Social Security funded?
    4. Why may 'intergenerational pressure' arise in relation to Social Security?

  d. The Great Society
    1. How did the Great Society expand the government's social policy responsibilities?
    2. What beliefs about the responsibility of the federal government for social policy are rooted in the Great Society?

  e. Social Policies Issues in the 1990s
    1. What impact did "Reaganomics" have on social policy and programs?
    2. What changes in political philosophy are advocated by the Democratic Leadership Council?
    3. What must a president do to accomplish changes in social policy?

  f. Health Care
    1. What are the three major approaches taken by the federal government in regard to health care?
    2. How much does the federal government spend on health care for the elderly, disabled and low income populations?
    3. What are the two principal methods of payment used by private health insurance providers?
    4. What are the six problems with the current U.S. health care system?
    5. What are five approaches to health care reform?

  g. Welfare
    1. What federally funded programs are part of welfare?
    2. What is the definition of 'public assistance'?
    3. What circumstances contribute to the 'feminization of poverty'?
    4. What are the most common welfare reform proposals?
    5. What are the appropriate roles of the federal, state and local governments for funding and setting of standards for welfare programs?

  h. Education
    1. Why did the 'founding fathers' give high priority to the education of children?
    2. What level(s) of government were given principal responsibility for public education?
    3. How did the Clinton administration translate the Goals 2000: Education for the Next Century program into goals and objectives?
    4. What arguments are presented for and against Goals 2000?
    5. What has been the federal government's role in public education?
    6. What four problems challenge public education today?

    i. Crime
        1. What four legislative actions comprise the federal government's comprehensive crime fighting program?
        2. What four anti-crime grant programs have been established since 1983?
        3. Why does crime fighting pose the biggest social policy challenge?
        4. Can crime be fought without violating traditional civil liberties?
        5. Is crime best fought by reducing poverty and the lack of opportunity which lead to criminal behavior?

    j. Social Policy in American Politics
        1. What programs should constitute the government's "safety net" for those who can't provide for themselves?
        2. How should the "safety net" be funded?

PART II — GLOSSARY

SOCIAL POLICY - The actions taken by government to meet minimal human needs in nutrition, housing, education, health care, and public safety.

MANDATE - The practice where one level of government (federal) requires another level of government (state or local) to offer a program or service without providing full or partial funding to offset the cost of implementation.

DEMOCRATIC LEADERSHIP COUNCIL - A group formed in 1985 to steer the national Democratic party away from the more liberal elements and policy positions of the party.

NEW DEAL - A series of relief programs established by the federal government during Franklin D. Roosevelt's administration to stimulate the economy and put people back to work.

SOCIAL SECURITY ACT - The original act (1935) and subsequent amendments established an insurance system supported by employee and employer taxes which provide pensions for retired workers, financial support for disabled workers and for children of deceased or disabled workers, and health insurance of retired and disabled persons.

ENTITLEMENT PROGRAM - Programs which provide a specified set of benefits as a matter of right to all who meet the criteria established by law.

TRANSFER PROGRAM - A practice which utilizes special purpose taxes currently paid by one segment of society to fund current benefits for another group. Today, Social Security taxes paid by young workers pay for benefits currently received by retirees.

GREAT SOCIETY - President Lyndon Johnson's mid-1960s broad based social and economic policies aimed at ending poverty and racial prejudice and making educational opportunities available to all children.

REAGANOMICS - President Ronald Reagan's early 1990s economic policy of tax benefits to the rich that would "trickle down" to help the poor and increases in defense spending which resulted in historic budget deficits and no money to try out new social policy ideas or programs.

MEDICARE - The national health insurance program for the elderly and disabled.

MEDICAID - A medical benefits program for low-income persons funded largely by the federal government but administered and partially funded by the states .

FEE FOR SERVICE - Health care provided by physicians of an individual's choice and paid for by insurance companies.

THIRD PARTY PAYER - The insurance companies which cover the costs of services provided by physicians and hospitals on behalf of insured individuals.

UNIVERSAL HEALTH CARE - The provision of health care for the entire population.

PART III — PRETEST

1. President Lyndon B. Johnson was successful in getting Congress to enact the Great Society's social programs because of all of the following *except*
   a. the growing restlessness within the country with racial injustice and poverty.
   b. his commitment to government programs as a means to address social problems.
   c. the winding down of the Vietnam War.
   d. the large majority of Democrats in Congress.

2. The New Deal included all but which of the following programs?
   a. Works Progress Administration (WPA)
   b. Comprehensive Employment and Training Act (CETA)
   c. Tennessee Valley Authority (TVA)
   d. Civilian Conservation Corps (CCC)

3. The clause of the U.S. Constitution supports a social policy role for the federal government.
   a. separation of powers
   b. due process
   c. equal opportunity
   d. general welfare

4. Social Security benefits are paid to Americans every month, while working Americans contribute to it.
   a. 40 million, 133 million
   b. 133 million, 40 million
   c. 20 million, 70 million
   d. 70 million, 20 million

5. Health care reforms would address all of the following *except*
   a. reduction of unnecessary procedures.
   b. rising costs.
   c. the quality of health care.
   d. increasing number of uninsureds.

6. Which of the following is not part of the federal government's anti-crime grant programs established since 1983?
   a. victim compensation
   b. drug enforcement
   c. hiring of more prosecutors
   d. alternatives to incarceration

7. Current debate related to public education has included all except which of the following issues?
   a. How much local control should there be?
   b. What standards and goals there ought to be?
   c. How much difference in local funding should be tolerated?
   d. Who will ensure that the needs of the poor, disabled, and minorities will be met?

8. The disparity between contributions to Social Security and the benefits paid is illustrated by Ida Fuller's contribution and receipt of in benefits.
   a. $200, $15,000
   b. $5000, $4500
   c. $22, $21,000
   d. $500, $500

9. "Feminization of poverty" is due to all of the following *except*
   a. male/female wage gap.
   b. fathers not paying child support.
   c. women entering the work force in smaller numbers.
   d. a rise in illegitimate births.

10. Brown vs. The Board of Education led to all of the following *except*
    a. school desegregation.
    b. incentives to improve schools for poor children.
    c. school busing.
    d. all of the above

PART IV — PROGRAMMED REVIEW

Knowledge Objective: To examine the role of government in social policy

1. President Clinton's social policy focuses on four areas: _____, _____, _____, and _____.
2. Actions taken by the government to meet minimal human needs in nutrition, housing, education, health care and public safety constitute _____ policy.
3. _____ favor private approaches to social policy and prefer that when necessary, social problems be addressed by state and local governments.
4. _____ believe it is the responsibility of government to provide some minimum standard of living and that the national government play a major role in setting policy standards and funding programs.
5. Governors are concerned about the tendency of the federal government to _____ social programs that states must administer with little or no federal funding.

Knowledge Objective: To review the history of social policy in the U.S.

6. The break-up of the _____ _____ has resulted in an increased interest in social issues in the United States.
7. Social policy debate today focuses on _____, _____, and_____.
8. The _____ was formed in 1985 to steer the Democratic Party away from the more liberal elements and policy positions of the party.
9. _____, a best-seller written by David Osborne, emphasized the need to reduce bureaucratic red tape, decentralize programs, rely on individual responsibility and the market approach.
10. The Railroad Retirement Act of 1935 was upheld by the U.S. Supreme Court because it was based on the _____ clause of the Constitution.

Knowledge Objective: To understand the nature of Social Security

11. _____, an entitlement program, is politically untouchable because everyone benefits, regardless of need.
12. Social Security covers _____ % of the American workforce.
13. _____ and _____ will cause 'intergenerational tension' over Social Security.

Knowledge Objective: To examine the federal government's role in health care

14. Federal health care policy focuses on three areas; _____, _____, and _____.
15. Federally sponsored research includes the following five elements; _____, _____, _____, _____, and_____.
16. In 1995 the federal government will spend $ _____ or cover _____ % of the national health care bill for 83 million Americans inclusive of veterans, the disabled, poor, and elderly.
17. The Public Health Service is headed by _____ and conducts research through the _____ and the _____.
18. Opposition to health care reform is based on the American opinion that _____.
19. Americans want universal health care coverage without _____ and lower costs without _____.

20. Health care costs have risen _____ % since 1973 and by 2030 are expected to represent _____ % of the GNP.
21. Of the 37 million uninsured Americans _____ % are employed full-time by employers who do not provide benefits.
22. If standardized forms and computers were used throughout the health care industry, a _____ % savings in health care costs could be achieved.
23. Canada, Germany, the Netherlands and the United Kingdom fund over _____ % of the national cost of health care as compared to the _____ % funded by the United States.
24. Experts believe that prevention measures related to the use of _____, _____, and _____ would diminish health care costs by _____.

Knowledge Objective: *To examine the federal government's role related to welfare*

25. The single biggest welfare program is _____.
26. The three welfare programs not traditionally seen as welfare are _____, _____, and _____.
27. Head Start provides _____, _____, _____, and _____ to approximately 700,000 children each year.
28. Public assistance programs encompass _____, _____, _____, _____, _____, _____, and _____.
29. In 1993, 37 million people fell below the _____ annual income poverty line for a family of four.
30. The majority of poor in the United States tend to be from four groups; _____, _____, _____, and _____.
31. The federal government funds _____ % of welfare program benefits.
32. _____, (D-NY) recommended the transfer of welfare programs to the Department of _____ to reinforce the importance of finding work and becoming self-sufficient.
33. _____ reward and supplement the wages of the working poor.
34. The failure of welfare programs is a result of a political system that _____.

Knowledge Objective: *To examine the federal government's role related to education*

35. _____ launched by the Soviet Union in 1957 facilitated the expansion of federal funding for education.
36. The _____ enacted after World War II has financed the education of 20 million veterans.
37. In 1954, the U.S. Supreme Court in Brown vs. The Board of Education declared _____ to be inherently unconstitutional.
38. The Goals 2000 program recommends three restructuring steps for public school education; _____, _____, and _____.
39. Advocates of _____ believe public schools would be improved because parents would demand better schools.
40. _____ % of college and university students benefit from Pell Grants and Stafford Loans provided by the federal government.
41. Public education has traditionally been under the control of the _____ governments .
42. The federal government provides _____ % of the $61.4 billion spent on education annually.

Knowledge Objective: *To examine the federal government's role related to crime control*

43. In response to current public concern about crime and violence, Congress established a comprehensive program of laws and funding to _____, _____, _____, _____, and _____.
44. In 1984, Congress overhauled the sentencing system to _____, _____, and _____,

45. _____ imposed a 5-day waiting period on the purchase of hand guns to allow background checks to be done.

46. The number of guns in the United States increased from 54 million in 1950 to _____ million in the 1990s.

47. President Clinton's crime control bill provides grants for an additional _____ police officers nationwide which will cost approximately _____ over a five-year period.

48. The _____ was established by Congress in 1965, provided $8 billion in grants over a twelve year period, and was abolished during the Carter administration because most of the money was wasted.

Knowledge Objective: To review social policy concerns for the 1990s

49. _____ coined the word 'safety net' to describe the social programs which are funded and provided by government.

50. _____ and _____ are 'safety net' issues for the 90s.

PART V — POST-TEST

1. The Democratic Leadership Council formed in 1985 advocates policies that
    a. encourage economic growth.
    b. redistribute wealth.
    c. place greater reliance on group responsibility.
    d. centralizes existing social programs.

2. Welfare in the United States was originally left to private charities and local government because America was a country
    a. based on "rugged individualism."
    b. seen as the land of opportunity.
    c. where government played a limited role in peoples' lives.
    d. all of the above

3. The social policy development process in the United States highlights all but
    a. the divergent roles of the president and Congress.
    b. continuing importance of federalism.
    c. the role of ideology and public opinion.
    d. the debate about the appropriate role of government in social policy.

4. If Congress does not enact changes to the Social Security system, funds may run out by the year
    a. 1998.
    b. 2010.
    c. 2030.
    d. 2050.

5. The Great Society program of the mid-1960s included all of the following except
    a. voting rights.
    b. pre-school for gifted children.
    c. health care for the elderly and indigent.
    d. housing for the poor.

6. The 'founding fathers' gave high priority to the education of children because they believed education, if widely shared, would provide the citizenry with
    a. a moral sense.
    b. an ability to reason.
    c. general knowledge of history and government.
    d. all of the above

7. In 1991, the FBI estimated that _____ % of household burglaries in the United States were reported to the police.
    a. 35   c. 70
    b. 50   d. 95

8. The United States generally has a decentralized criminal justice system except for the following agency(ies) which provide direct assistance to state and local governments.
    a. FBI   c. FBI and ATF
    b. DEA   d. FBI, DEA, and ATF

9. In 1983, Congress acted to place the Social Security system on better financial ground by all of the following reasons *except*
    a. raising the retirement age.
    b. increasing social security taxes.
    c. eliminating benefits for individuals who did not work.
    d. taxing 85% of social security benefits for upper income individuals.

10. Welfare reform proposals generally include all of the following *except*
    a. consolidation of programs
    b. employment of middle-aged females to provide day-care
    c. creation of privately administered and funded programs
    d. reduction in fraud

PART VI — POLITICAL DIALOGUE:
THE CLASH OF ISSUES AND IDEAS

1. President Bill Clinton's social policy reform agenda included health care, education, welfare and crime control. Legislative initiatives have been proposed in each area since he took office. Investigate what reforms the Clinton administration proposed to Congress. Were any of the President's recommendations enacted by Congress? If so, what strategies did the President use to garner Congressional votes? If not, did the initiative(s) fail because of the fundamental conflict between conservative and liberal philosophy regarding the appropriate responsibility of government for social programs?

2. In November 1994, the voters of California in a 59% - 41% vote approved Proposition 187. The law effectively denies public education, health and other social services to hundreds of thousands of illegal immigrants who are currently in the state of California. Gov. Pete Wilson indicated that it costs the state about $2.3 billion per year to provide the services for which there is no federal reimbursement. Immediately following the election, actions to delay implementation of the law were filed in state and federal courts. Both courts blocked implementation until issues concerning the constitutionality of Prop 187 were studied.

    Research the outcome of Prop 187. What constitutional issues were raised? What did the courts ultimately decide? What were the bases for the courts' decisions? Why did Gov. Wilson support this referendum? What social policy philosophy is embodied in Prop 187? What were the socio-economic characteristics of those who voted for the referendum? Is a Prop 187-like action the appropriate strategy for states that wish to rebel against federal mandates?

3. At present, Congress is not required to adopt a balanced budget. Interest in amending the Constitution to impose such a requirement re-ignited after the 1994 mid-term Congressional elections. One proponent of the measure, Sen. Robert Packwood, in a November 1994 address to the Republican Governor's Association, indicated that Congressional reluctance to curb the growth entitlement programs--Social Security, Medicare, and Medicaid- would result in massive reductions in federal aid to states should a balanced budget amendment be authorized. If you were a governor in a state with (a) a population encompassing significant numbers of African Americans, Hispanics, children and youth, and female heads of households and (b) a rising violent crime rate, what would your reaction be to such a change in federal social policy? Would your response be different depending on whether you are a Republican or Democrat?

Investigate the results of Congressional actions after the 1994 mid-term elections to authorize a balanced budget amendment, institute welfare and crime control reforms. Assess any changes in terms of their philosophical orientation. Is it the appropriate role of the federal government to set welfare and crime control criteria or should this be left to the states?

PART VII — POLITICAL SCIENCE TODAY

1. Despite the best efforts of the Clinton Administration to achieve a national health program over a 20 month period, the president and his congressional supporters admitted defeat in late September of 1994. Fierce attacks on Clinton's government-run, universal health care program by Republicans and the health-insurance lobbies eventually turned public support for Clinton's plan into a mixture of derision and apathy. However, Democrats promised that the fight for a restructuring of health care would begin anew in 1995, albeit the plan would be far more "incremental", i.e., probably far less than full health coverage for all Americans. But complicating matters was the Republican midterm election sweep in November, giving them control of Congress. In short, the future of major health care reform was uncertain.

What happened to Clinton's health care plan in 1995 or even up to the 1996 presidential election? Did Congress reach some kind of compromise regarding the extent of health coverage, the cost to employers, the extent of federal involvement, etc .? Or was the plan again postponed? Did President Clinton compromise considering the GOP-controlled Congress? Summarize your findings in a short paper.

2. The Clinton Administration was successful in passing a comprehensive crime bill in late July of 1994. The bill provided for 100,000 more police on the nation's streets over a six year period, banned a variety of assault weapons, allowed more funding for the construction and running of prisons, expanded the federal death penalty to other crimes (including carjacking), allocated billions for crime prevention/rehabilitation programs, and initiated college scholarships for students who wished to pursue law enforcement careers. However, there was some question among the GOP opposition as to how all of these programs would be funded. (After the November elections, some Republicans insisted that they would change the bill in 1995 since they now controlled Congress.) Some law-enforcement officials also doubted whether this bill would really reduce the crime rate in America. Research whether the bill was changed in 1995 and also why some law-enforcement officials doubted the crime-fighting efficacy of the bill.

PART VIII — DATA ANALYSIS

1. Social security is considered a political "untouchable" in Washington, D.C. Cuts in social security would definitely help in reducing the federal budget, but few politicians wish to propose such a course of action for fear of political retaliation at the polls. Interview your grandparents, senior citizens, other over-60 relatives, or even your own parents. Simply ask this "target population' whether they would accept cuts in social security payments and record their responses. Be sure to probe more deeply as to the reasons behind those individual responses. After completing your interviews, do you have a better idea as to why social security is considered a "sacred political cow"?

2. Using a similar interview approach used in Exercise #1, ask your classmates a series of questions about contemporary American education. First, would they favor or oppose the federal government establishing a national curriculum that would standardize educational standards and requirements in all 50 states? Second, would they favor or oppose extending the traditional 180 day school year to 220 or even more, a length comparable to educational practice in Japan? Third, would they favor or oppose extending the traditional three or four years in high school by at least one additional year before a high school degree could be achieved? Fourth, would they favor a new, expanded federal loan program, funded by an increase in federal income taxes, that would permit thousands of low-income high school graduates to attend the college or university of their choice? Once again, be sure to identify reasons behind those responses. Collect your data and use it in writing a short paper on American education.

3. Review the text material from "A Closer Look—Welfare Programs: Assisting the Poor. " If you were a member of Congress and felt compelled to cut welfare spending, which one of the six programs described would you target for those cuts and why?

PART IX — TEST ANSWERS

Pretest

1. c		6. b	
2. b		7. b	
3. d		8. c	
4. a		9. c	
5. c		10. d	

Programmed Review

1. health care, welfare, education and crime control reforms
2. social
3. Conservatives
4. Liberals
5. mandate
6. Soviet Union
7. what, how extensive, and who funds the programs
8. Democratic Leadership Council
9. Reinventing Government
10. "general welfare"
11. Social Security
12. 90%
13. Increased life expectancy, steady decline in the birth rate
14. research, cost controls, access
15. promote research, target particular diseases, regulate drugs, regulate health care providers, gather and disseminate information
16. $253 billion, 44%
17. Surgeon General, National Institutes of Health, Federal Drug Administration
18. the freedom to choose their own doctors
19. tax increases, additional restrictions
20. 325%, 26%
21. 84%
22. 15%
23. 70%, 42%
24. cigarettes, alcohol, drugs; $20 billion per year.
25. food stamps
26. financial assistance to farmers, national parks, loans to college students
27. educational, nutritional, health, and other social services
28. direct payments, food stamps, housing subsidies, transportation, job training, higher education, subsidized medical care
29. $14,000
30. African-American, Hispanic, young, female
31. 72%
32. Sen. Daniel P. Moynihan, Labor
33. Earned income tax credits
34. multiple goals, compromises and contradictions in response to demands, interests, and preferences to help the poor and eliminate poverty
35. Sputnik
36. G. I. bill
37. separate but equal school facilities

38. develop standards for student performance, curriculum content, and opportunities to learn; improve staff, curricula, assessment systems, and materials; and coordinate educational system with health and social services
39. vouchers
40. 50%
41. state and local
42. 8.2%
43. hire more police officers, make more crimes federal crimes, interpret federal laws more broadly, punish federal crimes more severely, increase spending on federal prisons
44. mandate minimum sentences for certain crimes, increase maximum fines for serious drug offenses, and create victim compensation programs
45. Brady bill
46. 200 million
47. 69,000, $3.4 billion
48. LEAA (Law Enforcement Assistance Administration)
49. Ronald Reagan
50. what programs, how to fund the programs

Post-test

1. a	6. d
2. d	7. b
3. a	8. d
4. c	9. c
5. b	10. b

Data Analysis

Responses to all three exercises will depend upon the specific opinions obtained by the student or the personal opinions/values of the student.

CHAPTER 21
MAKING FOREIGN AND DEFENSE POLICY

For nearly forty years all other U.S. foreign policy issues were dwarfed by our relationship with a super power Soviet Union. Eventually that fact dwarfed all other issues. And then suddenly, the entire edifice collapsed, along with its supporting ideology. Under Gorbachev and Yeltsin the Berlin Wall, which had separated East and West, fell and the Soviet Union itself crumbled into competing republics.

But the end result was not a world of peace and harmony. We fought brief wars with Panama and Iraq. The Middle East swarmed with conflicting interests. South Africa was aflame with racial discord. Latin America was restive with under-classes that demanded a fairer share of national wealth. Europe was drawing together into an economic bloc. Japan, China, and Pacific Rim countries had become our economic rivals. The Muslim world was a sea of unrest. The United States itself was weakened by our slumping economy.

In the face of these hard facts we needed a new comprehensive foreign policy if we were to aspire to world leadership.

In the last fifty years, defense goals of the United States have shifted drastically and the 1990s promise to be a period when our objectives will shift at an even faster pace. World War II left only two super powers - the United States and the USSR, who viewed each other competitively in every corner of the globe and outer space. That polarized world has disappeared, leaving at least five potential competitors for world power: Japan, Mainland China, the European Community, the United States, and the USSR. Both of the super powers appear to have overextended themselves militarily, while neglecting their domestic economies. Meanwhile, Japan, the Republic of China, and the European Community have growing economic power and potential military force that is formidable if not equal to the two super powers. This reality exists, while the Big Two seem to have arrived at a military standoff with no clear-cut victor.

In this atmosphere each is fumbling toward a reduction in its arms budget, and possibly disarmament. Leaders of the former Soviet Union and the United States must accept the reality that neither has the ability nor inclination to defeat the other or to dominate the world. A drastic cutback in nuclear weapons, a reduction of armed forces, and declining influence over former client states appear to be high on the defense agendas of the 1990s.

All predictions are blurred by several unknown factors. Will some of several "outlaw" nations such as Iraq or Algeria become nuclear powers? What about China, Israel, and South Africa?

What about new technologies of warfare such as nerve gas? Rather than massive armies, will terroristic tactics be the weapons of the future? Or will a greatly strengthened United Nations bring some respite in the search of all nations for workable defense systems?

PART I — GUIDEPOSTS

1. Vital Interests in the Post-Cold War World
   a. What recent changes outside the United States are affecting our traditional foreign policy?
   b. What are our foreign policy priorities for the 1990s?
   c. What is the basic objective of United States foreign policy?
   d. What are the new foreign policy challenges of the 1990s?

2. Key Players in Foreign Policy
   a. In what way does the State Department make foreign policy?
   b. What role is played by the National Security Advisor?
   c. What people compose the National Security Council? How much influence does it have?
   d. Why do activities of the CIA create special problems?
   e. How does the Foreign Service attempt to implement foreign policy?

3. The Politics of Foreign Policy
   a. How much influence does public opinion have on foreign policy? Why does it limit our actions?
   b. What impact on foreign policy is exercised by the media, interest groups, ethnic organizations, and foreign companies?
   c. Do political parties play a major role?
   d. How has Congress tried to redefine its role in foreign policy?
   e. Why do democracies have special problems in implementing foreign policy?

4. Foreign Policy Strategies
   a. What strategy does conventional diplomacy pursue?
   b. How does foreign aid fit into our policy? Economic sanctions?
   c. How have we used political coercion?
   d. How have we used covert action?
   e. When have we used military intervention?

5. The United Nations and International Organizations
   a. In which international organizations does the United States hold membership?
   b. What relationship does the United States have with the United Nations?

6. U.S. Security and Defense Objectives
   a. Who is responsible for our common defense?
   b. What are our national security objectives for the 1990s?
   c. Why is there debate over United States involvement abroad?

7. The Defense Department Leadership Structure
   a. Who participates in making our defense policy?
   b. How is the defense bureaucracy subdivided?
   c. How has technology made the traditional leadership of the armed forces obsolete?
   d. How was the leadership restructured in 1986?

8. Providing for Conventional Forces
   a. How has the draft evolved in our history?
   b. Why has the volunteer army become unrepresentative of the total population?
   c. Should women be allowed into actual combat? What problems of military life center around women?
   d. What is the military's position on homosexuals in the armed services?

9. The Politics of Defense Spending
    a. How has public support for the defense budget varied in recent years?
    b. To what groups can defense contractors appeal for support?
    c. Where have cuts been made in the defense budget?
    d. How has the Pentagon taken on a self-perpetuating life of its own?
    e. What do we mean by a military-industrial complex?
    f. How much of the national budget should be spent on defense?
    g. What is meant by a strategy of deterrence? How does Star Wars fit into that strategy? Why is it opposed?

10. Liberty and Security
    a. How do security and liberty potentially conflict?
    b. What shifts in Congressional attitudes are reflected in the present scene?

PART II — GLOSSARY

FOREIGN SERVICE - The government agency that, as an instrument of the State Department, develops and implements foreign policy.

NATIONAL SECURITY COUNCIL - The committee, composed of high-ranking officials, that coordinates major security decisions.

NATIONAL SECURITY ADVISOR - The person who directly advises the president on national security matters.

CENTRAL INTELLIGENCE AGENCY - The agency that gathers and evaluates information concerning foreign nations. It also carries out secret, covert operations.

BIPARTISANSHIP - The policy that stresses cooperation and a united front between political parties in foreign policy.

THIRD WORLD - Developing nations that are relatively poor.

JOINT CHIEFS OF STAFF - The heads of the various military services, who serve as advisers to the president.

DETERRENCE - The philosophy underlying our defense strategy, which requires a U.S. capability to survive a Soviet "first strike" and respond so massively that they would not attempt a "first strike."

*MILITARY-INDUSTRIAL COMPLEX - An alleged alliance between top military and industrial leaders, who have a common interest in arms production and utilization.

*COLD WAR - The post-World War II tension between the United States and the USSR and their respective allies.

SECOND STRIKE FORCE - The surviving military capability of a nation after it has suffered an all-out nuclear attack. In military strategy, this potential retaliation supposedly deters an aggressor nation.

PART III — PRETEST

1. State Department policy priorities for the 1990s include *all but*
    a. promote protective tariffs.
    b. promote democratic values.
    c. secure a global environment.
    d. work with allies against transnational threats.

2. In all nations, foreign policy-making tends to be concentrated in
    a. public opinion.
    b. the courts.
    c. Congress.
    d. the executive branch.

3. The secretary of state is *not* responsible for
    a. key statements on foreign policy.
    b. speaking before congressional committees.
    c. visiting foreign chiefs of state.
    d. deploying military forces.

4. A compromise modifying the ban on homosexuals in the military is described as
    a. pro choice.
    b. be seen, be quiet.
    c. shoot straight.
    d. don't ask, don't tell.

5. Much of the criticism of the Foreign Service is summarized in the statement that there are no _____ Foreign Service officers.
    a. old
    b. bold
    c. old, bold
    d. young, bold

6. The greatest checks on the president's foreign policy powers in recent years have come from
    a. the State Department.
    b. military advisers.
    c. Congress.
    d. the Foreign Policy Association.

7. In our all-volunteer forces there has been overrepresentation of
    a. women.
    b. middle classes.
    c. minorities.
    d. college graduates.

8. The decision-maker of last resort in our military system is the
    a. field commander.
    b. chairman of the Joint Chiefs of Staff.
    c. president.
    d. head of NATO.

9. The Reorganization Act of 1986 gave power to
    a. Congress.
    b. Secretary of Defense.
    c. Chair of Joint Chiefs.
    d. National Security Council.

10. The basic goal of our defense establishment is to
    a. preserve U.S. independence.
    b. reduce nuclear war perils.
    c. resolve regional conflict.
    d. spread our values and institutions.

PART IV — PROGRAMMED REVIEW

Knowledge Objective: To identify our vital interests

1. The chief objectives of U.S. foreign policy have been our national _____ and _____ well-being.
2. State Department priorities for the 1990s promote a more _____ and _____ world.
3. New foreign policy challenges include the _____ growth of the Third World; _____ wars with Japan; _____ to the former Soviet Union and eastern Europe; _____ traffic with Latin America; and _____ environment.

Knowledge Objective: To review the machinery of foreign policy

4. _____ domination of foreign policy has been consistent throughout American history.
5. The influence of the secretary of state is dependent on the _____ personal desires.
6. Most foreign intelligence information comes from _____ sources.
7. The most uncontrolled U.S. intelligence-gathering agency of the past thirty years has been the _____ .
8. The _____ _____ _____ attempts to integrate military and economic foreign policy.
9. In terms of personnel, the State Department is _____ .
10. The eyes and ears of the United States overseas is the American _____ _____ .
11. Critics of the CIA claim the CIA _____ the military strength of the former Soviet Union and _____ the threat of Islamic fundamentalism.

Knowledge Objective: To consider the politics of foreign policy-making

12. The general public has _____ voice in directly determining foreign policy issues.
13. Opinion makers _____ information and judgment on foreign policy to the American public.
14. The impact of interest groups on foreign policy appears to be _____ than on domestic policy.
15. Since World War II, political parties have normally played a _____ role in foreign policy.
16. In recent years, Congress has become more _____ on foreign policy.

Knowledge Objective: To describe the strategies developed by the United States to meet foreign policy issues

17. In general practice, presidents request foreign aid and Congress (increases, decreases) _____ these requests.
18. Economic sanctions as used by the United States normally consist of restrictions on _____ .
19. When the president uses secret CIA pressure to advance our foreign policy interests, the strategy is referred to as _____ action.
20. Military intervention as a strategy is most successful against _____ nations.

Knowledge Objective: To evaluate the role of the United Nations

21. For most of its history the United Nations was characterized by political _____ .
22. The United Nations gained respect by its role in the _____ Gulf and extensive _____ missions in Cyprus and Lebanon.
23. Critics of the UN declare that there is (little, too much) _____ relationship between member nation size, population, financial contributions, and voting power.
24. The United Nations is likely to play a _____ role in the post-cold war world.

Knowledge Objective: To examine our defense objectives

25. Both the _____ and _____ are responsible for the nation's common defense.
26. The U.S. defense program is to provide for the _____ of our country and protect American interests.
27. The United States (seeks, rejects) _____ multilateral alliances to provide collective security in the world.
28. We (are, are not) _____ committed to defending our allies and friends from armed aggression.

Knowledge Objective: To review the organization and operation of the Department of Defense

29. The headquarters of the Department of Defense is the _____ .
30. Many of the current rivalries among the joint chiefs of staff are over _____ issues, rather than traditional service rivalries.
31. General supervision of the various armed forces is under the jurisdiction of the Secretary of _____ .
32. The chair of the Joint Chiefs of Staff serves a two-year term to help ensure _____ control over the military.
33. The 1986 reform has made the _____ of the Joint Chiefs the most powerful peace-time military officer in U.S. history.

Knowledge Objective: To explore problems related to the recruitment of military personnel

34. Since 1973 personnel for the armed forces of the United States has been provided by _____ .
35. The volunteer army system has resulted in (overrepresentation, underrepresentation) _____ of minorities.
36. Under current policy women are barred from a(n) _____ role in the armed forces.

Knowledge Objective: To explore the politics of defense spending

37. Critics of high defense spending had (increased, declined) _____ by the 1990s.
38. Cuts in defense spending are opposed by local _____ interests.
39. The belief that business and defense now collaborate to encourage military spending is called a _____ complex.
40. Effective deterrence requires a survivable _____ _____ force.
41. The overriding issue of American military policy is to _____ the United States.
42. Our political system is designed to provide for_____ control over the military.

PART V — POST-TEST

1. Women now make up _____ percent of the armed forces.
   - a. fifty
   - b. thirty-seven
   - c. one
   - d. eleven

2. The headquarters of the Department of Defense is
   - a. the Oval Office.
   - b. Fort Myers.
   - c. the Pentagon.
   - d. Strategic Air Command.

3. The number of Americans who feel we are spending too much for defense has _____ since 1980.
   - a. declined
   - b. increased slightly
   - c. drastically increased
   - d. remained stable

4. The joint chiefs of staff are composed of
   a. representatives of the four armed services.
   b. a joint United States Senate and House committee.
   c. quasi-military organizations.
   d. the president's special aides.

5. Critics of the CIA claim all but one of the following
   a. The CIA inflated former Soviet Union economic strength.
   b. The CIA underestimated the threat of Islamic fundamentalism.
   c. The CIA intelligence is no longer needed.
   d. The CIA overestimated the military strength of the former Soviet Union.

6. Civilian control over the military does *not* include one of the following
   a. selection of commander-in-chief.
   b. commissioning of all officers by civilians.
   c. military strategy planned by civilians.
   d. military appropriations made by civilians.

7. Our basic goal in foreign policy has been
   a. the four freedoms.
   b. national self-interest.
   c. self-determination for all people.
   d. spheres of influence.

8. The Central Intelligence Agency has *not* been criticized for the
   a. Bay of Pigs invasion.
   b. keeping files on American citizens.
   c. coordinating information on foreign nations.
   d. overthrowing the Chilean government.

9. The coordination of foreign policy is assumed by the
   a. State Department.
   b. National Security Council.
   c. Senate Foreign Relations Committee.
   d. Joint Chiefs of Staff.

10. New foreign policy challenges include all areas *except*
    a. Fundamentalist Islamic Rule.
    b. Trade Wars with Japan.
    c. Global environment.
    d. water rights.

PART VI — POLITICAL DIALOGUE:
THE CLASH OF ISSUES AND IDEAS

1. In a recent best seller, *The Rise and Fall of the Great Powers*, Paul Kennedy reports that the United States has passed the zenith of its power and influence, which were at their height immediately after World War II. The task of American leaders is to adjust our foreign policies to reflect this relative decline. This is the central challenge to which our leaders must respond. Do you agree? Disagree? Why?

2. An international group of scientists (the Club of Rome) has projected a series of world disasters in the 21st century. Famine, pestilence, and pollution will rage uncontrolled over large sections of the planet according to the club, unless we immediately institute control measures such as contraception, changes in diet, and conservation of national resources. In this world-of-tomorrow scenario, the United States appears to be in a favored position.
   a. Assuming the predictions are true, how should we protect our future?
   b. How responsible are we for world problems?
   c. Should we share the world's resources equally, or should we "write-off" those nations with uncontrolled birth rates?

3. As editorial writer of a large newspaper, you have been concerned over the failure of American public opinion to support our military and diplomatic leaders. You believe that Walter Lippmann was right when he wrote in *The Public Philosophy* (Mentor: 1955) "The governors of the state must tax, conscript, command, prohibit: They must assert a public interest against private inclination and against what is easy and popular. If they are to do their duty, they must often swim against the tides of private feeling."
   a. What evidence exists to show that the American public has been wrong in its reaction to foreign policy?

4. Discuss:
   a. The United Nations will never play a major role in world affairs until its present lopsided voting strength is restructured.
   b. Foreign policy is best if it is bipartisan.
   c. Congress can never hope to play an effective role in foreign policy development.
   d. Conflicting assumptions regarding the importance of Central America to U.S. security.

5. The breakup of the Soviet Union, Czechoslovakia, and Yugoslovia into bitterly antagonistic fragments was one byproduct of the collapse of central communist domination. What role, if any, should the United States play to restore some order to the present ethnic hodgepodge? Can the United Nations pay a useful role?

6. "We need to break down the isolation from the civilian world that the armed forces now experience. The most honest, effective way is to reinstate the draft and use a lottery system to call up recruits, men and women, black and white." Is this proposal fair? Why should anyone object?

7. Non-proliferation is a temporary stop gap, rather than a policy. Sooner or later (probably sooner) nations outside the "inner circle" will gain nuclear weapons and use them against defenseless neighbors. Imagine if you can, Muammar al-Qaddafi with a nuclear arsenal. Or, if you prefer, substitute Yasir Arafat or the Israeli prime minister. Somehow, some way, the Great Powers must agree to prevent such power falling into the hands of minor states, or, if it does, how they will handle the situation. Do you agree? What would you propose?

8. How many billions should we cut the military budget and how should the cuts be applied equally to each part of the armed forces? Anticipate that each in turn will cry "Not me!" What would you do with the savings? Cut the deficit? Create and further American industrial policy? Produce a national health program? What else?

PART VII — POLITICAL SCIENCE TODAY

1. In the aftermath of the Soviet Union's disintegration, the liberation of Eastern Europe from communism, and the reunification of Germany, proponents of defense cuts argued that money could be saved from the defense budget and applied to social programs, i.e., the so-called "peace dividend." Opponents of defense cuts argued that the world was still a very dangerous place, with international threats ranging from terrorism to regional civil wars, to irrational dictators to trade frictions. The Clinton Administration became involved in such far-flung areas as Haiti, Rwanda, Bosnia, Iraq, and North Korea. Also, the American military publicly worried that American cuts in military readiness would jeopardize American security. Consider the question of defense cuts and their implications. Jot down your own conclusions.

2. What is your own opinion on whether all American men between the ages of 18 and 26 should be compelled to serve in the armed services through a compulsory draft? Would you see such a program as a violation of your civil liberties—why or why not? You may wish to debate the issue with fellow classmates. As a corollary, do you believe women should be drafted as well and eventually face a possible combat role? Consider the pros and cons in class discussion or through a short position paper.

3. While the exact relationship between military spending and economic growth is debated, it is probably true that cuts in defense spending affect procurement, i.e., a multiplier effect that creates jobs not only with defense corporations but also with defense sub-contractors. Some economists argued that the Clinton's Administration's cuts in defense spending hurt the economy. Research the merits of this argument.

PART VIII — DATA ANALYSIS

1. Most Americans are uninformed about foreign policy, not only about the reasons behind a particular policy but who the people are that decide which policy this country will pursue overseas. A successful foreign policy must have the support of key decision-makers in the executive and legislative branches, the military, the public, and other influential opinion-makers. Using an appropriate library source, fill in the names of those men and women who *currently* occupy the following offices and/or positions.

   The U.S. Secretary of State _____

   The U.S. Secretary of Defense _____

   The President's National Security Advisor _____

   The Current Head of the Joint Chiefs of Staff _____

   The Current Director of the CIA _____

   Chairman of the Senate Armed Services Committee _____

   Chairman of the Senate Foreign Relations Committee _____

   Chairman of the House Armed Services Committee _____

   Current U.S. Ambassador to the United Nations _____

   Current U.S. Ambassador to the Soviet Union _____

Chief Editor of the *New York Times* _____

Chief Editor of the *Washington Post* _____

> **Note:** Some good research sources for the above exercise include the *U.S. Government Manual,* the *World Almanac, Information Please Almanac,* or *Taylor's Encyclopedia of Government Officials.*

2. The end of the Cold War and the disintegration of the Soviet Union have obviously affected the American public's views on foreign policy goals, the dilemma of "guns vs. butter" (especially true in 1992 with the unemployment rate being high and the recession continuing), and the problem of handling other threats from the international system. Scrutinize carefully public opinion polls, probably best found from the Gallup organization, beginning in late 1991 up to the present and collate what appear to be the main shifts in the public's mood on any or all of the above-mentioned foreign policy issues.

3. Two issues raised in the chapter involve (a) the gay ban controversy that became prominent in the early days of the Clinton Administration and (b) the influence of the military-industrial complex (assuming that it exists). With the help of your instructor, form debate teams and research the two issues. The presentation of debates in class should foment interesting class discussion. As an alternative, either debate topic could be covered in an outside research paper.

PART IX — TEST ANSWERS

Pretest

1. a
2. d
3. d
4. d
5. c

6. c
7. c
8. c
9. c
10. a

Programmed Review

1. security; economic
2. secure; democratic
3. population; trade; aid; drug; global
4. Presidential
5. president's
6. open
7. CIA
8. National Security Council
9. small
10. Foreign Service
11. inflated; underestimated
12. little
13. transmit
14. less
15. bipartisan
16. assertive
17. decreases
18. trade
19. covert
20. small
21. impotence
22. Persian; peacekeeping

23. little
24. greater
25. President; Congress
26. protection
27. seeks
28. are
29. Pentagon
30. technology
31. Defense
32. civilian
33. Chair
34. volunteers
35. overrepresentation
36. combat
37. increased
38. economic
39. military-industrial
40. second strike
41. defend
42. civilian

Post-test

1. d
2. c
3. c
4. a
5. c

6. c
7. b
8. c
9. b
10. d

Data Analysis

1. The specific individuals who currently fill these posts will vary over time, given personnel changes in presidential administrations. If changes have recently occurred in any of the designated offices/positions, try to find out *why* those changes occurred.

2. The general trends and/or impressions will depend upon which polls the individual student consults.

3. Debate presentations will vary depending upon the information selected and each team's fundamental organizational approach.

CHAPTER 22
THE DEMOCRATIC FAITH

The bed-rock foundation of any government is the set of assumptions upon which it is founded. Democracy has its own special beliefs about the ability of people in general, the role of leaders, and the goals of government. Too often, in our day-to-day study of government's nuts-and-bolts, we skip over the basic ideas underlying the whole system. American students find it especially hard to stand off and look critically at their own government's philosophical underpinnings. Yet this ability is at the very core of political wisdom. It is useful to remember that most people who have lived on the planet Earth have been subject to authoritarian rulers. Our government is one of the rare exceptions, constantly faced with the question as to whether "this nation or any other nation so conceived and so dedicated can long endure."

Although American democracy is often described as "government by the people," we actually depend heavily on leaders to give focus and direction to the nation. Therefore, competent leadership becomes a key factor in making the political system work. The sources of this leadership, the way in which leaders make their way to the top, and the qualities that make for great leadership are basic questions which students of government must consider. In our history, who are the leaders that loom large? Do some periods call forth great leaders, or do great leaders make their own times?

In one sense the study of leadership is as old as politics, stretching back to such authors as Machiavelli or Polybius. In another sense, leadership is an unexplored aspect of the American political system, ignored because it does not easily lend itself to statistical analysis. In the vanguard of contemporary writers who have addressed this topic is one of the text authors, James MacGregor Burns.

PART I — GUIDEPOSTS

1. Philosophical Assumptions and Paradoxes
    a. Why is faith needed to believe in our system?
    b. Why do we need healthy skepticism?
    c. What assumptions did Thomas Jefferson hold regarding democratic government?
    d. Throughout history what form of government has been most common?
    e. What components of democratic government were blended in our Constitution?
    f. How did the Founders value efficient government as contrasted with safe government?

2. Participation and Representation
    a. What problems exist in participatory government?
    b. How are these problems lessened by representative government?
    c. How does Congressional representation reduce majority rule as reflected by the President?
    d. What is broker rule? Do we have it?
    e. Why do Americans have a love-hate relationship with politicians?
    f. Describe the gap between our idealized politician and reality.
    g. Why are politicians necessary to make democracy work?

3. Leadership
   a. What function is performed by politicians who are agitators; coalition builders; office holders?
   b. What role is played by politicians as brokers?
   c. How do leaders differ from managers?
   d. Distinguish between power and authority.
   e. Why is American dissatisfaction with their leaders a built-in fact?

4. The Democratic Faith
   a. How is dissent built into the democratic process?
   b. What relationship exists between democracy, education, and information?
   c. What non material beliefs are part of the American dream?

PART II — GLOSSARY

PARTICIPATORY DEMOCRACY - Direct citizen involvement in decision-making.
BROKER RULE - Mediation by politicians between organized interest groups.
AGITATORS - People who initiate movements.
COALITION BUILDERS - People who compromise the aspirations of conflicting interest groups.
OFFICE HOLDERS - People in elected positions who legislate the proposals of coalition builders and agitators.
POWER - The authority to enforce decisions.
AUTHORITY - Power that is recognized as legitimate.
ACTIVIST - Citizens who are alert in their demands for accountability.
DEMOCRATIC FAITH - A belief that people can govern themselves.

PART III — PRETEST

1. The American people rank as least ethical one of the following groups.
   a. funeral directors
   b. bankers
   c. TV reporters
   d. politicians

2. American politicians tend to win their great acclaim
   a. shortly after election.
   b. while running for office.
   c. after death.
   d. when they win reelection.

3. Critics of broker rule believe all of the following *except:*
   a. election laws are too complicated.
   b. low income persons are less heard.
   c. parties do not offer meaningful alternatives.
   d. a bias exists for the status quo.

4. At the very heart of those personal characteristics that motivate politicians is
   a. ideology.
   b. ambition.
   c. selfishness.
   d. craftiness.

5. A Greek spokesman who declared that government was everyone's business
   a. Socrates.
   b. Pericles.
   c. Zorba.
   d. Heroditus.

6. The most important element in American government today is
    a. interest group.
    b. committed citizens.
    c. great leaders.
    d. obedient followers.

7. Our founders believed authority is controlled by
    a. official statements.
    b. exit polls.
    c. ideology.
    d. public opinion.

8. Direct democracy works best when
    a. an area is small.
    b. a society is pluralistic.
    c. people are well-educated.
    d. standards of living are high.

9. Participatory democracy works best in
    a. colleges.
    b. cities.
    c. states.
    d. the armed forces.

10. Broker rule is *best* described as
    a. compromises between conflicting groups.
    b. substituting interest groups for parties.
    c. regulation by the New York Stock Exchange.
    d. giving women greater power.

PART IV — PROGRAMMED REVIEW

Knowledge Objective: To analyze the Democratic Faith

1. According to democratic theory, the only legitimate foundation for any government is the _____ of the people.
2. The democratic concept in practice is a mixture of _____ and _____ .
3. In the full span of human history, most people have lived under _____ rule.
4. The great American champion and spokesman for democracy in the late eighteenth century was _____ _____ .
5. Jefferson believed that governments were bound to degenerate that trusted _____ alone.
6. Athenians wanted _____ more than liberty or freedom.
7. Leadership is important in a democracy, but even more important is an _____ citizenry.
8. American democracy needs both faith and _____ .
9. Jefferson believed that the only safe depository power in a democracy should be vested in the _____ .

Knowledge Objective: To review the basic guiding principles of American democratic government

10. _____ was the principle most valued by the framers.
11. The Constitution both _____ and _____ power to national, state, and local governments.
12. The Constitution distributes power between the _____ and _____ governments.
13. Efficiency (was, was not) _____ the main goal of the framers.
14. The framers tried to protect individual liberty _____ government.

Knowledge Objective: To examine the prospects for American democratic government

15. Individual needs and the needs of society must be _____ .
16. Negotiations between interest group within the Congress that result in compromise legislation is called _____ rule.
17. Democratic governments always have _____ groups that are free to speak out.
18. American citizens (are, are not) _____ normally critical of their government.

Knowledge Objective: To analyze American attitudes toward politicians

19. Leadership can be understood only in the context of both leaders and _____ .
20. Politicians are held _____ in public esteem.
21. Our ideal leaders are usually _____ .
22. We probably expect too (much, little) _____ of politicians.

Knowledge Objective: To define the various kinds of leadership

23. People who instigate movements are called _____ .
24. Coalition builders differ from movement catalyzers in that they are chiefly interested in _____ _____ .
25. As political brokers, the coalition builders try to work out _____ between divergent groups.
26. The heart of democratic politics is _____ .
27. Competing groups force most politicians to become _____ .
28. Managers and leaders (do, do not) _____ require the same skills.
29. Politics is the _____ of democracy.
30. Effective leaders rely on _____ rather than power.
31. There (is, is not) _____ a single effective style that all leaders should learn and practice.
32. The leaders who emphasize bargaining and compromise are called _____ .

Knowledge Objective: To review the Democratic Faith

33. The ultimate test of a democratic system is the legal existence of an officially recognized _____ .
34. Thomas Jefferson believed there is nothing in the country that cannot be cured by good _____ and sound _____ .
35. Our political system is far from perfect, but it is still an _____ system.

PART V — POST-TEST

1. The principal objective of the framers was
    a. efficient government.
    b. representative government.
    c. individual liberty.
    d. responsive representatives.

2. The virtues of our present political system include
    a. easy leadership.
    b. safeguards against tyranny.
    c. decisive action.
    d. quick response to majorities.

3. The framers were least interested in making the government
    a. moderate.
    b. balanced.
    c. safe.
    d. efficient.

4. In the last days of Athenian democracy, the most common aspiration was for
    a. liberty.
    b. freedom.
    c. security.
    d. equality.

5. One of the greatest spokesmen for the democratic faith was
    a. Alexander Hamilton.
    b. John Adams.
    c. Warren Harding.
    d. Thomas Jefferson.

6. The full operation of majority rule is slowed by all of the following *except*
    a. federalism.
    b. free elections.
    c. Bill of Rights.
    d. checks and balances.

7. Education is one of the best predictors for all of the following *except*
    a. voting.
    b. participation in politics.
    c. knowledge of public affairs.
    d. intolerance for different opinions.

8. In writing the Constitution, all of the following goals were sought *except*
    a. efficiency.
    b. competing constituencies.
    c. distribution of power.
    d. preservation of strong local governments.

9. Leaders who emphasize power depend on
    a. force.
    b. persuasion.
    c. eloquence.
    d. charisma.

10. To have a democratic society, one the following practices must exist.
    a. the right to dissent
    b. total press freedom
    c. no restrictions on obscenity
    d. government-funded abortions

PART VI — POLITICAL DIALOGUE: THE CLASH OF ISSUES AND IDEAS

1. Pericles, in his famous funeral oration, declared that the person who takes no part in public affairs is a useless person, a good-for-nothing. Is this true? How would he rate American democracy?

2. Near the end, Athenians floundered in a society where the chief values were individual greed, self-centeredness, smugness and private comfort. Does this sound familiar to American students in the 1990s? Have we traded in our basic values for a society that has no higher goal than private comfort, no matter what is happening in the nation or world?

3. Jefferson said that the only safe depository of power was the people. If this is true, should we declare national bankruptcy?

4. Participatory democracy is a good slogan, but it makes for poor government. Comment.

5. John Gardner said that from the ranks of the critics come troublemakers and cranks but also saviors and innovators. Do we have to take one to get the other? Or is some sort of screening possible?

6. What sort of leadership do we need today? How can we get it?

7. Politics is not something we can afford to leave to other people. Why?

PART VII — POLITICAL SCIENCE TODAY

1. Now that you have probably finished your course in American Government, do you believe that democracy can be renewed and even improved under the support and leadership of *your generation of Americans*? Are your classmates and friends concerned about participating in public affairs or are they generally apathetic or uninformed about political life in America? Finally, has this course in American Government sensitized you to a need to be part of an "active, committed citizenry" - why or why not?

2. Given the disintegration of the Soviet Union and the liberation of Eastern Europe, do you believe you will live to see the eventual triumph of democracy everywhere in the world, even in such places as Cuba, North Korea, China? Why or why not?

3. Jefferson once stated that a "nation which expects to be ignorant and free expects what never was and what never will be." While it is true that there are more American citizens attending colleges and universities than ever before, would it help to strengthen democracy if the federal government subsidized even more citizens, particularly the poor, to go on to college than is the current case? In other words, would a population in the United States that was mainly college-educated vote more often, be less susceptible to political demagoguery, and keep a closer tab on the potential excesses and frailties of their elected officials? Conversely, would increasing the educational level of the populace really make a significant difference? After all, how do you explain the fact that while great numbers of Americans have gone to college, the voting turnout in presidential and congressional elections has been inexorably declining?

4. The New England town meeting is perhaps the most famous example of direct participation in political life. See if you can research how these meetings are conducted and implemented. Are there any aspects of the town meeting that could be transferred to communities with large populations? If so, how? If not, why not?

5. The chapter makes the point that majority rule may not always be an infallible guide to correct public policy or proper decisions for society as a whole. Reflect on how you, as a member of the American political community, could judge when the majority was wrong and the minority right? Can you think of any case studies from recent American history where the majority view was eventually exposed as being deficient and perhaps even dangerous? If you cannot think of an example, look back through the text for some ideas relating to this question.

6. In your own words, and from the perspective of the course, write your own definition of the term democracy. Share it with other members of the class.

7. Which definition of a politician - typical or ideal - fits your own judgment? Try to articulate why you chose one or the other.

8. Scan the newspapers, current journals, TV news documentaries, etc. and try to derive a topology of current American political leaders who fit the agitator, coalition builder, and office-holder categories. After each type, explain why you chose the particular individual(s) within each category.

9. In your own mind, what qualities make a leader effective? Try to think about the personal or intellectual traits of leaders on your own campus, in a fraternity or sorority, in local government, and

at the state and federal levels. One interesting question you might pose is whether leadership in nonpolitical spheres such as corporate or academic can easily be transferred to the political arena, i.e., governmental service.

10. Can an individual go into political life and remain true to his or her ideals? Try to view a video-tape of the famed political movie, *The Candidate* starring Robert Redford. In the film, Redford plays the son of a former California governor who decides to run for the U.S. Senate against a formidable incumbent. During the course of his campaign, he emerges from the underdog role through clever, slick TV commercials and eventually wins the race. At the very end of the film, he turns to his campaign manager and asks the question "What do we do now?" In other words, in winning he has so compromised his original values that he is morally and substantively lost. After viewing the film in its entirety, rethink the relationship between political compromises and individual integrity.

PART VIII — DATA ANALYSIS

1. Look at the text insert listing the reasons "Why People Run for Political Office" and "Why People Shy Away from Running for Public Office." Imagine you were contemplating a run for a political office and had to sort out the pro and con reasons surrounding such an effort. From the lists below, prioritize or place in rank order, from first to last, the most to least important reasons you *would* run and the most to least important reasons you *would not* run. Of course, you may add reasons which do not necessarily appear in the list. After you are finished, think about what the rank order tells you about yourself and your likely success or failure in the political arena.

2. Reread journalist Charles McDowell's proposed "Proud to be a Politician" oath. Assume that this oath, or one similar to it, was publicly used by every new member of Congress in the future with the media heavily publicizing the meaning of the oath. Over time, would this oath break-down the biases which exist against politicians or not? Cite reasons behind your opinion.

Why People Run for Political Office

✔ To solve problems and promote the "American Dream" — enhancing liberty and justice

✔ To advance fresh ideas and approaches

✔ To "throw some rascal out" whose views you dislike

✔ To gain a voice in policy making

✔ To serve as a party spokesperson

✔ To acquire political influence and a platform from which to influence public opinion

✔ To gain prominence and power

✔ To satisfy ego needs

✔ To gain the opportunity to learn, grow, travel, and meet all kinds of people

✔ To be where the "action is" — involved in the thick of government and political life — campaigning, debating, drafting laws, reconciling diverse views, and making the system responsive

Why People Shy Away from Running for Political Office

✔ Loss of privacy for you and your family

✔ Less time to spend with families or favorite pastimes

✔ Less income than in many business or professional occupations

✔ Exposure to partisan and media criticism

✔ Campaigning involves many things most people would rather not do— like marching in countless parades, attending county fairs, going to endless political dinners, banquets, service club meetings, and so on

✔ Rewards of serving in office appear meager

✔ Fear that one may have to compromise one's principles because of the complexity of our adversarial system

✔ Campaigning can often be expensive

✔ Some people don't want to show their ambitions, and they don't like conflict and divisiveness

✔ Some people think the constitutional structure and the party systems we now have make it nearly impossible to exercise meaningful leadership

PART IX — TEST ANSWERS

Pretest

1. d	6. b
2. c	7. d
3. a	8. a
4. b	9. a
5. b	10. a

Programmed Review

1. will
2. faith; skepticism
3. authoritarian
4. Thomas Jefferson
5. rulers
6. security
7. active
8. skepticism
9. people
10. Liberty
11. grants; withholds
12. national; state
13. was not
14. against
15. balanced
16. broker
17. minority or opposition
18. are
19. followers
20. low
21. dead
22. much
23. agitators
24. winning elections
25. compromises
26. compromise
27. brokers
28. do not
29. lifeblood
30. authority
31. is not
32. brokers
33. opposition
34. newspapers; school masters
35. open

Post-test

1. c	6. b
2. b	7. d
3. d	8. a
4. c	9. a
5. d	10. a

Data Analysis

1 and 2 - Answers will vary according to the reader's own values and reasons selected behind the opinions expressed.